WORKS BY RAÏSSA MARITAIN

Lettre de Nuit, La Vie Donnée, poems (Desclée De Brouwer).

Au Creux du Rocher, poems (Alsatia).

Portes de l'Horizon, poems, with an English translation by the author (Regina Laudis, Connecticut).

We Have Been Friends Together, memoirs (Longmans, Green and Co.).

Adventures In Grace, memoirs (Longmans, Green and Co.).

Le Prince de ce Monde (Desclée De Brouwer).

Histoire d'Abraham ou les premiers âges de la conscience morale (Desclée De Brouwer).

Chagall ou l'Orage Enchanté (Desclée De Brouwer).

The Angel of the Schools : St. Thomas Aquinas, with illustrations by Gino Severini (Sheed & Ward).

Notes on the Lord's Prayer (P. J. Kenedy & Sons).

IN COLLABORATION WITH JACQUES MARITAIN

Prayer and Intelligence (Sheed & Ward).

The Situation of Poetry (Philosophical Library).

Liturgy and Contemplation (P. J. Kenedy & Sons).

TRANSLATIONS

The Ways of God, an opusculum attributed to St. Thomas Aquinas. Translated by Raïssa Maritain and Margaret Sumner (Basiliam Press, Toronto).

Les Dons du Saint-Esprit, by John of Saint Thomas (Éditions Téqui).

SELECTED TEXTS

Léon Bloy : Pilgrim of the Absolute (Eyre & Spottiswoode).

Raïssa
Bagnoles, 1932

Raïssa's Journal

presented by Jacques Maritain

(enlarged with new matter for this translation)

Preface by
RENÉ VOILLAUME
Prior of the Little Brothers of Jesus

MAGI BOOKS, INC.

33 BUCKINGHAM DRIVE — ALBANY, N.Y. 12208

Library of Congress Catalog Card Number 72–95648
ISBN 0–87343–041–7

CONTENTS

———————

Illustrations

PREFACE

PREFACE

"The style best suited to the truth of spiritual things is perhaps one of purity and transparency and a certain lofty impersonality, rather than one marked by too much originality."

(*Les Grandes Amitiés*, p. 110.)[1]

IT is with a feeling of humility and with a heart full of gratitude that I am writing this preface to the collection of notes published under the title of *Raïssa's Journal*. First of all, let me be permitted to say to what an extent the reading of these intimate notes of Raïssa's allows us to share in an authentic spiritual experience and one which is particularly significant for us, the sons and daughters of Brother Charles of Jesus' family, and for others vowed like ourselves to the religious state, as well as for several lay men and women who have had the opportunity of reading them before publication. The present volume now makes them available to a wider circle. In their sober clarity they reveal to us the whole unfolding of the hidden life of a soul in love with God, and yet interested – and with what untiring charity – in the life of the world, especially in the new intellectual and artistic movements which characterised her times.

---

1. English version by Julie Kernan, *We Have Been Friends Together*, Doubleday, Image Books, p. 84.

Raïssa's Journal

Obviously it is not without a sense of inadequacy that I approach the delicate (and frankly superfluous) task of writing an introduction to a work which is its own recommendation. Faced with such an undertaking, how can one not feel somewhat clumsy? In deciding to attempt it, I was helped by the bond of friendship between myself and Jacques Maritain and, still more, by the wish to testify, as to a fact I can ascertain, to the radiance of the life which is expressed in these pages and to the very profound good they have already produced in many other lives.

Those men and women who have been brought by a grace of contemplation to "experience" the infinite mystery of God, his love and his mercy, are people who have something to teach us. Ever since God entered into a dialogue with man, and from the time of the Old Testament Covenant, he has been wont to instruct us through the lived experience of certain souls. No doubt, a great number of those who have thus experienced the divine mystery will remain forever unknown. The entirely secret work of their union of love with God has been sufficient. But some seem to have in addition a destiny to teach us, as it were without their knowing it, by letting themselves be revealed as they are, in their transparency: for they have received from Providence the gift of expressing simply, and in self-effacement, their relations with the Lord exactly as they experienced them.

The lines we have put as a chapter-heading to this preface were written one day by Raïssa when she was asking herself why the reading of Pascal, when she was still an unbeliever, had not moved her. What was positively Christian in Pascal, she wrote, *"scarcely touched me,"* and *"was veiled for me, no doubt by my ignorance, but also, I believe, by the very beauty of that admirable style which in itself, after a fashion, stopped me short and diverted my attention from the meaning it was intended to convey."*[2] *Raïssa's Journal* does not divert from these things: it leads one deep into them. The beauty of its style is of a quite different kind; I would say that it is created by the effacement of self in light. It derives a singularly striking force and freshness from a lofty simplicity and an invariable humility. . Moreover this stark simplicity corresponds to the needs of our time which no longer tolerates the floridity and the pious clichés which pleased our forebears. In reading these pages one feels as if one were being given direct access, through an astonishing sobriety of expression, to the world of Truth and of the Kingdom of God. It is precisely this quality of objectivity, of "impersonality", which gives a written work a universal value.

*

Nevertheless, one might hesitate to undertake such a publication. Were not these notes too private? In writing them, their author had never dreamed of publishing them. Had one the right to hand over so personal a "diary" to the public, without betraying a secret? Furthermore, could it interest those who knew nothing of its author?

Nevertheless, it is very useful to us to be guided on the path of contemplative prayer, on the path of secret love, of the "mad", boundless love for God by the knowledge of these spiritual experiences. And how could we know

---

2. *Ibid.*

them, if those who have lived them had not the candour to tell us about them? Or else to leave open, in case they had expressed something of them for themselves alone, the possibility, the implicit authorisation for another to bring this supreme testimony to our knowledge? It is by basing himself on such implicit authorisation, essentially in keeping with Raïssa's vocation, that her life's companion felt himself justified in publishing the *Journal*.

Another objection occurred to other minds. Raïssa's personality, the nature of her activities, the background of her life – were not all these too exceptional for her testimony to be received by contemporary readers at large? This would be to forget that, in the degree in which a soul's spiritual experience takes place on the level of dialogue with God, this experience transcends the multiplicity of concrete situations. On the other hand, it is clear that a book such as this is not addressed to everybody: it is addressed to those who are already somewhat accustomed to the ways of the spirit – and to those who are dying of thirst because they have not come across anyone who summons them towards the path with sufficient force. And both the former and the latter – perhaps more especially the latter – are more numerous than one might think.

It is striking, moreover, to note the marked parallel between Raïssa's spiritual way and the teaching of St Thérèse of Lisieux and that which is revealed to us in the whole life of Brother Charles of Jesus. Yet one could not imagine three people more unlike each other in character, social background and human destiny! I think it may be interesting to point out a few characteristics of this genuine kinship of spirit.

*

The dominant feature of this spiritual movement seems to me the anxiety to restore the contemplation of God to first place and to bring it back into the very midst of the world, into the very midst of the misery of the world, as a vital necessity for the normal flowering of the Christian life as the laity of our time is called to live it.

The holy Carmelite of Lisieux, while remaining in the cloister, received the mission to teach a path to contemplation and holiness accessible by its very simplicity to all who live in the world. On the same lines Père de Foucauld, a hermit in the desert and waiting in vain for companions, lays the foundations of an ideal of religious life whose essential is to give oneself up to contemplation in the framework of the life of Nazareth, of the daily working life of the poor. Raïssa knows that she is called to a contemplative life in the world, in that very setting – the realm of artists, poets and philosophers – where all that is best and most disturbing in the world is at its peak point of attraction and danger.

The fact is that, if the fire of contemplation and of a heart-to-heart relationship with God is not at work – in its full intensity in some, in a more or less imperfect and latent way in many others – in the very midst of the world and not only in the religious Orders, the Christians of our day will not be able to "stand fast" in their daily life and activities, nor to exercise a really fruitful apostolic influence. And God appears to be urgently inviting them through this whole line of spirituality and testimony. The source of it is certainly in the doctrine of St Thérèse of Lisieux, for in her the Church has recognised and confirmed the divine origin of this teaching.

*

The more man gives proof of intelligence and genius in the conquests of science and applies his reason to organise his existence on earth, the more he needs to know Him who is the beginning and end of all things, to be guided by the Lord and comforted by his love. This increase of knowledge and love can only be communicated to him by the very action of the Spirit in its gifts of light, wisdom and fortitude. On this level, which is that of a participation in Christ's very wisdom, man always remains the same throughout the ages, however great the changes and improvements in his human knowledge. The more man conquers the universe and instals himself in it as in his home, the more he needs the graces of contemplation, the more he needs to learn to pray. It is significant that souls, in their experience of the mystery of God, all meet beyond and above their differences of culture and civilisation, whatever their earthly calling and their different modes of expressing this supernatural experience.

The contemplative prayer of Raïssa, whose life was above all dedicated to intellectual work, and who was called on to testify mainly in the world of thought and of art, is but one with the experience of a factory girl or a woman wholly occupied in domestic tasks in a poor neighbourhood. I have known some such who, by these paths in appearance very different, have found the same simplicity of gaze on God and endured the same acute ordeals of purification, to achieve a more complete union with the supreme object of their love.

No doubt, at the outset of her spiritual life, Raïssa, whose health was very frail, was able to benefit by long periods of prayer: this was a grace granted her. Others will have to yield themselves up to the divine love in the monotony and harassing pressure of incessant manual labour (need one recall the classic example of Marie de l'Incarnation, a servant in an inn?). God guides each one according to the designs of his mercy. After all, later on we shall see Raïssa – and this is very much in accordance with a general law of spiritual development – being as it were torn between a constantly more and more urgent call to the life of silent prayer and the rush and bustle of a daily life eaten up by solicitude for her neighbour and for all the sufferings of the world. All around her she came into contact with so much spiritual and moral distress, perhaps even more appalling than material distress. *"My time is split up into tiny fragments,"* she writes in 1943, *"frittered away by a host of little occupations which leave no possibility of* recueillement *and no hope of silence in which thought and expression are nourished."* And, nevertheless, it is then that God's work is perfected in her and that she takes into herself, in order to transform it into supplicating love, the sorrow of mankind as it is revealed to her by a war in which God seems "to have abandoned us" and the massacre of millions of innocents.[3]

In its early stages, the life of prayer still remains dependent on the concrete conditions of existence, with the cares, the pains and the joys they comprise. But when a soul experiences in itself that mysterious action of God which makes his intimate Presence more or less manifest, then the differences between the paths are gradually effaced: in the end the soul is transported into a desert where there are no beaten tracks and where God alone is the guide.

---

3. Cf. in *Au Creux du Rocher*, the long poem "Deus Excelsus Terribilis" which emanates from the interior experience I speak of here.

Is this not why all contemplative experience, in so far as it is genuinely the work of the Holy Spirit, becomes, as the soul progresses further towards union with God, more and more marked by a truly universal character? All the souls who have been the intimate friends of God invariably recognise each other among themselves.

*

I had collected together several passages in Raïssa's notes which seem to me to illustrate her spiritual kinship with either St Thérèse of Lisieux or Brother Charles of Jesus, meaning to quote them at this point. Nevertheless it is better that they should be discovered of themselves in the course of an attentive reading of the *Journal*. I shall therefore confine myself to a small number of quotations.

I have said above that Raïssa was fully conscious of her vocation to be a contemplative in the midst of the world. *"It is an error,"* she writes, *"to isolate oneself from men because one has a clearer vision of truth. If God does not call one to solitude, one must live with God in the multitude; make him known there and make him loved."* (10th March 1919.)

"We walk in darkness, risking bruising ourselves against a thousand obstacles. But we know that 'God is Love' and trust in God is our light. I have the feeling that what is asked of us is to live in the whirlwind, without keeping back any of our substance, without keeping back anything for ourselves, neither rest nor friendships nor health nor leisure – to pray incessantly and that even without leisure – in fact to let ourselves pitch and toss in the waves of the divine will till the day when it will say: 'That's enough'." (December 1933.)

Thus the need of solitude with God which spurs the soul of every contemplative did not lead Raïssa to quit the world. But, in this intimate relationship with the Lord, she is going to learn two things: first of all to know how to use every experience the world brings her, whether of beauty or of misery, as so many occasions of nourishing her love of God; then to see the men and the civilisation of her time with an eye full of a sympathy, an understanding and a lucidity which only divine love is capable of infusing into the heart of a creature.

Like all those whom Jesus has specially called to be his disciples, she understood that these have to share, through suffering, in the redemptive work of their Master, and to "fill up those things which are wanting in the sufferings of Christ" (*Col.,* 1,24). She refers very often to this text of St Paul's, and comments very justly on it.[4] And she observes: *"There is also a fulfilment of the Passion which can be given only by fallible creatures, and that is the struggle against the Fall, against the attraction of this world, as such, against the attraction of so many sins which represents human happiness. That gift Jesus could not make to the Father; only we can make it. There is a mode of redeeming the world, and of suffering, which is available only to sinners . . ."* (25th November 1934).

What strikes us first of all about Raïssa – without any of those adventitious elements and "extraordinary" aids which are in no way essential to the mystical experience – is the very pure simplicity of a contemplative prayer in the depths of which God does not spare her harsh spiritual ordeals which make her penetrate "into the depths of the

---

4. Cf. *Loose Leaves*, Fragment 53, p. 246.

Cross". *"But I do not wish to remove myself from the Cross. Every day I abandon myself to whatever suffering God wills. And the Cross of Jesus carries me over all the abysses."* (30th August 1925.) And it is also the passionate ardour of her love of truth, truth of the natural order and truth of the spiritual order. So it is that she could attain to a rare and perfect unity between intellectual life, theological faith and contemplative experience. Everything is simplified in a vision full of wisdom whose unity generates peace, as well as a kind of supernatural understanding when confronted with the problem of error and evil in Creation. *"Error is like the foam on the waves, it eludes our grasp and keeps reappearing. The soul must not exhaust itself fighting against the foam. Its zeal must be purified and calmed and, by union with the divine Will, it must gather strength from the depths. And Christ, with all his merits and the merits of all the saints, will do his work deep down below the surface of the waters. And everything that can be saved will be saved. For our God has chosen to reign in humility, and it really seems as if he wishes to show himself only just as much as is necessary in order that the visible Church shall endure to the end and the gates of hell shall not prevail against it."* (7th March 1924.)

"I am coming now to take humanity quietly for what it is, without exclamations – regrets – sighs – and groans. In a quite different way from that of Leibnitzian optimism – all is for the best. God knows what he permits.

"He is not like a man who regretfully permits what he cannot prevent. He has let men go their own way armed with their freedom, – and they go it. They go, gamble and work, risk everything, – win more or less, and perhaps will end by winning everything. God has simply reserved for him-

self in humanity one Man who is his Son. And this Man-God calls to himself for his own work – which he also has to do with men's freedom – calls a small number of men, a handful in every century, to work in his own way." (Brief Writings, 16th February 1935.)

I cannot resist the desire to quote another note, written much later, in which Raïssa expresses a truth which I hold to be essential concerning Christian contemplation. *"Certain spiritual writers think that the highest contemplation, being free of all the images of this world, is that which does without images altogether, even that of Jesus, and into which, consequently, the Humanity of Christ does not enter. That is a profound error, and the problem disappears as soon as one has grasped how truly and how deeply the Word has assumed human nature – in such a way that everything which is of this nature: suffering, pity, compassion, hope . . . all these things have become, so to speak, attributes of God. In contemplating them, it is therefore attributes of God which are contemplated, it is God himself who is contemplated."* (Brief Writings, 1958 or 1959.)

*

I have insisted on the kinship which exists between the spiritual experience of St Thérèse of Lisieux and Brother Charles of Jesus and that of Raïssa. This kinship does not prevent each one from having his own special mission and a spiritual physiognomy as unique as the hidden name which in heaven will be revealed to each one of us. It seems to me that what is special to Raïssa's testimony is that it proceeds from the combination – which is rare – of an authentic experience of the mystery of God as well as of purely human realities, with an invariable rigour of thought. The clarity of an extraordinarily alert and truth-loving intelligence is always present. This no doubt explains how it is that, in notes written only for herself, Raïssa has been able to answer a number of questions which arise more and more as one advances in the Christian life and which sometimes pose themselves agonisingly to those who are seeking union with God. It is this, in my eyes, which makes the importance of this *Journal*.

It is good for us who are working, without always seeing very clearly, in the turmoil of human things and human events, to be enlightened, reassured, set back on the path of hope, by souls who, in virtue of graces of illumination, have been raised above the multiplicity of that which passes to the simplicity of that which remains eternally. These souls, though there are very few of them, have an irreplaceable mission among men.

Fr. René VOILLAUME

Prior of the Little Brothers of Jesus,

Marseille, Saint-Julien, 24th June 1963.

FOREWORD

FOREWORD

THE present collection is made up from the diaries, notes and fragments which I found among Raïssa's papers. It is composed in the first place of four notebooks covering the period 1906 to 1926 (or rather 1925, for there are very few pages for the year 1926); secondly of a green exercise book containing the "diary for 1931" and a number of separate pages; thirdly of notes and fragments which I found in another exercise book (a red one) and in various envelopes and in notebooks (all very incomplete) which cover the period from 1939 to the last years of our stay in Princeton; and finally of some pieces of her writing, her letters, and beginnings or rough drafts of essays which it seemed to me preferable to group separately.

This material is somewhat disparate and refers mainly (but with large gaps, due to lack of time and also in all probability to the fact that Raïssa destroyed many of her notes) to the years which followed the death of Père Clérissac and to certain moments which were particularly significant to her, first in the period between the two wars (1931, 1934, 1935, 1939), and then to what she was able

in spite of everything, to note here and there during the
period 1940 to 1960 when our life became a wandering one,
crowded and jostled by external events, and was burdened
with heavy duties and anxieties. Many things are missing,
and very often Raïssa was only able to mention, in the
briefest possible way, events about which she would have
had much to say. The fact remains that with all its gaps
and its sporadic nature (or perhaps because of it) it seems
to me that this collection bears a testimony which is remark-
ably coherent and of singular value.

On certain envelopes containing scraps of writing or
sketched-out essays, Raïssa had written "To be preserved,
perhaps" and "For Jacques to revise". I thought that such
an authorisation might also apply to her notebooks although
she had always kept them strictly to herself.[1] My task has
consisted of choosing the pieces of writing which in my
opinion were most significant, and in transcribing them
into this "Journal". Without mentioning the recollections
they stir up in my heart about the life of Raïssa, her sister
Véra, and myself,[2] what makes them so precious to me is
that they give some idea of the history and progress of her
spiritual experience, of her vocation to the contemplative
life and to silent prayer, of the deepening of her thought,
of the *martyrdom of the heart* and of the total gift of self
which God asked of her.

With absolute faithfulness, Raïssa was able to follow the
contemplative way and to testify to it, in the very midst of
the beauty and the distress of the world and of the incessant

---

1. Once however she let me see some passages of them (February
and March 1934, cf. *Loose Leaves*, Fragments 26, 27 and 28).

2. See J. Maritain *Carnet de Notes* (Desclée de Brouwer 1965),
esp. pp. 255 ff.

worries imposed on her by compassion for souls. In no one (and certainly not in myself) have I known such strength and such unflinching courage of will, nor such lucidity. She has written that God does not want "dead offerings",[3] that he wants offerings that are "human and pure".[4] What the soul offers then are things dear to nature which have been neither killed nor blighted, but which keep their human life and warmth more than ever, and can only be offered because they have been *transfigured*. And this requires a hard and most radical form of dying to self.

Many people nowadays seem to realise that the offering should indeed remain "human" and living, but they go astray because they do not know *the price that must be paid* if it is also to be "pure".

*

In a sense, Raïssa has said everything in her poems.[5] Were they not born there where, in the strange way things flow together, all sources join within the soul, and where the creative experience of the poet is only the pure mirror of his spiritual experience? It suffices that they have sometimes been compared with the classic example of

---

3. Cf. *Loose Leaves*, Fragm. 38; see also Fragm. 36.

4. Cf. the poem *Transfiguration* (in "Lettre de Nuit, La Vie Donnée"), translated by a Benedictine of Stanbrook as *"Patriarch Tree*, Thirty of Raïssa's poems"*, (Worcester, Stanbrook Abbey Press, 1965). "Bearing human gifts made free from stain", "Portant des offrandes humaines et sans tache".

5. For her collected poems, some of which she translated into English herself, see *Poèmes et Essais* (Desclée de Brouwer, 1968).

St John of the Cross. Nevertheless, the two cases are very different. St John is a master and a doctor of wisdom, whose poetry, skilfully elaborated according to the most perfect models of his time, conveys by means of allegories and symbols what he has suffered ineffably in contemplation. Taking care not to raise its voice, Raïssa's poetry is no less refined and no less skilled, but with a humbler, more hidden excellence which is but one with feminine grace, and which wishes, as it were, to efface itself in a rigorous stripping away of all superfluity, so that nothing remains but that which perfectly expresses what the heart feels. Hence there is no longer any need of allegories and symbols. Poetry transposes directly into a work of words, so fragile, precise and delicate that all is now transparent of what has been suffered ineffably in contemplation. It was to this that Pierre Reverdy referred when he spoke of that "ascension" which rises "to the point where the movement of the soul ends by imposing almost absolute silence on words."[6]

In this same precious letter to Raïssa, he goes on:

> That is the true magic of words, they are nothing in themselves, absolutely nothing, but they evoke the thing with such intensity that they transfigure it and re-create it, clothed in a resplendent beauty. Obviously this demands at least talent, and at best genius, but what is marvellous about yours is that it is produced with the most admirable simplicity, never a word put there for its own sake, always the thought, the feeling hold sway in the flow without, on the other hand, ever

6. Letter to Raïssa, 11 June 1955, about *Au creux du Rocher*. (Cf. *Mercure de France*, January 1962.)

coming to a stop or swelling to produce some effect. Hence, no doubt, that simplicity, that lightness of blood, that purity, and that flexibility of rhythm, which pulses from the heart to the soul and the spirit in such a sure, regular beat. . . . In fact, what I think is that, by raising poetry to its highest degree by the simplest possible means, you have made use of it as the ladder which your sensibility needed in order to follow your soul up to its level of mystical purity.

So, in one sense, yes, everything has been said in her poems. Nevertheless, inevitably, whatever the transparency of the poems may be, there remains in them the transposition proper to poetry, which carries us away into a world where all things are swathed in the mysterious *otherness* and the kind of fleeting happiness induced by music and beauty. In the face of such a world, the naked direct testimony of the *Journal* retains a unique impact. I, who cherished Raïssa's poems so much, and who had the privilege of seeing them born (and more, who witnessed her life and her sufferings) read the notes transcribed in this collection and it has been like a revelation of what I knew already, and knew very well, but knew only in a way, bordering on futility, which is inherent in human sight. This revelation has left me, as it were, dazzled now and somewhat bewildered.

> With no other light or guide
> Than the one that burned in my heart.[7]

7. *The Collected Works of St. John of the Cross*, trs. K. Kavanaugh and O. Rodriguez (London 1964), p. 69.

Why, oh why, many weeks before our fateful departure for Paris on 30 June, 1960, was she struck more than ever by those two lines of St John of the Cross which from then on she kept repeating to herself or writing out again, as if she could not lose sight of their mysterious message?

*

If I have had this journal printed, though it is in itself wholly private and personal, it is because I am persuaded that what has been thus lived and directly experienced ought to be known. I believe that these pages are of a kind to help and enlighten many souls, and that the testimony they contain is important, and able to renew and vivify our approach to certain eternal truths, and to enlarge our horizons. The Gospel tells us that everything which is hidden must be brought to light. As Raïssa herself has observed, the contemplative's mission, which is accomplished in silence with God, nevertheless demands (if he has received the gift of self-expression) that what has been suffered and learnt, through love, should also be communicated, however imperfectly, in words; this surplus as it were is needed to make the mission bear forth its full fruit.

I also want justice to be done to Raïssa. If there is anything good in my philosophical work, and in my books, this has its deep source and light in her contemplative prayer and in the oblation of herself she made to God. And her sister, Véra, too, played her part, a contemplative also, but entirely wedded to silence in sustaining us both by her never-ceasing devotion and by the singular strength which she received from her union with Jesus.

But there is still something else, which is not easy to

express and which, nevertheless, I want very much to add. This concerns God's mode of action. At a moment when everything collapsed for both of us, and which was followed by four agonising months, Raïssa was walled up in herself by a sudden attack of aphasia.[8] Whatever progress she made during several weeks by sheer force of intelligence and will, all deep communication remained cut off. And subsequently, after a relapse, she could barely articulate words. In the supreme battle in which she was engaged, no one here on earth could help her, myself no more than anyone else. She preserved the peace of her soul, her full lucidity, her humour, her concern for her friends, the fear of being a trouble to others, and her marvellous smile (that unforgettable smile with which she said *thank-you* to Père Riquet after Extreme Unction) and the extraordinary light of her wonderful eyes. To everyone who came near her, she invariably gave (and with what astonishing silent generosity during her last two days when she could only breathe out her love) some sort of impalpable gift which emanated from the mystery in which she was enclosed. And throughout that time she was being implacably destroyed, as if by the blows of an axe, by that God who loved her in his terrible fashion, and whose love is only "sweet" in the eyes of saints, or of those who do not know what they are talking about.

It was that implacably *sacrificial* manner in which God treated her in her last illness (and which was like a seal on her whole life), which signified in my eyes that, with a very special will, he wanted her to be more than ever wholly given, wholly delivered to Him, and in ways I should never

---

8. Loss of speech due to cerebral affection.

have conceived of earlier. He has taken the tunic, let us give him the cloak. Everything has been broken, what remains to be kept to oneself? The ordinary rules of discretion concerning the secrets of spiritual life have been destroyed at one and the same blow. Raïssa herself would have had a horror of publishing the notes in which she spoke of such secrets.[9] It is for me to make them known not without conscientious examination and anxious self-questioning. Nevertheless, the more I re-read the writings assembled here, the more clearly I see that it would be unforgivable to try to keep them "hidden under a bushel". The encouragement of certain friends in whom I have particular confidence, and to whom I gave a first privately-printed edition to read, has also contributed to my decision. I have set out earlier in this foreword the reasons which influenced me and finally decided me. In an epoch which abounds (and I do not complain of this) in so many documents which reveal the depths in which the poor human being, redeemed by the Blood of Christ, is at grips with the attractions of evil, it is good that something should also be shown of the depths of *love* accessible to this same human being when he seeks God at all costs, and struggles

---

9. Even concerning far less serious things she was convinced that "no man in the world is strictly worthy of the confidence of another man" (see entry for 24 October 1931). At first she did not want to publish her poems; it was under pressure from Véra and myself that she consented. And to get her to make up her mind to write *Les Grandes Amitiés* (Gilson, one day, in Toronto had been the first to urge her to do so) it had needed our goading as well as that of various friends. Among those was a friend in exile, a refugee in the United States during the war, the Austrian socialist Edmond Schlesinger, in no sense a Christian but a great humanist who, from the moment he heard of this project, never ceased to egg her on. I would like to thank him here.

and suffers for the salvation of his brothers, while being, like them, involved in the world's conflicts and in man's adventures in intellectual research, art and poetry.[10]

*

Raïssa kept her deepest life well hidden. What was apparent to all who knew her was the graciousness of her welcome, her gaiety, her vivacity, her exquisite delicacy, her ardour for all the things of the spirit, the compassion and kindness with which she *listened,* her intuitive penetration, and the charm of her conversation. Very few suspected what she had to suffer and in what remote places her heart dwelt.

The truth is that she passed with extraordinary ease and lightness from profound solitude to the realm of every day life. She was one of those souls of whom St Philip Neri, I believe, provides us with the highest example, who come and go freely between two planes of vital activity, amazingly remote from each other. Père Dehau realised this from the first, and he has often told me that in contemplative prayer she was so completely absorbed, and descended to such a profound level (to the depth where crucial choices are made at the very sources of life and where suffering is experienced, unmitigated) that, when she returned to the surface, she needed to be surrounded

---

10. The *Journal* is essentially to do with spiritual life; external events only play in it an altogether secondary part. If, nevertheless, the reader wished to put it in the framework of the events of our life, he would find a certain number of indications in *Les Grandes Amitiés* (*We Have Been Friends Together*), and also in a book, *Carnet de Notes*, which I published after the *Journal*.

C

by all the human activities which she loved, as poets do, and in which she found the element of playfulness and gaiety demanded by her nature. Not that she sought in them a mere opportunity for relaxation and "distraction"! For it is the peculiarity of these souls that they share in the work and the dreams of men with as much fervour and intensity (but purified of all worldly interests) as those whose entire existence is fixed on that level.

Thus it was that later on, in Rome, she was able to bear the burden of her obligations at the Palazzo Taverna so cheerfully and with such serene elegance.[11] Furthermore, as Père Faber points out, anyone accustomed to living in the presence of God, is hardly embarrassed before the great ones of this world. And later still, when the increasing trials of fatigue and illness had darkened our horizon, and she had to remain often confined to her bedroom, it was by incessant reading that she kept herself informed of what was going on in the world, about the new movements in art and in science, and took pleasure in the echo of the vast human clamour of the great country in which we were living. She never tired of looking at the reproductions of pictures she loved which lay scattered on her bed. There were also others at which she looked much, those of many fashionable works which she mockingly laughed at. She endlessly studied photographs, cut out of magazines and newspapers, of those rare children she called *beings,* because none of those psychological grimaces (dear to adults) appeared on their faces but only the naked gravity of the mystery of existence. And right up to the last, she found help and comfort in the precious exchanges which

---

11. See Preface, p. XVII.

delighted her, in conversation with her friends, and in those talks which she knew so well how to direct and animate from her corner of the blue sofa in the living-room at Princeton – that place where I always see her and which I cannot think of without a stab of pain.

And, dominating all the rest, there was her concern for my philosophical work, and for the kind of perfection she expected of it. To that work, she sacrificed everything. In spite of all her physical and mental suffering, and, at certain moments, of an almost total exhaustion, she succeeded by a hard effort of will (and because the collaboration I had always asked of her was, for her, a sacred duty) in revising in manuscript everything I have written and published, both in French and English. It is due to her tears that I have corrected, as was necessary, certain pages that were wrong at the end of the last book I wrote in America (on *Moral Philosophy*). Physically shattered by Véra's death, she wept, less over her bereavement, than over certain passages in my first draft where I had allowed subjectivity with its bitternesses and its anger to intrude. This she rightly judged unworthy of philosophy, and her mind, bless her, was not set at rest until philosophical objectivity had won the day. . . .

*

At my age, one is not afraid of saying all one thinks. Looking back on our past, one thing stands out more clearly for me about our life during the period between the two wars, in particular during the years at Meudon. It is that the work naïvely undertaken by us consisted in reality (like all work which tries to open the world of profane culture, of art, poetry and philosophy, to the energies of the Christian ferment) in attacking the devil on his own territory. It was a matter of dislodging from their positions those whom St Paul calls *Principes et postestates, mundi rectores tenebrarum harum,* and *spiritualis nequitiae,* and against whom he tells us the Christian has to fight more than against flesh and blood.[12]

Raïssa was well aware of it – she wrote *The Prince of this World.* I see better now why she had to suffer so much. It was she who bore the heavier burden of the conflict – in the invisible depths of her prayer and her self-sacrifice. I see better too why the battle was so ruthless and so swift – the baptisms rained down, so did the blows. Conflicts of this kind can be only fought in raids carried out at full speed. And the territory gained is not gained for long. For where the prince of this world has his kingdom, the Christian cannot establish his permanent dwelling as on definitely conquered soil. On such a domain, what he should hope to see, at certain particularly propitious moments in the course of history, is the flaring up of a kind of cultural blaze – what matters is less the result that can be expected of the blaze than the work of the flame itself while the blaze lasts.

I add that the order of the means corresponds to the order of the ends. Every founder, whether of a religious Order or of a lay institution, dreams of founding for eternity. But the Holy Spirit is not at work only in the

---

12. *Ephesians,* 6, 12. "For we wrestle not against flesh and blood, but against *principalities, against powers, against the rulers of the Darkness of this world, against spiritual wickedness in high places*" (Authorised Version). Italics indicate translation of Latin in text.

durable institutions which go on for centuries, he is also at work in ventures which vanish overnight and must always be started afresh. Doubtless one has founded nothing, one sees everything go up in smoke. But one's pains are repaid by what is best in this world, the marvel of those friendships which God induces and the pure loyalties he inspires, which are like a mirror of the gratuitousness and generosity of his love.

J. M.

Toulouse, March, 1963.

Revised for English edition February 1970.

15

I

FOUR NOTEBOOKS

1906 — 1926

Raïssa's Journal

FOUR NOTEBOOKS

1. First Notebook: 1906—1917

[THE first 78 pages of this notebook are filled with prayers, psalms and litanies copied out in her hand, with the most loving care.

In the middle, her *Consecration of oneself to Jesus Christ, Wisdom Incarnate, through the hands of Mary* (according to Grignion de Montfort), Heidelberg, 25th March 1907.

Two prayers, in the form of humble little hymns:][1]

Plombières, *June 1906.* –

> My God I am here before thee
> I crumble into nothing before thee
> I adore thy greatness
> My need is immense
> Have pity on me
> Let thy spirit dwell in me
> Let the Holy Spirit live in me

---

1. Raïssa would not allow these hymns, naïve songs which sprang straight from the heart, to be regarded as poems. They remain outside her poetical work. But they marked happy moments

The love of the Father and the Son
So that I may love thee and thou me
My God let my heart be pure
My intention be upright
My body be chaste
My God, let no one suffer through me,
May thy truth enlighten me,
May thy will be done.
      Amen.

Versailles, rue de l'Orangerie, 1909.[2]—

1.   If I were sure of pleasing
    Jesus, my sweet Saviour
    On earth I should have already
    A paradise in my heart

2.   And if Mary protects me
    Her blessed Son will receive me
    In the company of the Saints
    Who walk with Him in his Paradise

3.   Like a wandering sheep
    Whose shepherd is seeking it
    Seek me, merciful Mother
    Bring me safe to my Lord

---

of great significance to her—as well as to Véra and myself who were very fond of them and sang them for many years. (J.)

Since any attempt to render them in English verse would destroy their simplicity, it seemed best to give a plain, literal translation. The second is in rhyme which would involve artificial inversions and distortions of the original. (Translator's note.)

2. The original, written in rhyming quatrains, was designed to be sung to a tune of César Franck's in the "Hundred Pieces for Organ". It was published later in a collection of hymns edited by Abbé Roblot.

4. I have nothing that can please
   This God of Majesty
   And yet all I can do
   Is love Him and call to Him

5. All my being desires you
   Most perfect Truth
   O Wisdom that draws us
   And no resistance is possible

6. I am a stranger on earth
   Teach me your Law
   Teach me the fear that hopes
   And the love of your Cross

7. Saint Veronica, you whom the Lord
   So richly repaid for your kindness
   By leaving you, dearest of Relics,
   The print of His face on your napkln

8. Ask one thing for us incessantly
   Ask for a love so generous
   That in our souls will at last appear
   The true image and likeness of God

9. Victorious St. Michael
   In praising the Lord
   Join us to your angels
   "Who is like to our God?"

10. May you be blessed in heaven
    May you be blessed on earth
    You who praise the Father
    The Son and the Love of them both.
                        Amen.

*

26th November 1914. – Dates that have been important for us up to now.

Léon Bloy receives our first letter on the feast of St. Barnabas, June 1905.

Baptism of Jacques, Raïssa and Véra: 11th June 1906, St. Barnabas.

Raïssa's first confession: 22nd July 1906, St. Mary Magdalene.

First Communion of J., R., V., at Sacré-Coeur: 3rd August 1906, Finding of the Relics of St. Stephen.

Conversion of Jeanne, J.'s sister; baptism of our niece Éveline: 12th November 1906.

Confirmation of J., R., V., at Grenoble, after some days passed at La Salette: 6th July 1907, Octave of the Holy Apostles SS. Peter and Paul.

(Beginning of daily Communions, 27th June 1907, at La Salette. – Dedication to Our Lady as her "slave": 25th March 1907.)

Baptism of my father: 21st February 1912, Ash Wednesday. Confession, First Communion and Extreme Unction: Thursday, February 22nd.
Confirmation, by Monseigneur Gibier: Friday 23rd February.
His death: night of Friday-Saturday, 24th February.

Conversion of Ernest Psichari: Tuesday, 4th February 1913 (Shrove Tuesday).

Reads his confession of faith in front of the statue of

Our Lady of La Salette, in our little oratory in the rue de l'Orangerie. Père Clérissac, Jacques and I were present. Then makes his first confession.

Saturday, 8th February 1913: Confirmation at the Bishop's residence in Versailles.

Sunday, 9th February 1913: First Communion at Versailles, Chapel of the Holy Childhood.

This conversion is shortly followed by that of Massis.

J., R., V., become Oblates of St. Benedict: 29th September 1912, feast of St. Michael, at the abbey of St. Paul at Oosterhout, at the hands of the Father Abbot, Dom Jean de Puniet.

Permanent vow of J. and R.: 2nd October 1912, at the Cathedral of Versailles, feast of the Holy Guardian Angels.

21st November 1913, feast of the Presentation. Death of our friend, Père Baillet.

From October 1913 to July 1914, Père Clérissac said Mass in our home every time he stayed in Versailles; thus we had Mass all through Christmastide, the 3 Masses on Christmas Day and all through the month of May. During this time J. often heard him preach in Paris, at Notre Dame de Lorette; I only heard him the last day which was Whitsunday; in the morning he had said Mass in our home and blessed some roses. Ernest Psichari served Mass; unforgettable day; in the evening he, Ernest and all of us, including Mother, came back together to Paris and had dinner together.

In June 1914, Père Clérissac arranges with the Father Abbot

of Solesmes our stay near Quarr Abbey for the month of August.

1st August 1914, we land at Quarr; stay there for two months.

2nd August, declaration of the war which soon involves all Europe.

22nd August 1914: Ernest Psichari killed at Virton (Belgium).[3]

5th September: Charles Péguy killed at the Marne.

Death of Pius X, 20th August 1914.
Jacques had received a letter from him on January 8th 1914 with a blessing for his book on Bergson.

Death of Benson and of Miss Baker.

16th November 1914, feast of St. Gertrude, death of our beloved Père Clérissac, within about 5 days of the first anniversary of the death of Père Baillet who introduced us to Père Clérissac. Both were treated with great gentleness, both died in their sleep without having known the torments of the last agony.

The 6th of November 1914, Jacques began his course at the Institut Catholique.

These years which were not lacking in graces have also been abundant in all kinds of suffering; we have almost never been without suffering, either each of us on his own behalf or for one of the two others. Recently our dearest

---

3. Virton was the place indicated in the first news of Ernest's death. In fact it was at Rossignol that he was struck by a bullet in the temple. (J.)

friends have been taken from us, their souls ripe for heaven made this life too sweet.

Now what remains seems almost worthless and the horrible war which is raging, with its accompanying hatreds and atrocious miseries, would make this earth hateful if one did not know that in some way all is well because there is divine will and permission. There remains nothing for us but to ask more than ever for the perfecting of our souls, so that by aspiring to nothing but Heaven, they too may be worthy to be admitted there the day God wills!

1915

Versailles, *12th September* (in the Russian calendar, 31st August in the year 1883), – my 32nd birthday. Sixteenth Sunday after Pentecost (feast of the Holy Name of Mary). – The liturgy of this day is in accordance with my most constant petitions and reminds me of everything I love.

19th October. – Abbé Combe sends me a relic of Mélanie, three and a half lines written in the hand of the seer: "He wounds in order to heal, he does everything, my beloved. There has to be response from us and again it is God who prompts it. It seems to me that it is a good thing, when the Beloved has made himself master, to keep one's eyes fixed on God, the sun of justice."

27th October. – Visit to Abbé Millot (Vicar-General of Versailles). "My line is simplicity," he says, and it is true. I even think that it is the simplicity of a saint.

Mid-November. – Someone has slandered Jacques to Canon Gaudeau, denouncing him, and also Bloy, as a *satanist.* Good cross.

J.'s little article on Père Clérissac appeared in the *Couronne de Marie.*

29th November. – Began to read, or rather to translate, the *Summa contra Gentiles;* on the second page, this text: "Jucundius est (sapientiae studium) quia *non habet amaritudinem in conversatio illius, sed laetitiam et gaudium.*" (Wisdom VIII, 16).

30th November. – Resumed reading the *Summa Theologica* in Père Pègues' Commentary. Q. 35 a. 5. And promptly, in the *sed contra* I find the same text.

Is it not God inviting me to emerge from the weariness of spirit induced by many petty preoccupations and to fix my gaze only on Him as He has so often told me to, and now again through Mélanie: "It is a good thing, when the Beloved has made himself master, to keep one's eyes fixed on God, the sun of justice."

1st December. – Jacques brings me a book by Abbé Sandreau, *Les degrés de la vie spirituelle.* I open it at random and I find what I need pp. 514–563. "To tell you the truth, during the thirty years in which God has done me the favour of attracting me to a more interior life, I have found no more effective method of making great progress in it than this general cutting-down of reflections on the difficulties one encounters and on everything which does not tend towards God or to the practice of the virtues" (Letter of Venerable Marie of the Incarnation).

5th December. – Important conversation of J. and myself with Père Dehau, at the Church of St. Augustine.

9th December. – Adore – adhere.

The same disposition which makes us annihilate ourselves
before God is that which He exacts from us to unite us to
Himself. It is thus that "the last shall be first". The joy
of adoring! Because, in annihilating oneself, one finds
Him whom one loves. The ego is an obstacle to vision and
possession.

10th December. – Today everything seems to me so difficult that I feel I could have said to God in all sincerity:
"Don't be afraid to help me by giving me the grace of
renouncement and other virtues, for I see my impotence
so clearly that never again will I attribute to myself the
least of the good you will have worked in me" – always
with the help of divine grace.

The other day I dared to present myself before God and
show him my soul in all its ugliness, with the confidence
that He was willing to heal it and beautify it, He who can
and who alone can!

Do not poor invalids attract mercy by showing their
wounds?

Seek perfection, why? Our Lord wishes it: "Be ye perfect
as your heavenly Father is perfect." And why does he wish
it? Oh! It is because it is justice itself! Sursum corda.
Habemus ad dominum. Dignum et justum est.

Vere dignum et justum est, aequum et salutare, nos tibi
semper et ubique gratias agere, and this is perfection.

And if we do not desire justice itself, we are not truly
men! What do we desire then?

★

Humility, annihilation before God, that is only too easily understood! But the humility of a saint before all creatures? I understand it like this: the creature, even when holy, is of itself *that which is not,* as God said to St. Catherine of Siena. In thinking oneself above some other soul, one thinks oneself something and therefore one lacks the humility due to God, which is to recognise our own nothingness. Whereas if one does not esteem anything in oneself but recognises a grace as coming from the mercy of God one is not lacking in humility, nor in justice, for one attributes nothing to oneself. Thus St. Paul was able to enumerate a great many graces which had been given him. Usually, when one recognises some good in oneself while comparing oneself to one's neighbour, one behaves like the pharisee. We should never look except at God and ourselves and only concern ourselves with our neighbour to render him service. "It is I who am the judge," said the Heavenly Father to St. Catherine of Siena, "it is not you." And even if we were to discover nothing to find fault with in ourselves, we should not on that account be justified, St. Paul says.

1916

In November 1915 we made the acquaintance of Père
Dehau, whom the war had brought to Paris.[1] Master of
Père Garrigou-Lagrange and coming, on his recommendation, to hear Jacques at the Institut Catholique. I saw
him again on December 5th at the Church of St. Augustine,
and since then he has come several times to Versailles,
and in spite of all the need I had of a guide, I did not think
of addressing myself to him. – A little time before meeting
him, I had ardently prayed to Père Clérissac to send us
someone from heaven to guide me in silent prayer

---

1. How I wish I could one day speak more adequately of this
exceptional man, who united powerful intellectual genius with
the deepest spiritual experience and whose influence affected
many minds, than I have done in one of my first essays in which
I used him as my inspiration in sketching the chracter of *Théonas*
in my book of that name. He was an incomparable help to me in
going deeper into the riches of St Thomas' metaphysics and
theology. (J.)

("*oraison*"),[2] but it was some time before I realised that my prayer had been answered.

All the same, I was at a difficult moment, of dryness, weariness and bareness. I was struggling alone. At first I took to reverting to a longer time of silent prayer; it began by quiet absorption ("*recueillement*"),[3] lasting half an hour or a little more.

At the beginning of Lent this year, I had made the Lord the sacrifice of a very legitimate feeling, but one which seemed to me to take the place of his Love. He readily rewarded me by making my interior life easier – but after

---

2. The word *oraison* signifies in general silent prayer, the prayer of the heart. More specifically, and in the way Raïssa uses it, it signifies, not meditation in which the soul is occupied in considering ideas, concepts and images, but a wordless, intuitive and quite simple prayer, a loving attention to God in which the soul is primarily occupied in letting God have its way with it, and in which, as St Thomas expresses it, it suffers divine things, in silence void of words, concepts and images. Raïssa explains herself on the subject of this, so to speak, experimental knowledge of divine reality, in faith and love and dependent on the gifts of the Holy Spirit, in the letter "On Contemplative Prayer (*Oraison*)" in "Brief Writings" at the end of this book.

3. As to the word *recueillement*, it indicates an inner state which, far from being "concentration" due to voluntary effort, is rather a gift received, a quiet absorption of the soul which, far from being inertia, is a secret and unifying activity too deep to be perceived; such, for example, is the case of *recueillement poétique* and *recueillement mystique*. (On the subject of these, see Raïssa's study "Magie, Poésie et Mystique" in *Situation de la Poésie*. English translation, *The Situation of Poetry*, New York, Philosophical Library, 1955.)

It is difficult to find a satisfactory English equivalent of these two words *oraison* and *recueillement* which are currently used in French and which so constantly recur in *Raïssa's Journal*. "'Mental prayer' and 'recollection' have neither the simplicity nor the flavour of the original French. Moreover they risk giving a wrong im-

Easter I fell into a great sadness, having the desire to occupy myself only with God and being unable to.[4] Finally on May 3rd, 1916 a conversation with Père Dehau changed my life in a remarkable way.[5] I am copying out again here notes taken from day to day.

Versailles, *Wednesday, 3rd May*. – Visit of Père Dehau: resolution on his advice to give all my mornings to resting

---

pression to readers unaccustomed to the technical vocabulary of theologians." Such at least is the very decided opinion of Jacques Maritain, who has earnestly implored me not to use these terms. After we had both gone into the problem very minutely, we decided that the best solution was to use alternative expressions when the context demanded it, such as, for *"oraison"*, *silent prayer*, *wordless prayer* (or, often, simply *prayer*); and for *"recueillement"*, *absorption in God* or *quiet absorption*. The reader can thus refer back to this footnote in order to understand the precise significance of the terms *oraison* and *recueillement* in the original French, which, moreover, it has seemed advisable to use themselves in a few cases. (Trans.)

4. I remember the state of trouble and helplessness she was in then: seeking on all sides what God willed and coming up everywhere against blank walls. (J.)

5. It must be thoroughly understood that it was not in virtue of a general theory applicable to any soul attracted to God, but by reason of the particular exigencies of the particular vocation in an individual case, that Père Dehau gave Raïssa the advice which changed her life. To Véra, whose spiritual life he held in singularly high esteem, he never gave the same advice.

I may add that the help and devotion of Véra, who in her quest of union with God had assumed – and with what vigilant charity – the rôle of Martha in our home, allowed Raïssa to *live*, and to live according to her vocation, but never dispensed her from the burdens imposed by the service of souls and the service of truth, for it was her vocation itself which demanded she should load herself with such burdens, as it were in addition.

With particular reference to the years at Meudon, see Olivier Lacombe's letter at the end of this book. (J.)

in silence with God, according to what God will ask. Not to let anything disturb me unless someone comes to fetch me.

Friday, 5th May. – Silent prayer fixed at ten o'clock. *Obliged* to begin it about 10, very strong inducement to quiet absorption (*"recueillement"*).

6th May. – Silence (*"oraison"*) lasts an hour and three-quarters. Absorption in God very deep. Who can prevent God from having mercy on me? Read St. Thomas.

Sunday, 7th May. – First word of the Mass: *Misericordia.* Seven o'clock Mass. We had barely returned when the same quiet absorption took hold of me; inner retirement; the five minutes my sister stayed with me seemed to me very long. Lasted nearly all the morning in strong, successive waves. Continued even during Massis' visit between 11 and 12. Short moment of absorption towards evening, after which my soul was calm and refreshed.

Monday, 8th May, St. Michael. – Mass at 6 a.m. As soon as I was alone (at home) could not even say Prime; absorption in God for twenty minutes; then Prime, silent prayer, Terce, a little St. Thomas, prayer, and so on till about quarter past ten. After lunch, during my rest, wordless prayer for about thirty or forty minutes.

9th May. – Still the same prayer of absorption (*"oraison de recueillement"*) without preparation.

14th May. – Mass at 7.30. Then absorbed prayer in successive waves till midday.

22nd May. – Prayer less vehement in character, more transparent.

25th May. – "Be still and know that I am God." – Precept of the Sabbath or of Sunday. *Be still*, leave all occupations and *know*, know God, contemplate him, give him your thought and your heart; give thanks to him. Impression that this is what is demanded of me each morning; this seems proportionate to my strength, since it is a simple and easy thing which all men ought to do at least on Sunday – and they do not do it.

Saturday, 27th May. – Mass and Communion. Two hours in prayer. The second time, gospel of St. John, ch. 20, particularly verses 15–17. Mary! That one word, and Mary sees and gives herself wholly. Rabboni! My master! But Rabboni is a tenderer word, it has the ring of "Beloved Master".

During this prayer, delicious tears.

30th May. – Mass and Communion. More than two hours of contemplative silence.

1st June. – Ascension of Our Lord. Reading; quietly absorbed at these words: ". . . by applying their lips to the blessed side of their Redeemer." Contemplation of the Saviour's sacred breast, our rampart, our tower. Contemplation of the filial Heart of Jesus, the delight which the Father takes in this purity, this innocence, this trust, this abandonment, this infinite adherence. Contemplation of the love manifested in this adorable Heart. The Word, like a giant, has stridden over the infinite distance between God and the creature. Henceforth nothing can stop the Saviour's love of us. He has bridged the infinite to take on flesh like ours.

2nd June. – Visit from Père Dehau who assures me that "omnia clara, omnia consonant".

5th June. – Paris. Prayer in the train.

27th June. – Mass and Communion. Between 9 and 12, almost uninterrupted *oraison*. First of all, without definite consideration, then, trying to say the Litany of the Sacred Heart, at the first invocation, *Kyrie eleison,* obliged to absorb myself, my mind arrested on the Person of the Father. Impossible to change the object. Sweetness, attraction, *eternal youth* of the heavenly Father. Suddenly, keen sense of his nearness, of his tenderness, of his incomprehensible love which impels him to demand our love, our thought.

Greatly moved, I wept very sweet tears and I prayed the Heavenly Father to be willing to accept all the time I can give to *oraison* to make up for the forgetfulness of so many others. Joy of being able to call him *Father* with a great tenderness, to feel him so kind and so close to me. Never before have I felt that, and it was so sudden and unexpected.

(Once though, in 1907 or 1908, I was seized with a feeling of familiarity with God, with Jesus, with Mary. I wept and exulted. It was as if there were a perpetual spring

35

of joy, of sweetness, of happy certainty welling up in me –
it lasted a long while – and the memory of it has not been
effaced.)

28th June. – Mass and Communion. Silent prayer almost
without interruption, rapture of love.

29th June. – Absorbed prayer, a long time with short
intervals. "If thou didst know the gift of God."

1st July. – Meditation on the Blessed Virgin. The
Blessed Virgin is the spoilt child of the Blessed Trinity. She
knows no law. Everything yields to her in heaven and on
earth. The whole of heaven gazes on her with delight.
She plays before the ravished eyes of God himself. The
Father did not behave like this to his beloved Son; because
the latter is his Equal, condescension towards him is not
possible. Everything in his task here below happened with
the rigour of justice. He who took on the sins of the world
paid for the sins of the world.

2nd July. – *Oraison* full of sweetness on the Blessed Virgin.
. . . She is the calm lake of celestial Peace; the very pure
mirror of the eternal Light; the white, sweet-scented rose
on the breast of the benign Trinity.

15th July to 7th August. – Wordless prayer more difficult.
Nakedness of the soul. Fear of God. Tranquil melancholy:
feeling of having the heart filled with all the troubles
past, present and to come. Véra ill. Jacques tired, exhaust-
ing himself to earn our daily bread, having no time to
write. Mother who still seems so far from the faith. Still the

same need of my mornings in silent absorption, though these last weeks it is less pronounced, does not last so long and passes in a great barrenness of feelings and thoughts.

. . . Grace is something divine; by it we cry Abba! Father! The Father is he who gives *of his life*. The Creator gives only being, as the artist gives form. The statue is not the child of the sculptor. We are the children of the heavenly Father.

15th August. – In the midst of recollection, anxiety of the heart; desire for I know not what, spontaneous appeals to the Lord: my Lord and my God; my sweet Jesus; my *unique Jesus;* aridity of the soul, anxiety; need to stay there before God, "like a land without water". Aspirations and sighs into the darkness. Same state during Communion.

16th and 17th August. – Same anxiety. Where shall I find my rest? In silence. In abandonment to God. In annihilation. In humility, patience, wide charity.

18th August. – Quiet absorption which allows me to read St Thomas and to take notes. Ordinarily such absorption makes all reading impossible; the attention is riveted.

19th August. – Departure for Bourg-la-Reine.[6]

20th August. – Good morning. Absorption in God, peace, without images.

---

6. We spent some days there with the Bloys. (J.)

29th August. – Mass and Communion. Prolonged and very sweet recollection after Communion, and the idea that I would not be able to retire within myself later [in the day]; this was true.

31st August. – Jacques' departure for Pontaubert.

Still the same prayer. It seems to me that God is forming my heart to charity, to humility. . . . If I do not accept what my neighbour teaches me, God will not teach me either.

Life hidden in God. Not to see in my neighbour anything but the love with which God loves him, and his wretchedness as a creature which is no greater than my own wretchedness and which makes God himself pity us and draws down his mercy on us. All the rest is vanity and pettiness.

All the month of September, the same prayer. More frequent God-given absorption after Holy Communion.

Greater and greater obscurity in silent prayer.

Sometimes, during the time of *recueillement* the heart kindles more and more, up to the end. The love is well and truly felt. At other times, it is more diffused.

The body is in a state of great and pleasant repose, no matter what its position.

In this state of wordless absorption, necessity of isolating myself (I spend all my mornings in my bedroom), of closing my eyes.

Sometimes, however, a very sweet feeling of peace and love when reading St Thomas or some pious book.

One day I decided not to pray in silence the following morning, on account of some pressing work. The next day, I set out to say Prime; it took me an hour; the compulsion to silent absorption having been stronger than ever.

Père Dehau says that it is the prayer of quiet *(oraison de quiétude)*.

Wrote to the Father Abbot of Saint-Paul . . . "For five months now He has gently compelled me to devote all my mornings to Him. He does not say anything to me, the dear Lord, but he induces me so strongly to be alone with him that I prefer those moments of silence to everything in the world and cannot break them without regret. So I offer these long rests for those who do not observe the Sunday rest and are never still to know that He is God."

Beginning of October. – The truths of faith refer, some to the divine Majesty, others to the mysteries of the humanity of Christ, which St Paul calls (I Tim. 4) the Sacrament of Love *(Sum. theol.* II-II, 1, 3). – Thus the entire humanity of Christ is the Mystery of Love. Jesus crucified is the image of the Father offended by sin; crowned with thorns by the contempt of His will. The pierced feet of Jesus signify that the offended heavenly Father is prevented from running to our aid. – Jesus whose pierced heart signifies that what we had offended was Love itself.

Thursday, 12th October. – Intense absorption in God between 9 and midday.

People who do not want to set themselves to contemplative prayer before they have acquired all the virtues are like a little seed which would refuse to allow itself to be put in the earth before it had grown its root, stalk and leaves.

Oratio est "clarissima gratiae testificatio" (St Augustine).

1917

Long interruption in these notes on account of the aridity of the prayer, always the same, and the tedium of always noting the same things. Tiredness too and illnesses.

Versailles, *12th March*. – Long, ardent absorption in God.

13th March. – Have pity on your poor little creature.

14th March. – Long absorption.

15th March. – Long absorption. – Holy Heart of Jesus.

16th March. – Sudden absorption in the middle of reading. Mark (3:5): *Contristatus super caecitate cordis eorum.*

17th March. – Profound absorption in God.
I want my neighbour to have a shelter in my heart as I myself want to find a shelter in the compassionate Heart of Jesus.

Laetare Sunday. – *Recueillement* at Mass and Communion, then at home.

19th March, St Joseph. – Enthronement of the Sacred Heart in our home. By Abbé Richaud, in the presence of Mme Bloy. Abbé R. saw my mother wipe away two tears during the prayers.

In the evening, a little attack of enteritis declared itself which prevented me from going to lunch the next day with Mme. Ph[ilipon]; I may say that it is extremely rare that I can fulfil a promise to visit someone on a definite date. The obstacles nearly always present themselves in the form of grippe, sciatica or enteritis. Amen.

Jacques has to go before the Army medical board on 30th April.

25th March. – Sunday. Silent absorption nearly all the morning.

. . . The knowledge the Angels have of sensible things is entirely spiritual and detached, consequently it never includes any note of triviality. The things which are trivial in relation to man in the very special hierarchy of relations which they have with him cannot be so for the Angels who know them simply by their degree of being.

26th March. – Interior affliction.

In certain temptations the soul is as if suspended over an abyss of sensible delights and it has to resist giddiness by the entirely spiritual remembrance of the only true good. And although, in this state, the soul suffers much, it must not fear anything or think itself abandoned. It would not suffer in the same way if it were unfaithful.

In that case, it would not feel suspended, but fallen, and emptied, in an incommensurable way, by the departing of the grace of God.

I have observed two quite distinct kinds of *recueillement* (absorption in God).

In the first, the eyes remain open, the intellect is enlightened and the soul is in a kind of ecstasy.

In the second, the eyes are closed, the intellect receives nothing, all the affections of the will are, as it were, focussed in a single point and united to God. A union which is ardent, often delightful, but takes place in a kind of darkness.

Monday in Holy Week. – Long silence with God in the morning and afternoon.

Tuesday. – Peaceful absorption from 11 to midday. Lively affections, with words.

My ejaculatory prayers: O my God who created me, have pity on me, have pity on your poor little creature. Fiat cor meum immaculatum, ut non confundar. My Jesus and my God! My one and only Jesus! My one and only Beloved! Spirit of Love and Mercy. My beloved and blessed Saviour! Blessed and beloved Mother. O my Lord and my God, have pity on your little creature, infinitely wretched.

Wednesday in Holy Week. – Vivid awareness of affective union. An hour. Read *L'Abandon à la Providence Divine,* by Père de Caussade.

Friday, 13th April. – Between 9 and midday, almost

continuous absorption in God. In the afternoon read a few pages by Père Clérissac on the Church.

Saturday, 14th April. – At first, lively absorption, inspired by yesterday's reading. *O Altitudo, O Bonitas!*

Looking at the photograph of a sculpture in Chartres Cathedral, God moulding Adam, drawn to recollection by the thought that our very loving Father continues to mould us like that right up to the day when our perfection is achieved in Heaven.

Ah! to stay like that under his gentle hand, one's head abandoned on his *maternal* lap and let him do as he will with one, always.

I seem to realise that for some time a certain work has being going on in my soul, which, if I obediently co-operate with it, will lead me to the total abandoning of all my will to God. The things I read, fortuitously, revolve round this, at the very same time that my personal plans are regularly thwarted. . . .

To sum up, this year I have been led to be vigilant above all about humility, charity towards my neighbour (and on this point I have been helped interiorly by an inclination towards sweetness and suavity), the abandoning of my own will to the will of God.

A feeling which opens the heart towards God is good. That is why *true friendship* is good. What I owe to Jacques' holy friendship!

26th and 27th April. – Long absorption in God.

29th April. – Absorption being driven in a car, half an

43

hour. Then an hour at home. Tomorrow the Army medical board for Jacques. Gospel of this Sunday (today): "A little while and you shall not see me, and again a little while and you shall see me." I think of Jacques . . .

30th April, St Catherine of Siena. – Absorption, but anguished absorption. Praying like Our Lord on the Mount of Olives, I feel convinced that I shall be answered as Our Lord was answered, that is to say that it will be for me to adhere to the will of God.

Jacques declared fit for military service. It's a joke. But what torture for me. I said the *fiat* promptly without waiting for my heart to feel its full pain. St Catherine chose the crown of thorns, she is lending it to me for a while.

1st, 2nd, 3rd May. – Intense absorption in God, but in anguish and suffering. God and Jacques simultaneously present in my heart. Agony.

From now on, I can only consider myself as dead. What life for me if Jacques went away? Therefore little matters what may happen from now on. This thought strengthens me.

God wants this ordeal to increase my love. No doubt in the agony I am suffering the feeblest amen is worth more than the songs of praise in prosperity. In this ordeal there is a humiliation which is good, an apparent dereliction designed to strengthen hope and to unite us to the crucified Saviour. Our Good Mother in Heaven – it seems that she too has turned her heart to iron against us. But, after all, has she not kept us for three years out of the clutches of this hideous war? Must not this Valiant Woman graft us at last on the tree of the Cross so that we may bear the fruits of salvation?

During these days of silence with God in suffering, I understand these strange words in the Canticle of Ezekiel: *Ecce in pace amaritudo mea amarissima.*

Really, during wordless prayer, I am as if attached to my cross. May God make my will attached to his.

5th May. – *Recueillement* and immobility in suffering: then supplication addressed to the Blessed Virgin. I then receive the intimate conviction that Jacques will be spared, that I shall be let off with anguish. Appeasement. I write at once to Jacques' sister to comfort her.

7th May. – Still *recueillement* in torturing suffering. Serenity, humility of J. He suffers only because of my pain.

8th May. – Mass and Communion. The absorption begins a little before Communion, about quarter past eight, and goes on till midday, even in the midst of some occupations. This time it is a long rest in peace, without bitterness, which comforts me greatly.

18th May. – On returning to Paris, we find a letter posting Jacques to the 81st Heavy Artillery at Versailles; so Jacques will do his training at Versailles, our separation is deferred . . . it matters little, my life from now on has lost its security.

19th May. – Père Dehau orders me to keep myself at God's disposition for silent prayer, afternoon as well as morning.

25th May. – During prayer I seemed to be surrounded with an atmosphere of suavity, limpidity and rest. In the imagination, the impression of being quite close to the Saviour, of kissing his wounds. The suavity, the peace and the light remained for quite a long time. A suave attraction towards humility, towards love of only the will of God, towards a spiritual life without apparent graces.

Whitsunday. – If someone despises me, I ought to think they do well to; if someone misjudges me, I ought to be convinced they are right. And yet I ought always to be happy and at peace – because I have the right like other creatures to keep close to God, to look only at Him and to forget myself in forgetting all the rest. If I love the place where God puts me I have the right to peace, to joy, to the contemplation of my God. And in leaving all things and all personal cares like this, I shall not be acting out of contempt or out of spite but, admitting all the contempt people may have for me, I shall peacefully seek a refuge in the bosom of the divine Mercy, to which my very wretchedness commends me more than anything.

Oh! the good, the sweet repose, when one has left oneself along with all the rest, to remain at the Lord's feet and to gaze at him, adoring his slightest wishes.

My God, I ask nothing of you but charity and humility. You cannot refuse me them, they are necessary.

I would like to have a depth of humility which would be even greater than the baseness of my sins, so as not to be confounded.

"Beatitude begins with humility" (St Augustine).

Sunday evening. – Visit from Berthe G[ilbert]. The

thought that God has been willing to use me for her conversion consoles me; this soul will intercede for me before the divine Mercy.

Whit Monday. – Hard day. Everything lacking.

Tuesday. – At last! Long, ardent absorption in God. I felt as if I had found Jesus again after a very long absence. Visit to Bourg-la-Reine. God allows me to understand Jeanne [Bloy] when she talks to me of such delicate things in prayer. I feel my soul full of supernatural friendship for her, though our temperaments are very different, clash rather, and though I know she has said some rather hard things of me. So it is God who disposes my heart like this. I am happy about it.

Thursday. – Prayer in the train.

Friday. – Dryness, except for a brief moment.

Saturday. – Good morning. It seems to me that while I am recollected I make a continuous act of love.

3rd June, at Bures. – The necessity of lyricism for expressing love. Necessity of singing in the Church: singing of the choir; singing of the crowds; the music of the spheres. Speech is too arid, too narrow to express such Love. To do so needs either splendid singing or silence which is another lyricism, that of unifying love, uniting with the divine Jubilation itself.

Thursday. – Long recollection of these words of the Lauda Sion: *Quia major omni laude.*

Friday. – Learnt of the death of that poor Le Dantec. Keen emotion, and *recueillement* which lasts all the morning.

I never tire of reading and re-reading the little work of Blessed Albert the Great on Union with God; a unitive virtue emanates from every page.

The eternal beatitude with which God rewards the renouncing of all things for his love reveals, in a sense, the worth of the things one must abandon. Yet what they are is nothing compared with one atom of grace.

Saturday. – A good morning. Spiritual rapture in successive waves during two hours. In the interval a Kyrie eleison was sufficient to rekindle the fire of love which overwhelmed the soul.

After dinner, another happy moment of silence with God.

Sunday. – During the Procession, same state as yesterday but lasting a shorter time. I notice that, contrary to what happened during the previous years, I feel no need to look, on the contrary, and that I have difficulty in singing. Need to let my soul remain wholly in God-given absorption.

Afternoon, visit to our godfather Léon Bloy for the eleventh anniversary of our baptism (which is tomorrow).

Monday, 11th June. – I am ill. Eleventh anniversary of our baptism.

The mind and will thoroughly given to God, thoroughly fixed in him – the heart, the sensibilities can still experience various passions, and offer so to speak, the matter of an independent life but not the form, since the will does not consent. It is then, for the mind, like an external spectacle, which may cause it to suffer, more or less. Sometimes immensely. Echo of the temptation.

16th June. – Feast of the Immaculate Heart of Mary. – What do we ask of creatures, except a little love and a little happiness? But God is Love itself and essential Beatitude. No, they cannot regret anything, those who have left all for Him.

O Altitudo! O Bonitas! To sing them it would need endless songs, floods of harmony.

It seems that the Holy Spirit pours them into the heart that is recollected, silent and burning with love. This profound silence is lyrical; it praises, it pours itself out in a mysterious manner; it runs through all the gamut of humility, of joy, of love, without any expression in words.

Deep *recueillement* towards the end of the morning, in reading the Mass of the Immaculate Heart of Mary.

19th June. – Jacques receives his diploma of Doctor of Scholastic Philosophy.

24th June. – "And the Word was made flesh and dwelt among us . . ." and he wore himself out for us, in order to convince us.

I do not want his adorable and blessed Heart to bruise itself against mine as against an inert and stupid wall.

I want, in spite of the intensity of my pain – to believe him, to obey him, to follow him, to have confidence in his love.

I do not want to shut my eyes so as not to see that He has

shed all his blood to give testimony of the Truth. Jesu, fortitudo martyrum!

27th June. – Silent prayer in the train.

28th June. – Absorption in God begins early, I cannot finish dressing. At rest about a quarter to 8. Lasts, very strong and ardent, three-quarters of an hour. Forced interruption which is painful to me. Resumes about 10, lasts an hour and a quarter, very deep, very ardent, ardour of love, feeling of the presence of God. In a more diffused manner, till midday. Sadness of finding oneself alone again afterwards, without this felt presence which transfigures everything and fills the heart to the full.

The mercy of God is as great as the distance which separates the Infinite from the finite, and it stretches out to bridge this distance.

Tuesday, 3rd July. – Settled in at Bures, where the Van der Meers are.

4th July, at Bures. – Ardent absorption for three-quarters of an hour, then more tranquil. Departure of Jacques for Versailles (he is reprieved till the 31st July).

7th July. – Deep and prolonged absorption. *Tu es intus.*

11th July. – Silent absorption in successive waves, without ever entirely stopping, between quarter past 9 and past mid-day (prayed for Pierre Villard), and becoming stronger and stronger. Was not able to say Terce, or to read a word; at the mere thought of opening the Summa or the treatise of Blessed Albert the Great my heart swelled with the presence of God and could not bear any more.

Sunday, 15th. – Mass and Holy Communion. *Recueillement* began at Mass, resumed at home until midday; and again at lunch-time so that I had great difficulty in staying at the table and in eating.

Men do not really communicate with each other except through the medium of *being* or of one of its properties. If someone touches the true, like St. Thomas Aquinas, the contact is made. If someone touches the beautiful, like Beethoven or Bloy or Dostoïevsky, the contact is made. If someone touches the good and Love, like the Saints – the contact is made and souls communicate with each other. One exposes oneself to not being understood when one expresses oneself without first having touched these depths – then the contact is not made because being is not reached.

Wednesday, 18th July. – Visit to Bourg-la-Reine [to the Bloys].

For several days return of the torment of which I have already suffered two bouts, in March and June—but this time with incredible violence, amounting to a real martyrdom of the heart. Thanks to God, none of our friends while we were living together knew the suffering that was ravaging me and Bures has remained for them and, to all appearances for me, the delicious retreat whose atmosphere of sweet joy attracts guests. For me it is the place of my greatest sufferings. But Jacques often found me weeping during my prayer.[1]

Thursday, 19th July. – Confession, Mass and Communion. Nothing is so good as to weep before God.

20th July. – O Jesus, how necessary your Passion was. How necessary it was that your adorable heart should be pierced for me. O Jesus! O Jesus! your sorrowful and bleeding heart tells me not to be afraid and to have confidence, it tells me so so insistently. You know, O Creator of all things, what a living heart is, a heart of flesh and blood where earth and heaven battle. You know that the human heart which seeks you has to suffer, to die a thousand deaths, in order to find you.

And if you are all torn and bleeding it is not only because you suffer for our sins. . . . But you have also wished, in your infinite mercy, to show us that you have a heart *like ours* so that we can go to you with confidence, and that we can have faith in the Faith which you came to bring by your Word and to testify by your death.

---

1. I did not dare question her. And she told me nothing of what made her weep at Bures. I understood later, when I read *La Vie Donnée*, especially "Transfiguration" and "Douceur du Monde," how cruel to the soul of the poet is the conflict between the attraction of the *sweetness of the world* with all its beauties and the gift of oneself to God which such an attraction makes appear to be against nature. And, to tell the truth, it was a question of a spiritual rending much deeper still which was then being foreshadowed and of which she speaks more explicitly later on in this journal (see in particular 30th August, 1925) and which during her years of extreme interior suffering at Meudon, she was kind enough to allow me to glimpse. (J.)

That is why I open my heart to you without any fear. I cry out to you with all the strength of my being and I would rather die than offend you. I abandon my heart to you, ready to suffer it to be wholly consumed in a faithful holocaust until the fire of divine charity, inextinguishable, soars above the cinders of all my earthly forces.

I have an inexpressible confidence under your gaze, my Lord – and not because my heart is pure! But because your gaze is good; because your compassion is great; because your mercy is all powerful, O Jesus!

The Passion is a great effort of Our Lord to convince our rebel nature in time of temptation.

During all these terrible days it was given me to understand most deeply, by suave and incommunicable knowledge, that Jesus' sufferings are for the believing soul a passionate witness to truth; a most merciful effort to show us that he is like to us in the capacity to suffer, and that from similitude comes closeness; from closeness, confidence; from confidence, friendship and greater abandonment.

Sunday, 22nd July. – Separation of soul and spirit: a tearing out, a breaking off, an indescribable rupture. The soul rushes headlong toward the natural object which is pleasing to it. The spirit recognises in God its Only Love.

All this takes place each morning, for several hours, during silence with God. This persistent *recueillement* reassures me, and makes me vividly aware of the infinitely merciful benevolence of God. Often, during this time, I weep. And Jacques has seen those tears.

23rd July. – Christine [Van der Meer] asked me to read

her some chapters of the Revelations of St. Gertrude. I was profoundly moved by hitting at once on Chapter 1 of Book III, *On a special protection of the Mother of God*, and above all on Chapter VII, *On the Lord's Compassion for us*.

"If a soul sorely tried by temptation takes refuge with me, it is indeed of her that I can say: *Una est colomba mea, tamquam electa ex millibus, quae in uno oculorum suorum transvulnerat Cor meum divinum*. If I thought I could not help her in this peril, my soul would feel so deep a grief that all the joys of heaven would not be enough to mitigate my pain. In my humanity united to divinity, my loved ones ceaselessly find an advocate who forces me to take pity on their various miseries. But, my Lord, she replies, how can your immaculate Heart, which has never been subject to any inner contradiction, incline you to compassion for our so various miseries? The Lord answered: You would easily be convinced if you understood these words the Apostle said of me, *Debuit per omnia fratibus assimilari, ut misericors fieret* (Heb. 2: 17). He had to be like to his brothers in all things so that he might become merciful. Then he added: The single glance by which my beloved pierces my heart is that tranquil, assured hope which makes her realise that I can and will faithfully help her in all things. . . . Each one can force himself to say with his mouth, if not with his whole heart, those words of Job: 'Even though I should be plunged into the depths of hell, thou wouldst deliver me from it'. And: 'Even if thou shouldst slay me, still will I hope in thee. (Job 13: 15).'"

24th July. – *Recueillement*. Offered to God my heart

preyed on by sorrow; let it be entirely devoured by it if it must be, for the love of God, and purified.

If we had nothing to immolate, what should we have to offer?

For a very short time I had the intuition of being like a victim accepted by God, and that my poor torn heart was accepted as a sacrifice. This is indescribable; it was a very pure instant, in which, as in a lightning flash, my heart seemed to me pure; truly sincere, truly suffering, truly given and accepted. But perhaps all that is only presumption: Jesus, Mary, forgive me.

25th July, St. James. – Mass and Communion. Wordless absorption between 9 and 10. Gospel. "I came not to bring peace, but *separation*." The separation of the soul and the spirit, it is Jesus too who effects that.

Nature laments; she pleads her cause with prodigious eloquence, with a terrible power of seduction. She is not rebellious. She is not perverse. She is herself. And being able to desire only life, she has to consent to death; to a thousand partial deaths more cruel perhaps than total death, because one has to live while suffering them. It is a real mystery for the creature. One of its most dangerous reactions then is to put the Faith itself in question. The reasons for believing. Oh, how one has proof then that faith is a gift of God! For reasons, during this torment, are not worth much. But God is there, who keeps our faith.

The storm of temptation sweeps away all that is frail and lays bare the rock of faith. The soul lives then on humility, on obedience, in the absolute nakedness of faith.

It seems to me that my soul is calming itself and detaching itself. What joy to break oneself and to give something to Him who gives us all!

Thursday, *26th*, St. Anne and St. Joachim. – Mass and Communion. *Recueillement* during Mass. Tears over my misery and a vivid sense of God's mercy. I wanted to be gone, to die. . . . I thirst to know at last this adorable Reality for which one must leave everything – and to which the Saviour calls us by the voice of his Blood and His Death. But this desire for death is not pure. It is nature's spite at realising that she will be granted nothing, God helping.

27th July. – *Recueillement* all morning. In the middle of the morning, letter from our friend Louis Pichet, on active service in Salonica, to whom I have not written, who knows nothing of my interior life. This letter overwhelms me and consoles me. Here it is:

"Dear Madame, I am writing you this note about a dream about you which has troubled me greatly. I was among your community and very happy, I need hardly say, to be there; but you were being the target of fierce attacks from the devil, which you were enduring with constancy. So I must be becoming superstitious for since the beginning of the war, there have been any number of coincidences of this kind. . . . I implore you, do reassure the stupid old fool I have become, by sending me a little word to give me news of you. . . ."

28th July. – Mass and Communion. Long time of silence with God. "Christ was obedient unto death."

When we are carried along by abundant and sensible

devotion, we feel that we are not obeying, but running with our whole will towards the accomplishment of the Will of God.

But when this sweetness of love gives place to the aridity of trials we feel that it is not possible for us to go beyond the mystery of the divine Will. Its Law demands our obedience. Faith obliges us to obey. We come up against the divine Majesty which makes us aware that it has absolute right of life and death over us and over each of our wills.

Christ himself wanted to know this absolute submission of humanity to Divinity, and this is why he is praised for having been *obedient unto death*. The agony of Our Lord on the Mount of Olives is the agony *of humanity as such*, the multiple and one-by-one death of everything which could live and which has not the right to live without the consent of the Creator.

1st August. – Jacques begins his training in the 81st Artillery at Versailles. I am at Versailles for a few days. And I live in the anguish of what is going to come after.

6th August. – Mass and Communion. During silent prayer I am at last able to breathe again! After the overwhelming pressure of these last days of interior struggle, although prayer continued without interruption, I seem to feel my soul detached, freer, as if a bond had been broken. I imagine a kernel which has been turned round and round inside the pulp of the fruit, if that were possible, so as to make it lose its adhesions; it is that kind of work temptations operate in the soul to make it free, and detached from the world and from nature. . . .

In an acute temptation, the soul has a double intuition:

1) of *its absolute dominion* over the action to be decided, consequently of its free will;

2) of *its absolute impotence* to decide for the good action without the help of God.

9th August. – All these days, intense absorption of the soul beginning at 8 or 9 a.m. As long as it lasts, I have extreme difficulty in attending to anything at all.

All things are entrusted into the keeping of love.
We only really possess what we love.

The partial deaths, exacted sometimes, are appalling. What must death itself be – what an effort of nature to escape the annihilation of this life – what a sacrifice has to be accepted there. Sacrifice is not essentially an expiation, but a testimony, a homage. "If the grain of wheat..."

15th August. – Mass full of quiet absorption, of light, of tears, of consolation. At the end of my thanksgiving, I felt myself touched on the shoulder: it was Jacques, on leave, against all expectation.

A thousand *Ave Marias* for J.

16th August. – Day of suffering, anxiety, especially up to 3 o'clock. At that moment I became calmer and began to hope. At 5, telegram from Jacques, sent at 3.20: "Temporary discharge one year."

If we ought to be merciful and compassionate towards our neighbour, we ought to be so above all when we know his dominant fault. The first impulse is to bring all our severity to bear on it, but, on the contrary, it is on that we must concentrate all our charity: for it is a weakness which ought to be sacred to us for God alone can deal with it and cure it. These great defects of our brothers are like a nakedness we are not permitted to look at. But let each one of us bring his infirmities before the eyes of God, humbly imploring him to cure us. For this divine gaze may see all nakedness, moreover everything is naked before him, who heals and reclothes with light.

19th August. – *Recueillement*, varying in intensity, between 9 and midday.

Some days of arid quietude.

Saturday 25th, Sunday 26th August. – Very intense and loving absorption all through High Mass, Communion and thanksgiving. Impossible to sing.

– Sacrifice is an absolutely universal law for the perfecting of the creature. Everything which passes from a lower nature to a higher nature has to pass through self-sacrifice, mortification and death. The mineral assimilated by the plant becomes living matter. The vegetable which is consumed is transformed in the animal into sensible living matter. The man who yields up his whole soul to God through the obedience of faith, finds it again in glory. The angel who has renounced the natural light of his intelligence to plunge himself in the darkness of faith, has found the splendour of divine light.

30th August. – To love and understand one's neighbour, one must forget oneself.

F

31st August. – Visit from Père Dehau. He tells me to follow the inward attraction to contemplative prayer at whatever moment it occurs, unless there is an express indication that God wills otherwise. Also to follow the inclination to restrain and mortify my tongue wherever my neighbour is concerned. I must expect great interior mortifications destined to make me very supple in God's hands. Père D. tells me that, among the souls he knows, I am one of those for whom this is most marked (this work of "suppling" pursued by God in all fashions – and the necessity of living by silent prayer).

Contemplative prayer is a means, but with a certain participation in the end, that end which is the beatitude of the elect.

8th September. – Ever since morning, I seem to feel the presence of the Blessed Virgin (yesterday too). Exceptionally good, sweet, happy day.

Until the 19th September, habitual *oraison*. Heavy interior trial.

Bures, *18th September.* – If God did not exist, there would be no moral law either. Because the natural law would have no supremacy over the will of man if that natural law were not the reflection of the eternal law. Without the eternal law, foundation of the natural law, the will of man, being superior to things, can no longer seek anything but metaphysical good (the will to be, Nietzsche) which remains all there is, moral good having vanished.

19th September. – My heavy burden has been lifted from me since morning; radiant day, I feel sheltered, warmed, comforted interiorly.

6th October. – God-given absorption does not alter the underlying base of sadness, even of sorrow, of which I have been inwardly aware for several months.

Sunday, 13th October. – I no longer note down the silent prayer each day; it has the same character of quietude, more or less sweet, more or less arid, more or less intense.

24th October. – The good Lord has returned with force. O my dear beloved, O my unique beloved – dearly bought, all the more loved. I say dearly because I am at the moment I am paying, but when I shall be fully in possession of my treasure (like the mother whose labour in childbirth is over) I shall find that I have given nothing – that all I have given is nothing in comparison with what I shall have received. "If a man should have given all the riches of his house for love, he would despise them as if he had given nothing" (Office of the Immaculate Heart of Mary). We give him our heart, our mind, our life; and He – will he not give us his Mercy?

Friday. – Terrible night. During the morning, deep absorption with God, but in suffering. O Jesus! my God who is promised to me!

Saturday. – Long *recueillement*. I suffer so much, in spite of appearances. My soul is a continual lamentation, a perpetual *miserere*. – Today everything is suffering and lives by suffering, there is no earthly refuge; wherever one goes one encounters the Wrath of the Just Judge. To find his Mercy, one must withdraw into oneself and weep for one's exile and one's sins. How the desire grows to see at last Him who is promised to us.

October – 3rd November. – Illness and death of our beloved godfather Léon Bloy. We had practically not left him, Jacques, Véra and I, the last 8 days. On Wednesday morning, 31st October 1917, I was at his bedside. He told me he was suffering greatly. "You are paying for the conversion of your godchildren." He replied: "The baseness of my nature is expiated by. . ." I could not catch the last words. "It is very painful, the spirit cannot clutch on to anything, it slides." After a fairly long silence, he said to me: "I would like to have done something for you" (I believe, I *know*, that he prayed very much for Jacques on the 16th August; he had said to me emphatically several times this summer: *You have nothing to fear*!). I answered him: "You have done everything for me, since you have taught us to know God." A little while after, seeing he was suffering terribly, I said to him: "I wish I could suffer instead of you, my dear godfather." And he, emphatically: "You do not know what you are asking. Jesus said that, you do not know what you are asking" (allusion no doubt to verse 22, Mat. ch. 20). And he added firmly: "*I* have done it." His wife came close to him and murmured: "Ave O Crux, spes unica"; and he corrected sharply: "O Crux ave, spes unica."

End of November or beginning of December, letter to the Father Abbot of Saint-Paul:

". . . The Fatherland, the one where men will love each other! How can one not long for it ardently? Here below men have claimed to be dispensed from loving God (who, they say, does not need our love) and to make the human race happy by philanthropy alone – and God, abandoning them to themselves, shows them that, without love of Him, love of one's neighbour cannot be realised on earth. But who wants to understand this? Alas, how sad to be few when it comes to loving and glorifying the only one worthy of love and praise. I am particularly struck by these things in thinking of the new Russia and its leaders, bolsheviks or no. Atheism is the basis of their culture, the heart of their heart, their very life blood. So everything that is happening was foreseeable, and, as for myself, who well know the Russian temperament, I have experienced an immense sense of horror. The tragedy of the affair is that one cannot even regret the old régime. The unhappy Russian people is unformed material, rich in good and bad potentialities, which easily allows itself to be manipulated in the name of any humanitarian idea. . .

"You have doubtless learnt, dear and most Reverend Father, of the death of our godfather Léon Bloy. All the newspapers have spoken of him – at last! but piling up errors and calumnies in doing so; *l'Univers* is well to the forefront with this kind of story. Some of them have not hesitated to throw suspicion on the faith and the sincerity of a man who has brought back such a great number of souls to God. The ardour, the greatness, the unshakeable strength of his faith – truly we have been witnesses of it for twelve years, and so have others along with us, like the great Christian and great scholar Pierre Termier. We were present at his last agony and at his death – at his last Communion on All Saints' Day, while the Church was singing the Beatitude of the poor. He was surrounded by many friends who wept at the faith and humility of this dying man, summoning up all his strength to strike his breast and receive for the last time Him whom he had been receiving every day for thirty years. . ."[2]

Sunday, 30th December. – Death of little Jean-François van der Meer. He was born on the 17th September 1915, on the feast of the Stigmata of St. Francis. Baptised at the hour and on the date of the Apparition of Our Lady of La Salette, the 19th September at 3 o'clock in the afternoon. All this little life was marked by suffering. He was a

---

2. I found in this notebook a copy, made by Véra, of a letter I wrote to Leo Lutkie on Jan. 20, 1918; I take the liberty of transcribing it here:

"During this week of agony, all of us around him had the impression that he was struggling *alone* with his God, in a final purification by suffering, when it was no longer poverty or human injustice but divine love itself which was penetrating to the depths of his soul, in supernatural darkness. Bloy, who had so loved splendour, and images of divine glory, and the taste of grace, but who set the intuitions of individual feeling above the light of intelligence, and who, by taking everything in a literal sense, believed perhaps too easily that he understood God's intentions, died thus without any consolation of the senses, in pure Faith, in that pure and obscure Faith which was his virtue *par excellence* and his strength. It was like an act of reprisal by divine Transcendence, and at the same time an infinitely merciful operation of Love, for one sensed in it both the ultimate pardon and the ultimate test. One sensed also in him an admirably secure and tranquil conscience.

"*I am expiating the baseness of my nature* he said at one point to my wife; it was one of the few things he said during that time. He took his last communion on the morning of All Saints, while the holiday bells rang in the distance, and *Beati pauperes* was

luminous child and I often saw strange gleams of intelligence in his eyes. He truly held a very great place in our hearts.

Fell ill on the Octave of the Holy Innocents, laid in his coffin on the 1st January, the Circumcision of the Saviour, buried on the feast of the Holy Name of Jesus, 2nd January 1918. Dear little Jean whom I loved so much, and who the last time I saw you received me with such a loving smile and clasped your little arms so tenderly round my neck, dear little Jean, who perhaps, in Paradise, are a great and very helpful soul, pray for me.

---

sung in the churches. How can I describe the tenderness, the sweetness and humility of his responses to the Litany of her whom he described as his Lady of Compassion? He may have committed many practical errors but he truly believed in the Holy Trinity, and in the coming of the Lord Jesus, and he truly loved Jesus and Mary and truly loved the Church, he always possessed magnificent sincerity and generosity, and marvellous tenderness for souls. The Catholic press, as might be expected, did not know what to say of him except for dismal stupidities, and was not even capable of paying homage to his extraordinary gifts as a writer." (J.)

2. Second Notebook: 1918-1919

1918

2nd January, Feast of the Holy Name of Jesus. – In the train, going to the funeral of little Jean-François: the name of Jesus like a kiss on my lips. This reminds me of a grace received on the same feast, in Heidelberg, in 1908; during Mass and for a long time after Mass, the blessed name of Jesus filled my soul with an infinite sweetness and an exquisite savour. The memory of it is sweet as honey.

Versailles, *16th January*. – Impression that now God exacts of me a harder life – of sacrifice – of self-giving – of vigilance over all my intentions. Everything grows darker. The time of childhood is over. . .

23rd January. – I love the saints because they are lovable; and the sinners because they are like me.

Sexagesima. – To walk on the waters, that is the vocation of the Christian. With no human support, in pure faith, in hope and pure charity. With no feeling, sometimes, simply keeping one's eyes raised to God. . .

7th February. – In the morning, prevented from praying in silence. In the afternoon, having urgent letters to write, I thought I would dispense myself from prayer, but the good Jesus took all his time and I could not do a single letter in three hours.

9th February. – Prolonged prayer in the morning. Temptation, sacrifice. The benefits of temptation: it maintains the vigour of the soul and its vitality. Sustained virtue is a proof of will-power, not of poverty of nature and insensitiveness, as is the opinion of those who yield to all solicitations from below. The disciples of Jesus are just as capable as they are of feeling pleasure and pain to the full. But, having chosen to go to God through all obstacles, they trample on their own heart if necessary.

One can even say that the sensibility of the determined sinner becomes increasingly blunted; whereas it becomes sharper in the strong man. And, in the heart of the latter, temptation can acquire a degree of acuteness all the greater because God, who assists at the conflict in the soul of the just (or of whoever desires to become so), knows that he will triumph in it by His grace. The human heart is then probed in all its depth – down to the very foundations of human nature; it seems as if every one of its fibres is laid bare and all its lineaments revealed. The richness, the complexity of nature is something resplendent. And yet the man, tempted to this point, who resists, strong in faith, marvels at a still greater wonder. All this magnificent and shattered nature, he soars above it by the impetus of his spirit. Carried by grace, he rises above himself. In spite of the pathetic appeals of his suffering, the clamours of rebellious nature and its specious reasonings – everything which at that moment seems to constitute his very being – he tears himself away from it all, he dominates it, in the obscurity of faith, and in that peace which surpasses all understanding.

Saturday, 23rd February. – To Christine: ". . . Have you noticed, dear Christine, these words of the prophet Joel, allotted to the epistle of Ash Wednesday: 'Rend your hearts and be converted to the Lord your God, for he is kind and compassionate.' Rend your hearts for God is kind! So therefore it is God's incomprehensible love for us which wills all our heartrendings."

Sunday, 24th February. – Letter from Abbé Gouin (whose acquaintance Jacques made in connection with La Salette) announcing his nomination as parish priest of Vernie, in La Sarthe. Luckily, he says, there is a presbytery there which can house fifteen people! Is that the shelter Our Lady of Salette is reserving for us next summer? It is curious this letter arriving just after every hope of keeping Bures has vanished.

Sunday, 3rd March. – Sudden conviction this morning in the middle of prayer that Jacques and I ought to go to Rome in the Easter holidays. To take Jacques' work on La Salette there. This conviction is accompanied by great interior happiness. I seem to see as clear as daylight that the moment to take this step has arrived. Curious, for up to now I have always felt "there was no hurry"; and the execution of this plan seemed to me bristling with insurmountable difficulties.

68

Sunday 10th. – The journey is fixed – it will mean a great deal of hard work to finish the copy. Véra is taking it on herself.

Silent prayer full of joy which delivers me suddenly from the residues of a heavy grief which was weighing on my heart and undermining my physical strength.

We shall have to make a number of expeditions for the passports etc., in the midst of Big Bertha's shells.

Monday, 11th March. – Visit from the Gothas. It lasted three hours and a half – numerous victims in Paris.

Giving, giving! We *must* give our life to obtain eternal life. Give it a thousand times before death – and make death itself *voluntary* (although it be inevitable) by finding it *good* – which is impossible without faith, hope and charity. But faith is obscure, and grace cannot be felt – and hope itself seems to be drowned in the bitter floods which sometimes overwhelm our soul; *intraverunt aquae ad animam meam.*

On account of the Big Berthas and the Gothas and our approaching departure for Rome, Jacques has decided to send Mother and Véra to Vernie where Abbé Gouin has invited us. Preparations for the two departures. Great tiredness; I wonder how it will be possible for me to stand fifty hours of travelling and two nights in the train. In the morning, especially, I have hardly the strength to get up and I envisage the fatigues to come with anguished apprehension.

All our friends think that I am very rash to make this journey and that Jacques is too, that the Austrian offensive may begin and that it will be impossible for us to return to

France for a long while. When I consulted Dr. Mondain, he predicted eight months of illness if I made this journey in my present state of health. He has left it to Jacques to decide now, and Jacques has no hesitation. But on the eve of the day fixed for our departure I was refused my passport because my father was Russian! The following day, contrary to all hope, I was granted it.

26th March, Tuesday in Holy Week. – Departure for Italy. All the doubts and obscurities have vanished.

We feel under God's will, entirely disposed to obey him in everything though we still do not know exactly what we shall do in Rome. Only one thing is decided: to take the manuscript to Père Garrigou-Lagrange and ask his opinion on the theological value of Jacques' work.[1]

We shall go step by step as God will lead us.

It is one of those very serious moments in life when one must opt for God, although many forces and arguments militate against it with an appearance of rightness. Baptism, for us, was one of those moments. . . And now we must risk many things for love of the Blessed Virgin – Jacques' present position, the peace of his future. Today all hesitation has vanished and our hearts are joyful. Remains the frontier to cross with the enormous manuscript (or rather the typed copy that has been made of it).

For our stay in Rome and our activities there, see Jacques' notes.

---

1. The work referred to is one on La Salette which has remained unpublished. (J.)

Departure from Rome on the Monday after Low Sunday, postponed feast of the Annunciation. Arrived at Versailles Wednesday morning. Jacques took me to Vernie on Saturday April 13th and resumed his lectures in Paris on the 15th April, in the midst of the bombs and shells of the Gothas and Big Bertha.

Vernie. – The house is ravishing, in the shadow of the church; view on to a big garden and the open country. But rather difficult early days for me, because the cold does not permit me to occupy the little rooms on the second floor. So I totally lack solitude, all the more because our friends the Van der Meers are with us.

18th April. – Good *oraison* in my little cell.

19th April. – Silent prayer in the living-room, in spite of the presence of everyone.
The same on the 21st. *Lumen tuae veritatis.*

21st April. – To Jacques: "Yesterday I had a good morning. Once again when I recollect myself, I again find the same simple demands of God: gentleness, humility, charity, interior simplicity; nothing else is asked of me. And suddenly I saw clearly why these virtues are demanded, because through them the soul becomes habitable for God and for one's neighbour in an intimate and permanent way. They make a pleasant cell of it. Hardness and pride repel, complexity disquiets. But humility and gentleness welcome, and simplicity reassures. These 'passive' virtues have an eminently social character."

30th April. – A good morning of prayer. Peace is impossible if one is not united to God and if one does not see all creatures in him. In him they have the unction of the Holy Spirit and lose their bitterness; and the one who thus sees them in God loses his own bitterness. For all created things have been rendered bitter by sin. The purer the soul is, the more it is united to God, the more it also becomes sweet and the more it tastes in all things the sweetness God pours into them by admitting them into the plan of his Providence. To dwell in God for his love, for our joy, is also the best means of bringing the good odour of Jesus Christ to others, of keeping our creaturely bitterness away from them and letting the suaveness of the Holy Spirit go out to them.

3rd May. – Two years already of this prayer of passive absorption (*"oraison de recueillement passif"*). How slow the soul is in being transformed! How the Saviour delays in increasing my love! But already his mercy towards me is such that it can only be measured by the infinite. All my heart and all my life is his.

To Jacques: "For two days I have had the great joy of being able to isolate myself in my cell where it is warm enough now. Ah, how good they are, these mornings given to the Lord! Thank dear Père Dehau very heartily for me for the advice he gave me, two years ago already. *'Domine ostende nobis Patrem et sufficit. . .'* Truly it seems to me that this is what this so simple *oraison* is: the heart takes refuge with the Father, and that is enough. And these things which one understands so quickly (in prayer) and which one has to express at such length, are they not 'the secret and mysterious speech of the Father, that speech which insinuates itself gently, like a faint whisper, into the most intimate depth of our being' (Tauler)? These very simple things which insinuate themselves gently and impress themselves strongly, like a concrete experience – are they not a merciful and fatherly lesson? . . ."

Sunday, 12th May. – Today the savour of the good God has hardly left me. From this dear presence, I have derived the deep conviction of the utility, the necessity of contemplation. Not only for the (accidental) glory of God and our own joy – that is too obvious – but also for the spiritual life of other men. If they lapse, is it not because they no longer remember the relish of God and of his Light? To make them know them, such is the outward function of the contemplative: the uncreated Light, the eternal Wisdom which is Christ; the substantial Savour which is the Holy Spirit.

External works themselves, works of mercy, owe their excellence to the power they have of revealing God's goodness.

There have to be souls solely occupied in drinking at this heavenly spring. Through them, afterwards, the living water of love and its divine taste reach those whose vocation comprises more activity. Contemplation is like a waterwheel which draws up the water and makes it flow into channels. If contemplation ceased entirely, hearts would soon be dried up (because all love presupposes a contemplation of the desired object).

At the well of Jacob, at the feet of Jesus, this is "the better part". And no doubt the repose of John on the breast of the Saviour, and, even more, the deep and hidden union of the hearts of Jesus and Mary, were the means of making the Apostles better able to savour the ineffable sweetness of the divine Lamb.

Thus love of one's neighbour, as well as love of God, obliges the contemplative to remain close to the divine source. So let no one whom God attracts to the quiet of contemplation, befog himself in the affairs of the world and take on the bitter taste of created things, wounded by sin. Doubtless he will have to render a strict account of all his comings and goings, as well as of every petty personal act which is alien to the divine mercy, humility, and goodness from which he himself profits so richly.

... Contemplation must bear its fruit for one's neighbour, even though it often dispenses from external works. This fruit is the Relish of God which one makes known by loving every creature with a love of charity, by forgetting oneself so as to remember only God who is in all things – who despises nothing that he has made – who suffers patiently our offences, and who corrects us only in loving us. No pettiness. No turning in on oneself. No defending oneself. Above all, no discouragement. No abandoning of contemplative prayer.

Not to judge bitterly. Leave the office of justice for that of charity.

19th May, Pentecost 1918. – First Communion of little Anne-Marie van der Meer (five and a half). Ravishing feast. We were there in full force; Pierre and Jacques have come for three days. Marvellous weather, the dining-room all hung with hawthorn. And the overflowing joy of all our hearts. On such occasions, how one realises that "it is good for brethren to dwell together"! If only my dear mother were a Christian. I hope for it always from God's goodness: she will be converted.

6th June. – Security, simplicity of this silent prayer: God is in us by grace, it is enough to strip the soul of all other love to find oneself in the presence of God alone. To love him solely. That is the whole of my prayer and I know nothing else. There is no special light, except sometimes a kind of instinct which guides me in important actions. Relish of God and formation of the soul; gentle, progressive and, as it were, easy; tending above all to love of our neighbour, to humility, to simplicity, to truthfulness, to silence, to nakedness of spirit – to the love of God. In this way one experiences how the two commandments of charity make only one.

10th June. – Contemplative prayer is not a question of making God descend from heaven! He is already there, in us, by grace. It is a question of descending into ourselves, to the bottom of our soul, and that, once again, by sweeping away obstacles.

18th June. – I marvel at the possibility which has been given me to rest in silence with God and experience true peace. It astonishes me to think of the value the Lord attaches to our poor love. One would really think that possessing our hearts is the end he proposed to himself in creating us; and he seriously pursues what he has proposed to attain: "It's no laughing matter that I have loved thee!" Is there not in this, as it were, a metaphysical necessity? Uncreated love, in pouring itself out on creatures, remains love and consequently is not satisfied unless another expansion responds to its expansion and makes union possible.

Versailles, *8th July*. – Jacques is once again discharged for a year. I came here to be able to pray better, and to know sooner. A little before 2 o'clock, a violent impulse of the soul threw me on to my knees and made me pray out loud to the Blessed Virgin with a voice and supplications which startled me myself – it was exactly the hour when Jacques was examined. Grace? Telepathy? Or both?

I returned to Vernie thoroughly ill.

Vernie, *21st July*. – I have given to God, with the truly extraordinary help of his grace, things I loved more than myself (for my love was disordered). I must begin to give myself; this is indeed much easier.

I have learnt to love men more for God – and to esteem them much less in themselves. Their judgment matters little to me, at least fairly little. What matters to me from now on is to be with my God, and to learn to love him truly. To make his Love and his Mercy known, by becoming kind and merciful myself, by living only on his Love.

3rd August. – Twelfth anniversary of our First Communion, at Sacré Coeur; then, penetrated through and through by the sense of my immense poverty, I implored the Lord to "give me something", I wept copiously, and I did not dare raise my mind towards any particular grace, I left the choice of it to God, and he gave me a magnificent alms – he gave free rein to his omnipotent love which deifies souls. O my God, what sorrow to have so often offended you again in these twelve years!

5th August. – Collect of the Mass for the Eleventh Sunday after Pentecost: "Omnipotent and eternal God, who through the excess of thy goodness *dost surpass the merits and desires of those who implore thee*, pour down on us thy mercy."

Ardent prayer, I want to be all God's so as to love him. After two hours of peaceful *oraison*, a wave of love, a real spiritual rapture, and that during nearly an hour, in successive waves. It seems to me that one thing only is demanded of me, to love my God, to spend my life in loving him. Immense gratitude for the mercy of God, for these graces of love he grants me and which he grants to other souls in contemplative prayer. All good belongs to him, to him be all the praise.

Humility which the graces of God imprint on the soul: the more he shows His generosity, the more evident our poverty appears; the more clearly, too, shines out the gratuity of God's gifts.

To *me*, these gifts? – Everything is easy to God. Who can prevent him from showing mercy? Who can prevent him from manifesting himself in the soul that he has made, that he sanctifies, that he dwells in, that he loves. Amator noster. In me or in the saints, it is always he who acts; to him be the love of all hearts.

6th-7th August. – How useful it is to recognise the graces God grants us. Humility and love grow together. Grace impresses humility on the soul as the seal prints the wax.

Love not only loves to pour itself out, it also *demands* to be received. . .

The Holy Spirit becomes more familiar when one knows

that it is he who acts, through the intermediary of the gifts, in the soul which contemplates.

The love of God becomes consciously felt in the heart. It presses on it; it seems as if it wants to burst out of the breast, to appear, to shine out in splendour – and this is an ecstasy of love!

This time silent prayer overflows into the afternoon; in spite of all my efforts it is impossible for me to remain at table, to eat; on the pretext of feeling sick I go and shut myself up in my bedroom till the end of this inexpressible rapture of the heart.

It is sometimes one aspect of God and sometimes another which ravishes the soul. Each of his Names, successively, unites one to him. It was Truth – Wisdom. It is Love.

16th August. – Letter from Père Dehau (dictated by him to a kindly secretary).

"My very dear child, your letter touched me very deeply. I bless the Lord for having made you so keenly conscious of the sweetness of his blessings and having at the same time put before your eyes a doctrine which confirmed and illuminated everything. There is not the slightest doubt either about this truth or about its application to you. So go forward, always as much and as fast as possible, giving the Master all the time he asks in a great peace and a sweet joy."

5th September. – After having been to Communion, I said to the Lord that he did not seem to me to be disposed to grant me the lofty graces of *oraison* (how I could have said such a thing when I deserve to be entirely ignored in the distribution of these very precious graces!). – The immediate response in my soul was the question about the Chalice: "Can you drink the Chalice?" I did not reply *I can*,[2] – alas, I feel so much that I cannot. I am terrified of the ordeals they say one has to pass through to achieve a great union with God. My soul is frightened and becomes sad: "Quare tristis es anima mea. . . Spera in Deo!" It does hope in God. It implores him to give it a generous heart. I feel that God leaves us free to choose between a measured love and a measureless one. But it would be a great misfortune to choose spiritual mediocrity – yet there is nothing but that or total immolation of oneself.

To love one's neighbour as oneself. What does one love most in oneself? One's own will. To love one's neighbour as oneself is to come out of oneself and to live in one's neighbour as in oneself, in other words to make our neighbour's will our own will – to love and do everything according to that will.

God is, in the highest sense, our neighbour.[9] Our love for him ought to be an *ecstasy*. Going out of ourselves, we ought to transport ourselves into Him, so that, no longer having any will but God's will, we should always love it, whatever it does with us.

We have no peace except when our will is accomplished. If we are united to God to the point of no longer distin-

---

2. But neither did she reply *no ;* she did not shirk what God demanded. As the rest of the entry shows, she accepted in full God's will for her – in fear and trembling, and without daring to demand the chalice, but without refusing it; and is not this how pure humility and equally pure generosity go hand in hand? And she had reason to be frightened. It was after this that the great agonies came. (J.)

3. *In via eminentiae,* and in this sense that, while being Other than we, he is more intimate to us than ourselves, by his presence of immensity and by his presence of grace. (J.)

guishing our will from his, we have found peace, and joy too, in a certain, more or less conscious, way.

This grace: to have no other will but that of God is the only one we can desire, demand unconditionally, seek with diligence – hope for without presumption.

As long as we remain capable of wishing something else obstinately, and of making anything whatsoever, even if it were the most precious graces, a kind of end in itself for our desires – we are imperfect, presumptuous or miserly. We are not in an absolute heart-to-heart relation with God; from this comes the greater part of our depressions, our fears and our failures.

I do not want to weary of asking God that his will should be accomplished. – Thy will be done! With that I shall have all the rest, even courage, even generosity – even that ecstasy of love in which one no longer lives by one's own will. But the peace which will result from this will perhaps be that peace which, "surpassing all understanding", leaves our nature in sorrow, travail, darkness, almost disquiet.

And it is of that I am frightened.

It seems to me that I no longer know what God wants of me and I am frightened of what he wants. All I can do is moan and implore and expect everything from a mercy that is infinite. I am truly too poor! suspended between heaven and earth by the mediocrity of my desires. Will the Lord will to change my feeble heart into a generous heart that is uniquely his? Do so, O all-powerful God, that there may be one more heart to love you wholly.

6th September. – It seems to me that what happened yesterday was meant to show me that my heart is attached to many things and that, seeing this clearly, I can disengage it by appealing more ardently to divine mercy. A disposition of the soul is required of me, and not exactly any change in my life. I must always act from within. I take courage, hoping that God will give me sufficient help in each particular case.

But I am discouraged in another way. All this morning intense absorption in God. – I was able only to read a little in Father Lambelle where he speaks of the highest mystical states. And the sight of the infinite distance which separates me from the goal causes me to lose courage once again. I no longer experience the tranquil serenity which prayer has given me heretofore. My heart is shaken with burning desires, by the fear of not desiring according to God, and by terror in the face of the grandeur of the good desired, which has never before appeared so terribly great, and by the fear of not making progress, and by the temptation to abandon the attempt, to devote myself to active life (which would lead me quickly to despair), like an earthworm enamoured of the moon which realises one day the folly of its love and goes off to bury itself humbly in the ground.

May the light of Christ deign to illuminate and bring order to this chaos.

8th September. – It seems to me that one could characterise the phases of divine love in a soul which has reached full spiritual development in the following way, under the seven Gifts on which the mystical life depends:

The Master:

> One considers God as Master and obeys His commandments.

The Friend:

> One seeks out His friendship by a pure life and by the desire to know Him better.
>
> One frequents the divine Friend by means of silent prayer.
>
> One makes Him one's Unique Friend by means of the prayer of union.

The Lover:

> In the purifications which follow this prayer one experiences all the torments of love.

The Fiancé:

> The Lord goes to the soul which He has embellished and contracts a spiritual engagement with her. The soul is wholly innocent.

The Divine Spouse:

> And the mystical marriage is consummated and maintained by an indissoluble union. The soul is wholly deified.

9th September. – A good morning.

A return of confidence. During absorption in God (*recueillement*), the impression that the Lord will help me forward. My desires these days have been largely good, I think, though tainted with an entirely natural attraction to happiness, where the will of God is not taken into account clearly enough. Furthermore, the demon has made use of these desires for spiritual perfection to discourage me by showing me the immense distance which separates me from the goal. Which proves that nothing is good except abandoning oneself to Providence and the Mercy of God. . .

> God the Creator also maintains us in
> existence every instant.

God the Redeemer also purifies us of evil
    every instant.
God the Sanctifier begins, continues
    and completes the sanctification
    of the predestined.

And this is "the act not of him who wishes, nor of him who runs, but uniquely of God who is merciful". (St. Paul.)

But to whom is God merciful? To those who place their hope in Him:

"Ad te Domine levavi animam meam. Deus meus in te confido, non erubescam." (Ps. 24.)

This divine confidence is an infinite grace, and we must work every day to plant it in the soul. Confidence is the only weapon of the humble, the poor and the weak.

"Noli timere, vermis Jacob," said the Lord. (Isaiah, ch. 41.)

11th September. – Departure of the Van de Meers for Paris and Holland.

16th September. – I get nowhere by looking at myself; I merely get discouraged. So I am making the resolution to abandon myself entirely to God, to look only at him, to leave all the care of myself to him, to practise only one thing, *confidence*; my extreme wretchedness, my natural cowardice leaving me no other way open to go to God and to advance in good. So, thoroughly convinced of my total inability to do anything good whatsoever by my own strength, I must think of myself as a little fledgling bird in the hand of God, as in a nest which I cannot leave, having only very feeble wings. I must not even worry about this extreme weakness, but devote myself only to praising and loving the very gentle hand which warms me.

Trust is the form grace takes in the poor one who is striving towards God.

19th September. – Reading *The Castle of the Soul* disturbs me. Is it that the translation is bad? Is it the manner, material rather than formal, in which St Teresa expresses herself that worries me? Definitely I ought not to leave Blessed Albert the Great, through whom the Lord seems to want to provide for all my spiritual needs.

4th October. – Departure of Jacques and Véra for Versailles. During their absence I am ill, absolutely without strength, and immensely anxious about them on account of the terrible epidemic of an unknown illness which is called Spanish influenza for want of a better name.

But this anxiety was not groundless: Jacques and Véra return on the 12th, and on the 13th of October, Véra develops influenza with the beginnings of congestion of the lungs. Temperature of 104°, no good doctor, great difficulty in procuring medicines. In my own broken-down state I am absolutely beside myself with grief. I can already see my little sister dying. Père Dehau, who is there, cannot manage to make me listen to reason: but God's goodness grants me half an hour of *recueillement* which calms me and comforts me.

At last Véra reaches the convalescent stage, then M. le Curé falls ill. We take him into our house and Jacques nurses him. Mother is at the end of her tether, for we have been without a servant for the past month. I help her as much as I can but I myself can hardly stand upright. M. le Curé is not very ill. I am afraid of Jacques' catching the infection.

On the 1st of November, early in the morning, dear Dr Pichet arrives. M. le Curé, better, says Mass. I want to give thanks to God for this, but I have the feeling that all is not over yet. Indeed, in the evening, relapse of M. le Curé.

At last our invalids are getting up, but now the peace of Vernie is disturbed by the arrival of American soldiers who loot, steal and kill each other when they are drunk.

11th November. – Armistice. End of the nightmare of the war, at last! On the feast of St Martin. Everything has been miraculously quick since our offensive of the 18th July.

1919

Vernie, *1st January*. – I am copying out here what Père Dehau said for Jacques to pass on to me during Jacques' last trip to Versailles (October).[1]

"Let her take the portion the good God gives her. The good God *does not want* bodily mortifications for her. Above all, let her not attempt them, let her not even think of them.

"*Contemplative prayer, full stop, that's all*. She is not to think of anything else. Remain with Jesus. Offer as mortification all Our Lord will determine himself through the sufferings of *oraison* (no time for a lot of things which seem necessary, periods of aridity, anxieties, temptations). Accept all that in a spirit of mortification. And only that." (The dear father might have added our continual illnesses.)

"Not settle down in comfort and well-being? – Yes, to be sure, but one mustn't exaggerate. Quietude assumes a

---

1. We all three spent the scholastic year 1918–1919 at Vernie. I had obtained a year's leave from the Institut Catholique de Paris in order to prepare my *Introduction Générale á la Philosophie* and *Petite Logique*. (J.)

quiescent state. One mustn't aim to make the body suffer, but rather to *put it aside, in abeyance . . .*

"The generous immolation of oneself for the love of God; *or* a love that *above all* contains suffering.

"Virtual suffering is superior to actual suffering (*it is the suffering of Jesus in Heaven*); and it is found in love.

"Charity, the god of virtues, contains everything eminently. Ama et fac quod vis. It is love that does everything. Everything is drowned in love, transfigured, far above the order of moral virtues, in the celestial ocean of charity.

"Let her fear absolutely nothing. Let her never think about this matter of suffering. Contemplative souls are often frightened in advance at the idea of the crosses. But that will not happen, or not as we think. It will be transfigured.

"Mixed up with these fears are temptations of the devil who, being unable to destroy the spiritual edifice, tries by every means to make one come down to the lower floors, to make one go down right into the basement. He sounds alerts, he makes the sirens scream. Let her not bother about the diabolical sirens, let her never go down to the basement.

"If she is afraid, if she is terrified, let her *put herself straight away into love.* She feels herself repulsed by the divine excellence (terrifying centrifugal force of the virtue of religion). The only solution is love, the charity which alone can put us on the level of friendship with God. *Vis fugere a Deo, fuge ad Deum* (St Augustine). You are afraid of God, throw yourself into him by love.

"Double response to God: that of St John of the Cross: to suffer and be despised for your love. That of St Thomas: Lord, nothing but yourself. The first is inferior to the second, it is human, if not earthly. The other is angelic. St Teresa is not in the least an angelic type, she is a sublime woman but she is *wholly a woman.* Even with St John of the Cross, imagination and imagery – a glorified imagery, radiant with poetry – play an enormous part in his mode of thinking.

"With the angels, the problem of suffering does not arise since they cannot suffer. And thus the whole spiritual life (*in angels*) can exist without suffering. The angels die mystically, it is true. 'Let us die the death of the angels.' *Our* suffering has no other reason for its existence except to lead us to this death of the will. If love is sufficient, this death will be much better realised.

"Love does away with analysis. Not to think too much about St Teresa's distinctions; that impedes *the absolutely simple movement of love, which loses itself in the object and does not concern itself with the subject.*

"Religion says *you and I.* Love says *us.* Dilectus meus mihi et ego illi. And that is all.

"Hurry along the dead straight path of *oraison.* Let her look neither to right nor left, nor, above all, backwards. Hers is a soul which needs extraordinary limpidity. Not let a grain of dust disturb the atmosphere."

Beginning of February. – The Peace Conference makes one think irresistibly of the Tower of Babel. They will be scattered . . .

A fortnight in bed with an attack of sciatica. Distress of body and soul. All the same, I feel that, for four months, I have been tasting of the chalice foreboded on the 5th of September. My God, my God, how can I hold fast, with this frail body, without the help of *oraison?*

I would like to translate some of the smaller works of St Thomas, beginning with the *Divine Ways* and to have them published by Rouart. Grolleau and Rouart accept the idea. Will the Lord allow me for once in my life to fulfil a project?

Sunday, 9th February. – Jacques leaves for Tours (he will be away for two days on the business of Pierre Villard's estate).

Two hours after his departure, I begin to shiver with fever. It came on suddenly, and with no apparent cause. Do I then have to be ill every time Jacques leaves us? It is strange.

I take pity on Mother and Véra, worried to death with anxiety. Suddenly the thought that I might die before Jacques' return pierces my heart like a sharp sword. An absolute pain, so profound, so keen that it seems to share in the immateriality of the soul. I implore the Lord to have pity on Jacques; I take a little La Salette water; my soul becomes calm again. The fever makes me alternately shiver and burn. It lasts till morning. At midday, there is not a trace of it left. I am not at all ill, only tired. And I cannot help thinking that it was sent to me to procure me that moment of pure and acute suffering, offered to God, for an end I do not know.

Mid-February. – Copied out a few little notes on art (1917).

Art is an intellectual virtue which permits the soul to impress a sensible and spiritual human imprint on a given material; strictly speaking, it is the faculty of creating a new form, an original being, capable in its turn of moving a human soul.

The work of art is the living fruit of a spiritual marriage, a marriage which unites the activity of the artist and the passivity of a given material.

It is this creative faculty which gives the artist the sense of his particular dignity.

He is like an associate of God in the making of beautiful works: by developing the powers implanted in him by the Creator – "every perfect gift is from on high and cometh down from the Father of lights" – he creates, so to speak, in the second degree, using the power and the matter created by God.

Artistic creation does not *imitate* God's creation, it continues it. And just as the traces and the image of God appear in his creatures, so the human imprint is impressed on the work of art, the full imprint, not only of the hands but of the whole soul; hence the power to move us which great works have. They are mirrors of the spirit and the passions, of human greatness and human misery.

Merely to imitate, in the sense of *copying* nature, is to be outside the pale of art. To paint a landscape which resembles nothing is to violate, not art, but a material condition of art; this can be simply a folly; but it can also be an artist's folly and one which will sooner or later be turned into wisdom.

Thus cubism can be regarded as an effort to escape from the crude sensibility of the impressionists. It is abstract sensibility somewhat as mathematics could be regarded by some (such as Auguste Comte) as abstract natural sciences.

Art proceeds from a spontaneous instinct, like love, and it ought to be cultivated like friendship.

Ash Wednesday. – From a letter to Mère Marie-Thérèse:

"My heart feels sore all over by dint of suffering and sympathising; I hope the Lord will accept the offering of it, however poor it is . . . .

"One day, forgive me for being so naïve, I imagined that I had got rid of myself at a single stroke by becoming a Carmelite (yes, a Carmelite, because it is more austere); it was over, I no longer bothered about myself; then my soul opened great wings and breathed deeply and freely in God. As a result, I felt lighter for a whole morning. Oh, my good Mother, how I envy you!"

(In December 1918, I wrote to Mère Marie-Thérèse about Père Clérissac's book on *The Mystery of the Church,* and a letter of his[2] that we had published:

"On the subject of St Teresa, what can I say to you, my dear Mother? The poor oblate, attracted to contemplative prayer by her on the very day after her baptism, has always, quite simply, cherished and admired in her the beloved of God.

"Père Clérissac's aim, no doubt, was to issue a warning against a distorted interpretation, perhaps too common among 'those daughters of St Teresa whom other directors, prevailing over the spirit of their Mother, have made into introverted souls,' and who seek a pretext for their self-centred spiritual attitude in the misunderstood writings of the Saint. On account of this very thing, and of the pain you have felt, my dear Mother, we deeply regret having published this letter without the few necessary clarifications. But, taken very generally, it is so typical of the

---

2. This letter of Père Clérissac's was reprinted by Raïssa in *Les Grandes Amitiés*, 9th Edition, p. 237 (p. 239 in earlier ones; p. 201 in the pocket edition). (J.)

H

spirit of our dear Father, that this explains our wish to make it known.

" . . . Most certainly Père Clérissac was not thinking of St Teresa when he talked of those for whom 'the simple life of the Church was no longer sufficient'; how could one think that of any saint, least of all St Teresa? No. But when 'the simple life of the Church was no longer sufficient for men', God in his infinite mercy gave them saints, who, by explicitly describing the marvels of the interior life, were to arouse souls from the torpor into which they had sunk in the midst of a society which had forgotten the great liturgical life. On that point, we are certain of Père Clérissac's thought.")

10th March. – I seem to see in every man someone under torture. The happiest are happy only in hope. Some truly are so but these are (almost) angels. Some appear happy but these are hardly men.

There is no prayer of union except in passive contemplation.

It is an error to isolate oneself from men because one has a clearer vision of truth. If God does not call one to solitude, one must live with God in the multitude; make him known there, and make him loved.

But if one establishes one's life in the city, one must not saunter about with one's hands in one's pockets. One must take part in the life of the city and try to "establish all things in Christ".

Many pious Catholics have been far too fastidious and withdrawn, too ready to leave activity to those who understand neither its principle nor its end. Or else they have involved themselves in it with no knowledge of the things they are dealing with and their specific requirements. One must do everything well, especially if one has the perilous honour of serving Truth. Above all one must do no disservice to charity. Christianity is not only a force which makes for order – people have been a little too conscious of that particular aspect of it.

It is a dynamic driving force, in virtue of the charity and zeal which animate it.

The very order it establishes, and guarantees, is not for the good of the few; it is for the good of the greatest number, the common good.

Catholics have too often been the servants of what is least worthy of being served – the servants of those who invoke "order" only in their own interest.

Two things manifest the spirituality of the soul: the nature of the intellect and *pudeur*.[3]

Pudeur, in the human compound, is a spiritual instinct which reveals the *real* (and not conventional) superiority of the spirit to the flesh. It is a strictly human instinct, being

---

3. "Modesty", or "sense of decency", by which one occasionally translates the French word *pudeur*, gives only a very incomplete rendering of its meaning. No English word or expression seems to suggest the idea (contained in the word *pudeur* and used in this sense in the passage) of a very delicate degree of "modesty" – owing far more to inner chastity than to any social convention – which causes certain things, in particular involving the human body (but also the soul and sometimes its noblest and most cherished feelings), to appear as things which ought to be protected from the gaze of others, not because they are impure in themselves but because they might risk being in some way injured or soiled or profaned in the thought of others. In the circumstances, it seemed best to use the French word *pudeur*. (Trans.)

an assertion of the rights of the spirit over the domain of the animal nature. A specifically human instinct. It is found neither in the angel nor in the beast. But the more man lives like the angels, the more delicate his *pudeur* becomes – (the child, being still too little developed as man, is unaware of *pudeur*); it grows in proportion as the spirit fortifies itself against the flesh. Thus *pudeur* is not related only to innocence: the child is innocent but is ignorant of *pudeur*; it lies in the instinctive consciousness which the spirit develops of itself and of the part assigned to it in the human compound.

Pudeur and prudery are opposed to each other, are in inverse ratio to one another. A soul anchored in innocence by the grace of God and the purity of life ignores prudery to the point of sometimes seeming to be destitute of *pudeur*. Anyone who knows that God has done all things well is not ashamed of any of the things God has made when he relates them to the wisdom of God.

But as soon as man feels that any subversion threatens the hierarchy of beings: God, spirit, animal nature, and especially when the flesh enters into conflict with the spirit, *pudeur* raises its voice all the higher when the spirit is freer and more vigorous and behaviour more innocent.

Pudeur is commonly more accentuated in woman because woman is to some extent above and below animal nature: above, by the greater purity of her life – I am speaking in general;[4] – below, because her maternal functions are

---

4. Raïssa wrote these lines in 1919. – After the second world war she might have added (it is something she often said to me) that when woman thinks she has emancipated herself by rejecting what is characteristic of her nature "in general", her immodesty becomes worse than that of man. (J.)

vegetative rather than animal. For these two reasons it is more repugnant to her to be recalled to her carnal functions.

A true and total love, a Christian marriage, idealise even the flesh because they unite not only two bodies, but two humanities. They are good because they are willed by God. They are innocent and pure. Do not let us be more spiritualistic than the Holy Spirit.

Shame is not always a sign of a bad conscience. If I realise that someone has an impure thought about me, it is I who will blush.

If anyone lies in my presence, it is I who will lower my eyes . . .

*

Art draws all its objective value from its civilising power. It contributes works of goodness, of delicacy, of intelligence, of reason, – in a word of all the gifts which are the dowry of human nature, – it contributes to spiritualising man, to making him more ready to receive the natural and supernatural contemplative life, and to bear, through grace, savoury fruits for eternal life.

And certainly God does not need our preparation to make us divine – He can "make children of Abraham out of these stones". But He did not create nature for the purpose of despising her powers; on the contrary He likes to see these powers act within a framework of order, and to make Nature the collaborator of his omnipotence.

The Catholics of today, when they are sound on doctrine, are as a rule narrow-minded as regards the proper domain of art and its civilising function, the function of natural spiritualisation it has in humanity. They are hard on artists. And the latter may well wonder whether their natural gifts are a sign of their being among the reprobate. It seems to me that Catholics ought to possess a genuinely informed doctrine concerning everything which is human, a doctrine which conforms with truth, taste and intelligence. No timidity. No pharisaism. No ignorance. No prudishness. No Manicheism. But the full and luminous Catholic doctrine.

24th March. – Jesus, so many sinners who ignore you! All this disorder. All this hotchpotch of necessities whose end is uncertain. Only one thing is necessary, absolutely – to love You. And it is the only necessity which is almost universally ignored.

. . . Will you let everything go adrift? Come to our aid lest we fall by the wayside.

You will that the saints should constitute a great capital of merits and love – with which every soul leaving this world will be able to pay for its salvation.

You let sinners go their own way, you stir up the just to love you more – and you levy in advance the share of the poor people who only recognise you when they are dying.

This is the way the world goes, and you show that your kingdom is not of this world. This is how saints grow. This is how the Redemption is accomplished.

Brief method of *oraison.*

Put oneself in the presence of God.

1. *O my God who seest me.*

Purify oneself under God's gaze.
2. *O my God who created me, have pity on me.*

Enter into union.
3. *My Sole Beloved.*

25th March. – To Jeanne Bloy: "What has happened to
Mme. Erlanger? I have wondered whether she might not
derive much good from reading St Thomas, especially the
treatise on the *Law*. For me reading that was milk and
honey – it is true that the very abstract, very stark language
of St Thomas does not put me off. In that treatise he shows
the extraordinary tenderness, the really motherly care of
God for the chosen people and how 'all things happened to
them figuratively'; and that nothing could happen to them
which was not related more or less closely to Our Lord –
is not that an unheard-of privilege? So it seems to me
that this treatise on the Law is on the mercy of God
towards Israel and, as I read it, I did not know how to give
thanks enough for such a choice, such a predilection. But
since their motivation and aim is Jesus, if, being a Jew, one
denies Jesus, one denies having been chosen, loved, predestined and the *Law,* if it is not seen as a preparation
for *grace,* is no more than the severe revealer of sin. . . ."

Same day. – Art is a fruition: when the sap will be once
again Christian, the fruits will be so too, of necessity, and
without the artist having acted on purpose.

But there is a period of transition during which unity
is not yet achieved between the will of the man and the
sensibility of the artist . . .

People must not think that devoutness is enough in
itself to make a Christian artist.

They must realise exactly what pure and genuine art demands. The artist has, as it were, moral obligations to art. He has strict duties towards the work he has conceived: abneget semetipsum. If he seeks to please, he fails in his duty. But he has the right to try to make himself understood. Purity of intention is necessary to the artist. An artist who has integrity as an artist is very near to being a moralist. He has the feeling of a certain purity in himself. Rouault. – Cf. Cocteau's *Le Coq et l'Arlequin*. This angel of whom the artist must be the guardian is precisely his integrity as an artist.[5]

28th March. – Profound state of *recueillement*.

5th April. – Unusual *recueillement*.

My one and only Beloved, to whom shall we go?
You alone have the words of eternal life.
And you have, in addition, those of temporal life
Which are the Ten Commandments,
And the one to love You, which sums them all up.
The Truth and all it reveals:
Our beginning and our end. And the value of all beings.
And all the virtues that you love.

Whatever happens, my Only Beloved,
And whatever must be suffered
We shall have known happiness

---

5. In this notebook there are many other notes on art which I have not transcribed here and whose substance, like that of the fragment dated mid-February, has also passed into *Art and Scholasticism*. (J.)

(And grant that I may know it eternally in your Love)
The infinite grace of faith
The incomparable sweetness of your presence,
Your Light, O Christ!
Which enlightens every man in this world
Makes visible good and evil
Puts order into chaos
Points out the way,
Reveals all truth
And gives eternal life.
– This joy shall not be taken away from us
My one and only Beloved.

*

There is a joy suited to our animal nature and as perishable as it is.

There is a beatitude proper to our spiritual nature which reaches its full height in the blessed, in whom it is as immortal as the spirit.

There is a beatitude proper to the divine nature, infinite and perfect as God.

Who does not see that the other kinds of joy are only images and attenuations of this?

And that, far from carrying things to excess, we are, on the contrary, satisfied with very little when, in order to express spiritual and divine joy, we use words which express the sensible and earthly ones.

"Let him kiss me with the kiss of his mouth; thy breasts are better than wine" (Canticle of Canticles).

When we think, we have a vague awareness of our brain.

When we love, we have a slightly less vague awareness of our heart; the human make-up explains this.

But our love for God is no more carnal than our thought is bodily.

All our values depend upon the nature of our God. He is the Archetype. He is the measure of all things.

Now our God is Spirit.

Spirit therefore will be first in the scale of values.

And matter, bodies, will be last.

To progress, therefore, is to go from matter to spirit, from animal to man, and from man to God by the ladder of reason and grace.

To civilise is to spiritualise.

Purely material progress can assist in this if the promoters of this progress aim at relieving humanity of the heavy burden of material necessities and at procuring it the leisure necessary to the spiritual life.

But material progress which serves only to satisfy ever-increasing covetousness, all the concupiscences of the flesh, and the will to power, is a return to barbarism, that is to animality, to matter, to chaos.

Art, like the sciences, draws its social value from its civilising power. It is also a test of civilisation.

6th April. – Dr. Amieux is bringing us his eldest son René. A child reputed to be incorrigible, who has at last decided to turn over a new leaf and to come here for his religious instruction.

13th April. – Beauty of nature greater still, more appealing to the heart, more revealing to the intelligence when men know that it is the work of a Person, in other words of God (of three Persons, one should say).

So it is with the instinct of animals; it reveals itself as intelligence, justifying the naïve impression it makes on us, when we know that, in fact, it is the divine intelligence which has endowed animals with the instinct necessary for self-preservation.

It is God who hatches the chickens, and it is He who builds the nests of the little birds by an act of his Intelligence, which has once and for all provided for the needs of creatures destitute of reason.

It is the Lord who stretches himself out like a dead leaf over the eggs the hen is sitting on.

What did Jesus do for us? Did he not open his arms, stretch out his arms on the Cross, where he exhausted himself to the last drop of his blood, to brood over our souls till they hatched out in his Love?

Sub umbra alarum tuarum protege nos . . .

He said: "I have greatly desired to eat this passover with you!"

And our hen wanted to brood on her eggs, and became depressed and her comb went pale, because they took her eggs away from her.

And it was at the moment when our salvation was about to break out of the shell that Jesus immobilised himself on the Cross.

And in the last days of sitting on her eggs, when the hen felt the chickens stirring, she no longer moved, even to eat.

This humble creature has been a vivid image to me of the touching mercy of our God. And surely if we could perceive for one single moment that infinite mercy as it actually is, we should die of love, and we should enter into eternal Beatitude.

16th April. – Remark of Michel Rouault, Jacques' godson (aged 7): "If God is everywhere and we don't see him, we are looking through him all the time" (Letter from Marthe, 14th April).

Maundy Thursday, 17th April. – Véra gives me this very precious piece of news: Mother has taken to reading the Gospel which has been on her table for the past seven months!

I am not forgetting that Mère Marie-Thérèse has been praying for her specially these last days, during her retreat.

From the 10th to 20th April. – I made a kind of retreat. Sweetness of the quiet absorption which no other sweetness can equal.

23rd April, Wednesday in Easter Week. – Arrival of Charles Henrion. Another real friend. We have not seen him for nearly five years, and before that we had only met him two or three times – and we feel that we know him like a brother – and this is how we love him in the love of God.

12th May. – Various ways to God.

Souls familiar with the thought of God fly with a marvellous swiftness from the created to the Uncreated, if the perception of the created has been really profound, has reached the deepest foundations of being. They are like the diver who touches the bottom of the sea, and with a kick of his heel rebounds to the surface and comes up into the light.

From a particular truth, some leap to the idea of truth, and from there to the Truth which is God.

Others perceive good in this way; and others beauty.

Others still reach Our Lord through the awareness of a pure, acute personal pain, or through compassion.

Others, like St Francis of Assisi, through the knowledge of – and delight in – total deprivation, through which they feel they belong more intimately to Christ and possess all things in Him, etc.

We all have our limit. But, in general, we are not limited by a curved line. We are, rather, polygonal figures: beware of your neighbour! And let him beware too!

22nd May. – Resolutions. *Veni sancte Spiritus*.

Self-examination every day, at a set hour.

Very frequent short and fervent prayer.

Total abandonment to God.

Free my heart from everything it clings to most, such as following Jacques in his work, and helping him. Free it from prayer even, when prayer is impossible because of illness. For I continue to be ill in spite of taking all possible precautions.

Consent to be completely inactive and useless better to allow God to work in me, and to desire only what He desires.

Be attentive to divine impressions.

Be attentive to all the movements of my heart.

See to the purity of intention of all my acts, to perfect sincerity.

Mortify all bad inclinations.

Don't believe that everything will be accomplished in a short time.

Pray with confidence.

Value only the love of God.

Beseech Him every day to make me know and do His will.

Offer all my actions to God.

Do everything in union with Jesus.

Permit myself to be inactive (in the case of illness) and to read for pure recreation only when my conscience clearly allows it.

Request the grace of being able to make a general confession soon to an experienced priest.

Beseech the Holy Spirit to make me humble, and very obedient to his promptings.

Place all hope in divine mercy.

29th May, Ascension Day. – René's First Communion, surrounded by his father, Jacques, Véra and myself. I had just enough strength to arrive at the church at the moment of Communion, in the middle of the High Mass.

2nd June. – When we write the promised article on art for "Lettres", not to forget that nothing is higher than contemplation because nothing is higher than the love of God.

7th June. – Jacques' mother spent a few days with us and told us about one of her friends who was led to God by spiritualism. In the course of a conversation with Mother, whose heart I could feel completely softened – at last, after so many years – I had the chance to talk to her a little about myself. And since we had got on to the topic of rather extraordinary things, I told her that, a little more than thirteen years ago, before I even believed firmly in the existence of God, I heard in my sleep, just by my left ear, a voice so loud that it woke me up, and this voice said to me, a little impatiently:

"You are always asking what you ought to do: the only thing is to love God and serve him with all your heart."

My dear Mother, very moved, said to me: "Happy those whom God himself leads into the true path!"

Then she added this, which melted my heart:

"Why don't you talk to me about all these things, *since I believe in God?*"

And then my mother began to weep very sweet tears; I was just thinking those tears were sweet and at that very moment she told me so.

"There are tears which hurt," she said, "but these are doing me a great deal of good, they are good." And we parted very happy . . .

1st July. – Omnis homo mendax. Every man is a liar, either because he does not keep the promises he has made us or else because he keeps less than he seems to have promised.

Our friends fail us, and let us be sure that we fail them too, since we are men, as they are.

One deserts us because of an involuntary cowardice; another for some reason of prudence; another from simple indifference; this one has not understood . . . that one is too busy with other things . . . yet all of them love us and seek to please God.

So what can one say of enemies and of the envious?

God alone is faithful.

Prophecies. They rarely admit of exact dates. This is because time, which is almost everything for man, is almost nothing for God who binds together the past, present and future in his eternity. Let us clothe ourselves in the divine sentiments. In true prophecies, let us attach no importance to the date of their realisation. When they announce a good thing, let us ardently desire it. Let us remember that, for centuries, Patriarchs and Prophets sighed after the coming of the Messiah. – And from the moment of the Lord's death, the Apostles began to hope for and expect his glorious return.

St Vincent Ferrer and the Blessed Grignion de Montfort prayed for the coming of the apostles of the latter days whom the Blessed Virgin mentioned at La Salette. Perhaps we are asked to pray fervently for such an advent, still very far away but none the less desired by God, which we must therefore desire and hope for without wavering.

We are spending all the summer at Vernie before returning to Versailles.

3. Third Notebook: 1919-1923

1919 (continued)

Vernie, *11th July*. – Nowadays it seems more than ever that real good can be done to only a small number of souls. Because the world is being swept along by monstrous forces it can no longer resist. Men have unleashed forces they can no longer control.

So, more than ever, we must love truth and justice. Pray, love God more than ever, hope for miracles.

Nowadays the political positivism of Maurras seems awfully limited.

My Unique Jesus, in the midst of this new deluge which does not drown the impious but increases their number, preserve the unique Ark of the Church. My Unique Beloved, keep the souls whose sweet duty is to know you and love you safe in the shelter of your love. Increase the courage of those who wish to serve you.

Raise up great Shepherds who will be capable of giving their life for sheep.

Sweet Lord, everything is possible to you! Save this world which is perishing.

– The mercantile civilisation which is the civilisation we

have had since the fifteenth century is a pseudo-civilisation, lacking as it is in concern for the true good of the human and divine *city*.

Since the advent of Christianity, there is no true civilisation except that which, through the earthly city, *aspires* to the heavenly city.

Aiming at human and divine good through virtue, work, politics, the sciences, the arts, sanctity.

Holy Spirit, Spirit of Love, you are the guest of the soul not only because it receives you, but even more because in it you yourself receive the Father and the Son. You are the bond, the love-knot without which the soul could not unite itself to Jesus. It is you who draw down the Saviour by your unspeakable groanings and, by the infinite force of a love which is God himself, bring about the alliance and alloying of creature and Creator.

Purity of heart: I must free myself of all feeling of conceit about Jacques and the performance or the success, and even the intrinsic value of his work – so that nothing matters to me *in him* and in me but the love of God, "regarding *everything* as dung that I may win Jesus Christ and find myself in Him", with Jacques.

One single force can still be opposed to the general madness: intelligence enlightened by faith – to save what can still be saved.

15th July. – The disinterested search for truth and contemplation, and the love of beauty from which the arts derive *are not of this world,* because they are in the way that leads souls of good will to God, and serve to manifest the presence of God, as the visible things he has made serve to manifest it to upright souls.

16th July. – Among students there is generally more curiosity than love of truth. To know no matter what, to know as many things as possible.

The person who *loves* truth, seeks to know the first causes, an ultimate knowledge beyond which one cannot go.

What is a man who does not love truth?

Have always passionately believed in the possible knowledge of *that which is,* always aspired to the possession of absolute truth.

At the Sorbonne, disappointed by the sciences because partial.

Oppressed by determinism; distressed by relativism; liberated by the criticism Bergson made of all these theories. Comforted by the affirmation of a possible knowledge of the absolute.

Gripped at this moment by the divine Truth.

The realism and the faculty of disinterested contemplation proper to women make them lovers of metaphysics when they study philosophy.

I have always had the keenest desire to know the ultimate truths, not being able to base my life on uncertainties, not being willing to base it on feelings uncontrolled by reason.

God himself employs arguments *ad hominem*. He has a special argument available for every soul he seeks. Man must go to meet him by searching for truth. "We are incapable of not desiring truth and happiness" (Pascal).

"Truth is so obscured in these days and falsehood so entrenched that unless one loves the truth one cannot recognise it" (Pascal).

Avid of true knowledge, I did not know where to find it. At twelve, I thought it lay in medicine; at eighteen, in the natural sciences; at twenty, in metaphysics; at twenty-two, in theology. I know now that it does indeed lie there, and that holiness, when added to it, infinitely increases it, and that the wisdom proper to it can do without everything.

Know your religion, Catholics, know your greatness!

No science, no experiment can prove it wrong, it has the words of Eternal Life and also those of temporal life. "All that is true is of the Holy Spirit" (St. Justin). Everything that is true, everything that is good, everything that is beautiful is ours! And we alone possess the secret of happiness through the obscure and unifying knowledge of **love.**

As an atheist, I preferred metaphysics because it is the supreme science, the ultimate crowning of reason.

As a Catholic, I love it still more because it allows us to have access to theology, to realise the harmonious and fertile union of reason and faith.

It was not enough for me to live, I wanted a reason for living and moral principles which were based on an absolutely certain knowledge; God gives this unrest to those who do not know him in order that they will seek him. At that time I was not willing to allow any value to those *reasons of the heart* which suffice to indicate good and evil. I held these instincts to be invalid as long as the intellect had not justified them.

– Among all the sciences it is metaphysics which, after all, seems to me the best suited to a feminine mind with a gift for abstraction. I am not saying that women are gifted for cutting a figure as great philosophers – but only for understanding and assimilating the philosophy of great philosophers.

"Women who seek above all to please . . . who reflect little, who are quickly discouraged . . ." do not take up philosophy, and they do right.[1]

But those who seek to please God, if they have the taste for abstract truths, ought to cultivate their intellect humbly and fearlessly, for knowledge can only increase their charity.

A girl who studies philosophy, when she is gifted for it, exposes herself much less to "losing her simplicity, her freshness, her good sense, her faith," than a girl who frequents "the world". On the contrary, she finds in philosophy new reasons for being simple; it strengthens her good sense and her faith, while her *natural dowry* remains intact.

But young people of both sexes should be taught *true* philosophy.

---

1. I found here between the pages of this notebook a printed questionnaire sent by Père Peillaube on behalf of the *Revue de la Philosophie :* "Scientific inquiry as to the suitability of philosophical studies for girls". At that period girls were the best philosophy pupils at the Institut Catholique in Paris.

Père Peillaube had asked Raïssa to reply to his questionnaire. These are the thoughts aroused in her on that occasion which she has noted down in her diary. As far as I remember, she did not write a reply. (J.)

Women possess keenness of intellectual vision, but not *active* power of mind: they make excellent pupils but as a rule they do not create, either in the arts or the sciences.

They lack the self-control, the patience, the wisdom (in the speculative order where wisdom and power are synonymous) to order and co-ordinate, draw all the conclusions.

But they assimilate the great abstract truths extremely well.

"Metaphysics is the most abstract of disciplines", it is true, therefore very few men are capable of it, *a fortiori,* few women.

Yet, as it governs theodicy and ethics, a woman who is philosophically-minded is drawn to it by preference, in order to examine in this supreme light what her whole life ought to be. She regulates her whole conduct on these highest truths, even when she does not enjoy the supreme good of supernatural faith.

Woman's realism delights in the knowledge of ultimate realities.

Her sense of order – "she would tidy up God himself", Péguy said – is satisfied by being able to order her whole being in the light of intelligence. Her powers of contemplation enable her to love the truth she knows more intensely and, in certain cases, to increase her range of knowledge through the very love that she bears the Truth. Her great capacity for loving attaches her more strongly to the Truth and induces her to dedicate herself to it.

Faith has been attacked in the name of the Intellect. It is in the name of the Intellect that it must be defended nowadays.

One of the reasons for loving metaphysics is that it admirably disposes the mind, through the indubitable knowledge it gives it of its limitation, to that rational obedience which is receptive to faith (supernatural). "Rationabile est obsequium nostrum."

"Submission and use of reason, in which true Christianity consists" (Pascal).

Truth is the rule of the intellect and of the will, it has an absolute and legitimate power over the whole man. Not to follow the truth which the intellect shows us is to disobey God; for the intellect is, in us, a certain similitude of the uncreated light (St. Thomas).

"Philosophy is something cold and austere; it prefers truth to all the rest. . ."

Philosophy is cold . . . this is a prejudice. Philosophy, in its highest abstraction, is warm and burning!

The science whose ways all lead to God – how can one call it cold?

I give thanks to God who put in my heart such an ardent love of truth when, ignorant of the divine Truth, I lived among sceptics and atheists. That desire which the physical sciences could not satisfy because they are partial, and which modern philosophies completely frustrated by their relativism, was fulfilled by the revelation of Catholic doctrine and of Thomist philosophy.

Against them, no science has any arguments; no philosophy any advantages.

13th-19th August. – Visit of Père Garrigou-Lagrange. A few blessed days. Jacques Froissart arrives too, sorely tried by his mother's illness. Jacques reads Père Garrigou-

Lagrange his *Introduction to Philosophy* and his article on art.

Charity and humility of Père Garrigou-Lagrange. He does not despise the little religious congregations which have arisen in great numbers these last years, for he knows persons in them who are greatly privileged by God.

His admiration for the Carmelites of Avignon (he has just been preaching a retreat to them). The heroism of their penance; the great mystical favours of which some of them (Mère Marie-Thérèse in particular) are the object.

22nd August. – Illness, illness! I no longer leave my bed, so to speak. Impossible to be properly looked after here, the doctor has done me harm.

Annihilation of body and soul.

8th September. – Lying in bed, very ill, I was the victim of an excessively painful passive examination of conscience. It annihilated my soul little by little, showing it how utterly without merits, without strength it was. I could no longer find any refuge in myself, and I was, so to speak, driven to the borders of despair. Jacques, who was with me, seeing my grief which I could not hide though I did not talk about it – at least not at the beginning – tried vainly to comfort me.

If the feeling I experienced then were to persist in all its force, I think I could never again yield to a temptation of pride.

Up to the 24th of September, the date we return to Versailles, I get worse and worse. Terrible attacks of sciatica, etc. The morning of the day fixed for our departure, I do not know if it will be possible for me to get up. At last God allows us to leave.

At Versailles, I am already much better after two days – and then continue to get better and better, so much so that I soon recover my far from brilliant, but sufficient health of before the autumn of 1918.

I feel as if I had spent a year in Purgatory. My poor soul is quite shattered; it seems without life, without zest, without emotion. It seems fantastic to me that one can be moved by anything whatsoever in the domain of piety. I wonder how I can ever have been moved by sermons, services, devout reading, etc.

This lasts for some time, now I am slowly emerging from this dreary torpor.

Versailles, *8th November*. – Truly! Absorption in God would come back? But in how humbled a heart!

O Jesus, you are not like certain rich people who only give to those who know how to make money fructify. They do not help the sick or the old or the incapable.

But you, Lord Jesus, you give to all – and you only take back from him who lacks confidence in your limitless goodness and says to you: "Lord, I know that thou art a hard man."

A proud man envies the superiority which surpasses him.

A humble one, on the contrary, loves good wherever he finds it, and by this love, in some sense appropriates it to himself.

22nd November. – To Catherine van Rees:

"My very dear Catherine. Your letter overwhelms me. I marvel at the grace of God in your souls.

" 'I do not pray the Magnificat enough,' you tell me. But, poor victim of God! however little you do it, believe me, heaven is moved by it.

"Remember that Jesus himself cried out on the cross: 'My God, my God, why hast thou forsaken me!' And now he unites you to him so very closely in the very work of the Redemption.

"For if you expect consoling words from me, dear beloved soul, I have only this to say to you:

"That Pasch of which the Lord said: 'I have greatly desired to eat this passover with you'—you are eating it now with Our Saviour: the Pasch of the Passion and the Crucifixion, through which salvation comes to men. Through your sorrow and your patience you are co-redeemers with Christ.

"It is the sublime yet everyday truth of Christianity that suffering united to love works salvation.

"Believe that while your little Haditia was being born into the life of glory the reign of grace was being extended here below. Believe that while sorrow is immobilising you, torturing you, you are drawing hearts to God which needed your cross to raise them to the knowledge and love of truth.

"God has suddenly plunged you both into the very heart of this ultimate reality: redemptive suffering. And when one knows by faith (that is to say with all possible certainty) the marvels he works with our suffering, with the substance of our crushed hearts – can one coldly refuse Him?

"Dear friends, you who refuse nothing, you who bear such an extreme grief so humbly, I think you now have a greater knowledge and experience of all these things I am saying to you than I have myself and I ask you to pray

God for us, for we have often been wanting in patience in much lesser trials.

"May this terrible and blessed God make himself the comforter of your souls, he who has made himself like to us, St. Paul says, in order to be able to have compassion on all our miseries.

"Dear Catherine, with an infinite respect I kiss your heart in which I see Jesus present with his cross and his patience. In your heart and in that of your dear husband to whom I beg you to convey our brotherly compassion.

Your Raïssa."

*

"You believe because you want to be comforted."

– Yes, our faith comforts, as truth comforts, as love comforts, as the Paraclete comforts.

And you who think you owe your strength only to yourself, what do you know about it?

It is not because you do not love God that he does not love you – and it is not because you do not call on him for help that he leaves you to yourself.

And I tell you: you do not believe because it would hurt your pride.

1920

Versailles, *16th January*. –

> Heavenly and blessed Father
> See me here before you
> With Veronica's veil on my face
> The veil that bears the Holy Face.

> At the sight of the features of Jesus
> May your mercy be aroused
> And may it deliver me from evil.

> O you who created me, have pity on me.

*

Jacques on the *Revue Universelle,* philosophical editor. Extraordinary thing, this review which Père Clérissac so much wanted, which he spoke of to Massis, Jacques and Ernest, which Père Janvier was interested in – well! the project having been completely abandoned, now the review is being launched, and, as it happens, with Massis and

Jacques on the staff. It is the first time Thomist philosophy has had such a wide entry into the world of culture.

24th-27th January. – Jacques in Holland, seeing Father Abbot de Puniet, the Van der Meers and the Van Reeses again.

Abbé Cornuau is very ill.

2nd February. – Received from Rome, through the agency of Père Pègues, authorisation to have Mass celebrated at home as long as I am ill.

4th February. – A letter from the good Eugénie Marescot tells us of the death of dear Abbé Cornuau. The funeral will take place tomorrow. Jacques leaves for Montargis.

19th March. – Mass at home, intention shared with my friend Marie-Anne François: the conversion of the Jews.

21st March, Sunday. – Vitia Rosenblum brings Père Malvy, S.J. to see us. He turns out to be, like my friend, an ardent philosemite. I tell him about our projects, he wants to take charge of them.

He is seeing Mme François and her two converts in Paris. It is decided to have a Mass said for Israel on the 21st of April (Patronage of St. Joseph).

21st April. – Baptism of Odon-Jérôme-Jacques Lemaître (Jacques and I are his godfather and godmother). – As to the Mass for the conversion of the Jews, it did not take place, Mme François having been ill and myself too.

23rd May, Pentecost. – Père Malvy will come and say the Mass himself. We decide to have a meeting afterwards with our convert friends and it is Père Malvy who is taking charge of the instructions. Is this the path God destines for Mme François?

Père Malvy, more scientifically than theologically minded. Knows several languages. Simple; he greatly touches our heart.

I regret having broken off this journal as regards inner prayer. Certainly, it is always much the same, except that the duration of the dryness is longer (more frequent too). But however arid the *oraison*, the time given to it is no less; however arid it is, nevertheless I cannot replace it either by reading or by meditation which would do violence to my feelings and which tire me greatly; whereas arid silence with God sustains me, rests me and I would not give it up for anything.

I reproach myself for having too often tried to read in order to excite myself to devotion; it has only succeeded in tiring me.

31st May. – Letter from C. H. telling us about Éve Lavallière.

25th July. – Baptism of our godson Jean-Louis Barthe.

8th September. – Jacques Froissart enters the novitiate of the Carmelites at Avon.[1]

5th December, Second Sunday of Advent. – Death of Pauline Philipon after eleven days' illness. Very holy death.

---

1. In religion he took the name of Bruno de Jésus-Marie. (J.)

1921

Versailles, *17th February*. – To Émile Baumann:

"Dear M. Baumann, I want to give you my testimony on the subject of the expression of Léon Bloy's which troubles you; his exact words were these: 'The baseness of my nature is expiated by . . .' (I could not quite hear the words that followed, but I understood: 'by these sufferings'.) I cannot have the slightest doubt about this. The last words my godfather had the charity to say to me, because he saw me there beside him, quite overwhelmed with compassion, are forever in my memory; but I did not fail to note them down at the moment itself.

"I think that the plural, 'the basenesses' which appears more conformable with 'personal humility', could have added nothing to his own, profound and simple like all the sentiments he expressed in the last days of his sorrowful life. If 'the basenesses' had been the expression appropriate to what he felt, he would have used it, for you know that he never varnished anything. And, moreover, in the midst of all his cruel sufferings, he preserved all his lucidity, as I was able to observe when his wife came close to him, saying in a whisper: *Ave, O crux spes unica,* and he corrected sharply: *O crux ave. . ."*

12th March. – Total abnegation is my path (so badly followed by me).

All possible mortification, *interior*. In fact, it depends entirely on myself to create the "desert".

Jacques in Belgium since the day before yesterday, Sunday.

Monday, March 14th, lecture at Louvain on Ernest Psichari.

No date. – To Jeanne Termier-Boussac.

"Dear Jeanne, You well know that if I have not yet thanked you for the gift of your poems,[1] it is not because I have put off reading them. I have read them five or six times already and shall certainly often read them again with the same indescribable emotion.

"O you, the living, who, in books, only seek souls!

"Are we the 'living'? God knows. But you, Jeanne, you generously yield up the secret of a great and shining soul full of poetry and pain, of courage and faith.

"What would you have me feel, if not, above all, an immense respect?

"A feeling about you which is not new to me. It is what has always prevented me from showing you compassion in these years of mourning; forgive me if I have seemed to you indifferent. I saw your soul as a very precious work in the hands of God; watered by the bitterest, sharpest and

---

1. These poems, for which Léon Bloy has expressed his admiration, had appeared under the title *Derniers Refuges.* (J.)

most penetrating sorrow, but also 'standing at the foot of the cross'. And I felt too keenly the inadequacy of anything I could have said to you. And as to the 'words of eternal life', I knew that the Holy Spirit could not fail to insinuate them himself into the depth of your soul at the opportune moment, after the elapse of those evenings that God respects,

When there is nothing left in me in the black silence
But one vast cry, the ageless cry of Rachel. . .

"Today I can let myself say all that, dear Jeanne, because you yourself have spoken. And your words, poet that you are, have the admirable grace of being as beautiful and true as your heart."

No date (probably March 1921). – Our life is getting complicated, more and more people flock to Jacques; frequent visits, and very heavy correspondence.

How can I keep my time of silent prayer, already much cut into in the morning by illness and the fatigue that results from it – prevented in the afternoon by necessary work, visits, letters?

What is God's will?

If I could live like a recluse among my family?

But is not my duty to be at Jacques' side?

April-June 1921. – Illness. Numerous medical examinations. They have decided on an operation; however there is no hurry.

They are going to all lengths to cure me without an operation. They are sending me to Switzerland.

We have met the saintly Curé of La Courneuve, Père

Lamy – it was Dr. Vaton who brought him to see us on Easter Thursday 1921.

He said that day to Dr. Vaton and has since repeated it several times to Jacques and Véra that he had a very definite feeling that I should get better – and he is praying for this.[2]

Departure for Blonay, the 21st of June.

28th June. – *L'Ami et l'Aimé* (by Raymond Lull), p. 360.
"Where does Love die?
The Friend replies that it is in the pleasures of this world.
Where does Love live and nourish itself?
– In meditating on the other world."

And so once again: necessity of mortification and prayer. The saints have said that in all tones of voice!

My unique and adorable Jesus, it is because you are the Truth that I leave everything that is contrary to you for you; it is not because you reward the trouble one takes for you.

If I looked at the reward, perhaps I should not be able to prefer what is distant to the pleasure which is near.

---

2. I transcribe here, for mention, a note of Dr. Vaton's which I have kept among my papers.

"*30th March* 1921.—On the return journey in the car, only two sentences were exchanged, M. le Curé saying his rosary all the time as on the way there.

Question: 'Don't you think that Mme Maritain has something of Our Blessed Lady about her?'

Answer: 'Yes, I was *struck* by it!'

A few moments later and quite spontaneously, M. le Curé added: 'I have hope that she will soon recover.' These words were uttered very slowly and in a very positive tone."

I add that Père Lamy also told me (what at that time seemed completely improbable) that "she would make long journeys." (J.)

But to separate myself from the Truth – you would have to abandon me completely for me to consent to that.

That Truth which is Yourself, Being itself, and all Perfection – to separate myself from it would be to choose nothingness and truly to tear out my heart and soul.

13th July. – Of the difficulty of perfection in the world, where one is incessantly obliged to be busy with the management of oneself and of things – where one is at the mercy of all the occasions of acting imperfectly. The religious life is such a considerable help to renunciation.

In the world, in the midst of occupations, distractions and temptations of all kinds, what is there that can replace the boons of the religious life? We were talking about it this morning with Jacques.

Might it not be a greater humility and a more abandoned trust in the mercy of God who will take into account our good will, knowing all the various obstacles?

Yes, in spite of all the deficiencies and all the imperfections and all the sins, let us keep afloat by confidence and by the humble and constant recognition of our spiritual mediocrity.

Let us accept trustfully the state of life in which Providence has placed us. For God can sanctify us anywhere! And we, we might remain just as mediocre if we left the world.

To love. To abandon oneself. Nothing else is necessary to sanctification. No, nothing, not even silence with God if that is rendered impossible by real obstacles, interior or exterior.

The soul can be sanctified without, so to speak, realising it, and find itself at last united to God without having had the leisure to practise what it would have thought most necessary for this.

Avoid sin, humble oneself because of sin, never be discouraged. Love God, love, love.

That is the one thing necessary. All the rest can vary *ad infinitum*.

Wednesday, 10th August. – During silent prayer I feel inwardly solicited to abandon myself to God, and not only solicited but effectively *inclined* to do it, and do it, feeling that it is for a trial, for a suffering, for which my *consent* is thus demanded. I make this act of abandon in spite of my natural cowardice. . . And, in less than half-an-hour, the blood reappears, so it is not yet a cure, in spite of the air and the rest. Is it a serious attack which is threatening?

A month of illness. A month of convalescence. Jacques saves me by taking me out in an invalid chair.[3]

We have made the acquaintance of Ramuz.

19th October. – Versailles. Jacques is thinking of forming a society of the people who meet every month at our house to study with him this or that point of Thomist teaching. I propose that all those who join it should make a vow

---

3. Dear Père Garrigou-Lagrange, who visited us several times (he spent his holidays in Switzerland), sometimes took my place in pushing the invalid's wheel-chair along the roads. It was during one of these promenades that Raïssa had the idea of asking him if he would consent to come every year to preach a retreat to the friends we would gather together to hear him. He immediately agreed. That was the origin of the annual retreats of the "Thomist Circles". (J.)

of *oraison*, so as to emphasise the necessity of the spiritual life for those who serve God by intellectual work.

We are asking Père Garrigou-Lagrange to be the Director-General of the Thomist Circles and that the Circles should not be under the control of the Dominican Provinces.

Approval of Père Garrigou (letter of 2nd February 1922).

My suggestion for a motto has been accepted: O Sapientia.

1922

Versailles, *15th May*. – Understand this: Obedience is good not because of the goodness of the one who commands (provided he does not command evil things), but because of the benefit of self-forgetfulness it procures for the one who obeys.

For someone who has nothing at heart but to concern himself with perfection, obeying is necessary, and it little matters whom (naturally it is assumed that he has sought a director with the necessary prudence) provided that he obeys, that he forgets himself and is thus turned towards God.

Honestly, in these conditions, is one obliged to seek for a director among a thousand, or ten thousand? This seems to me simpler and easier.

17th May. – God and souls, there is no other interest in life.

God in the soul, there is no other aid.

18th May. – By uniting our small coins to the stream of

gold of the Passion of Christ we can repair the injury done by sin to the Divine Substance itself. Sin is *le mal de Dieu* (the refusal, the betrayal of God's love), the offending of God; in what manner can the Divine Substance, which is impassible and intangible, be touched by sin? It is a great mystery. But this offence is not a metaphor, since the divine Word became incarnate first and foremost in order to repair the deprivation inflicted upon divine Love,[1] "le mal de Dieu", sin, and glorify the Father; and only in the second place in order to save us.

Those who welcome Suffering make reparation through Christ and with Christ.

23rd May. – My only One, my Jesus, my God.
        God alone lovable.
        His love, the only happiness.
How to give myself up? What to do? Where to begin?
God, my God, deliver me from evil, that is to say from myself.
Root out self-love.
Plant charity.
Give me strength and purity.
Intoxication of love. It is not merit, but succour.

---

1. Our human concepts are absolutely deficient, there is in our language absolutely no word to express *what such a* "*deprivation*" (suffering, "*le mal*", metaphysically considered, is essentially a deprivation) *is in God;* this is something *innominatum*, for which there is no name. The only words we can use are merely metaphorical, yet what they designate is not fictitious, is not "a metaphor", it is real. Cf. above, p. 86 (Second Notebook, January 1st, 1919) what Père Dehau said to me about "virtual suffering" and "actual suffering". (J.)

You, Lord, give charity, increase love, the real, the substantial love.

Re-read Father Osende's article (*Vie Spirituelle*, July 1921). We ought to contribute actively to our sanctification. Passivity is given by God. Hence we ought to use all our faculties as well as possible unless God puts them at rest. The quietists put themselves at rest.

June. – At the request of Père Garrigou-Lagrange, Jacques and I have composed a little spiritual guide for the members of the Thomist Circles.

Mgr. Mariétan is willing to print it for us on his own press at Saint-Maurice, under the title: *De la vie d'oraison*. It will not be put on sale.[2]

The manuscript has been submitted to Père Garrigou who has approved it.

Wednesday, 28th June. – Pilgrimage to La Courneuve, with Jacques. Talked about C. H. with the saintly Curé. "It is daylight in that soul; when it is daylight, one sees clearly." "He has energy, he has heart, he has eloquence, he has everything!"

Thursday morning, departure for Switzerland.

Friday morning arrival at Val d'Illiez. I retire to bed.

Tuesday, 4th July. – Visit from Ghéon and d'Altermann.

Thursday, 6th July. – Silent prayer. Fire.

---

2. This edition was indeed distributed privately to our friends. It was later that we decided to publish the little work. (J.)

At Val d'Illiez we make the acquaintance of Charles Journet.

20th July. – It is evident that everything must be based on *the presence of God* and on his action by *sanctifying grace,* which gives the soul a special life, a *divine life*.

The divinely living soul attains its highest and most intimate simplicity in this divine life.

But it also lives a natural life which is multiplicity.

Contemplation requires the simplification of this natural life, and this simplification is obtained by active and passive mortification.

In order to be united with perfect Unity and Simplicity, the soul must itself become simple and unified.

To go further, I think a special action of God is necessary.

Mystical contemplation begins with this special action; this work of love is very particularly the work of the Holy Spirit.

31st August. – Letter to C. H. on contemplative prayer.[8]

Mother and I sorely tried by ill health. We are leaving Val d'Illiez as quickly as possible at the beginning of September.

Pilgrimage to Saint-Maurice d'Agaune.

Return to Versailles. Mother very ill with heart trouble. Preparation for our first Thomist retreat.

---

3. This letter is of particular importance. It will be found at the end of the book, among "Brief Writings". (J.)

Versailles, *30th September - 4th October.* – O Sapientia! First retreat of the Thomist Circle.

29th September. – Père Garrigou-Lagrange says the Mass of St. Michael in our chapel.

30th September, St. Jerome. – Beginning of the retreat. Mass in our chapel said by Abbé Daniel Lallement.

Instruction at 10 o'clock.

At supper: Père Garrigou-Lagrange, Abbé Millot. The latter greatly moves Père Garrigou by talking of Our Blessed Lady with a ravishing piety and simplicity.

Sunday, 1st October. – Mass at home said by Abbé Charles Journet.

Instruction at 10 o'clock.

At 2 o'clock, study meeting with Père Garrigou-Lagrange who talks of the natural desire to see God.

Then Ghéon reads us his "Sainte Germaine Cousin".

Monday, 2nd October. – Two Masses at home, the first said by Abbé Lavaud at which Jacques, Véra, Ghéon and I go to Communion; the second said by Abbé Péponnet.

After Communion, Jacques, Véra and I make the vow of *oraison* for one year.

Instructions at 10 a.m. and 3 p.m. I cannot go to them; Véra hears them.

At 4 o'clock Dr. Pichet brings us Père Lamy, Curé of La Courneuve.

In the afternoon here, he sees Frère Bruno, Altermann, Ghéon, Canon Rageth and Père Garrigou-Lagrange.

At supper: Père Garrigou-Lagrange, Père Lamy, Ghéon, Altermann, Canon Rageth.

Mother, who was ill, got up for supper with us. She listens with visible emotion to all that the venerable Curé of La Courneuve says to us about the Blessed Virgin and Our Lord. We have never yet seen him so expansive, so simple, so humble, so dignified and so moving. At first, Père Garrigou's face is stiff, but soon its expression visibly relaxes into confidence, and then emotion. At certain moments, especially when Père Lamy is talking of Our Lord's love for priests, we all feel a clutch at our hearts. Ghéon weeps; my heart is burning. I have to contain myself and this is painful: an hour of unique beauty. Wisdom, prudence, humility of our dear director, Père Garrigou-Lagrange, all radiant in his white habit. Majesty, charity of the humble Curé de la Courneuve. Great mercy of God for all of us.

Tuesday, 3rd October. – Mass in our chapel said by Abbé Dondaine. Ghéon goes to Communion with us.

Instruction at 10 on humility.

After the instruction, I go and talk to Père Garrigou, very good for me. He enjoins me to pray all this year for the Thomist Circles, and to ask very specially for *humility* for all; he is pleased with the retreat; he hopes that the work will bear precious fruit, on condition that it is well grounded in humility.

As to humility, I am bold enough to say to Père Garrigou-Lagrange that I admit what he says about the dangers of pride which lie in wait particularly for intellectuals and that I admit this in my own case, although I do not feel in myself motions of pride, properly speaking, but rather of vanity. But that I do not admit it for Jacques, in whom there is no pride; I am sensitive to the motions of pride – in others! (in my own case I am blind perhaps). But I am certain that there is no pride in Jacques (unless one is speaking of the innate seed common to all).

The Father did not think my outburst reprehensible. "You do well to say this to me. Perhaps it was the good Lord who inspired you. In any case, I was not alluding to any particular person, I was not alluding to Jacques; I was thinking more of girls."

I also took up the defence of girls. For women, vanity is more of a menace than pride, properly speaking. Vanity is a weakness and, as such, is often found in women. Pride is a strength; an evil strength, but a strength, and it is more an attribute of men.

These poor intellectual women! How people mistrust them! Yet, when they combine prayer with study, may one not hope that the light will abound through reason properly exercised and through the grace which is lacking to no one? And may one not hope that the light will preserve them from the silly pride, into which, to be honest, ignorant women fall at least as often as learned ones?

Ah, if they lost sight of prayer and its prime importance, above every kind of human knowledge, yes, then pride would be something to be very specially feared for them!

At 3 p.m. admirable sermon on prayer.

Wednesday, 4th October, St. Francis of Assisi. – Mass in our chapel said by Canon Rageth. Frère Bruno serves Mass. Véra and I are at it. Jacques goes to the general Communion of the retreatants.

At 10 a.m. last instruction, on Contemplative Prayer.

In the evening, Ghéon has supper with us. Then he reads us *Conte des trois jeunes filles à marier* (episode from the life of St. Nicholas). Thus ends our retreat. . .

Thursday, 5th October. – Père Dehau dines with us. Very sorely tried. We have never seen him so depressed, so overwhelmed. These trials can go to great lengths with contemplatives. And this particular one is so defenceless.

Monday, 16th. – Père Dehau.

These days *oraison* several times very deep in the heart, very ardent, still just as obscure, just as simple. Once it seemed to me that I was on the brink of an ocean of love, that it only needed a little, a very little for me to be engulfed in it – I was not engulfed in it, poor me! O my one and only Jesus, how delightful and painful at once is this state! When shall I be pure enough for you to unite me to you closely, and not let me ever again be parted from you! Jesus, my God, make me all yours! O my only Beloved, my repose and my life, my God and my all, have pity on me.

When you are there, making the soul rest in silence with you, drawing it to you and uniting it, there is no room for doubt. But when one finds oneself alone again, seeing how great is the poverty of the soul and remembering one's sins, one doubts the graces received on account of their divine value. One wonders how the Lord cannot weary of every day drawing to himself a soul which seems to make no progress in good. And yet it is indeed He, and without Him I most certainly could not live! Or I should live as someone in despair and so I could not live!

Lord, make haste to strengthen me. Give me a new heart, a generous heart, pure, forgetful of itself, beating only for you, triumphing, through the effusion of your Love, over itself, and over the sin of others, drawing them to you by firing them with your Love that is stronger than death. O my only Beloved, draw souls to you!

O blessed Jesus, how is it that so many saints with their heart on fire with charity have not converted the world? What a mystery! However tiny the spark of love you put in the heart of the least of your children, he feels as if he shared in your power; while you unite yourself to him he believes himself capable of overthrowing all heresies, if his love, if your Love, could appear before the eyes of all. But, alas, this love remains hidden in a wretched heart, you do not allow it to manifest itself – perhaps it can only be known by the very heart into which you infuse it? This love so powerful and so unarmed, is delightful and painful to the heart, for the more the soul loves you, the more it longs to see you known and loved by all.

It is a great torment, it is something almost inconceivable to one who loves you, the existence of all those people who do not know you, Truth so shining clear! Jesus, how is it possible! The soul cannot hold at the same time the deep knowledge of your Love and the thought of this world which is ignorant of you and seems to live without you. O Jesus, it would be easy for you to enlighten us all. Have pity on us.

12th November. – We leave for Louvain.

We are spending the month of November in Louvain where Jacques is giving a lecture on the 16th on Luther and afterwards six talks to the students on Descartes.

December. – Jesus, my God, you are my only love, truly, truly . . . The rest is my misery.

Have pity on a very miserable being, on the one You see, not the one I see, or the one people see in me, but the one You see.

For myself, I can no longer do anything; I do not even see how I could emerge from the chaos of my imperfections. Where to begin? And what exactly is to be done? I no longer see anything.

I can only weep.

I hope in You because you wish it, and even command it. But act quickly, my God, make haste to help me. I put myself at the feet of your Divine Mother, I embrace her knees. Act quickly, O Mother! and in such an effective way that light and strength will be given me both at once to fulfil God's will regarding me. For I no longer have either strength or light, barely a little light to see my destitution, barely a little strength to cry out to you: save me! Ah to love, to love God. Love Him truly, live only for Him! With an upright heart, a pure soul, a generous will. To love God, love his suffering creatures, live and die for Him! To hold my soul always in my hand and God always in my soul. Or rather that, once and for all, Jesus would ravish me out of myself and carry me away for ever in the bosom of his Love!

23rd December. – Jacques sees Miss V. S.[4] for the first time.

---

4. If I remember rightly, it was Louis Massignon who took me to see her; in any case Massignon knew her at this time and always preserved a deep respect and affection for her. (J.)

Jewess, converted 15 years ago. Ill ever since. Of whom Prince Ghika, Dr. Havet, of Louvain, and Canon Thiéry have spoken to us with admiration. Jacques had the shock of finding her living in the very flat our friends Christine and Pierre van der Meer had occupied at 16 rue Boissonade, where their little Jean died.

1923

Versailles, *1st January*. – I went with Jacques to see Miss V. S. She is altogether peaceable, altogether simple; so weak that you can hardly hear her voice. I saw two Japanese at her flat, one of whom is a doctor and studying theology at the Institut Catholique. He wants to be a priest and a missionary. With Miss V. there also lives an Englishwoman, dressed as a Franciscan, who leads a hermit's life there; and another Englishwoman who acts as their servant, or rather as a lay-sister, for she is a person of good family who has come there for the love of God. All these people belong to the Third Order of St. Francis.

9th January. – Jacques went to see the saintly Curé. The latter told him that he likes the Thomist Circles because of their spirit of liberty. That is what is needed, he says, that is how souls ought to be grouped. Jacques said a word or two to him about Miss V.

Sunday, 14th January. – Miss V. assures us that God

L

has given her the grace of recognising priestly hearts,[1] and those who ought to work with her.

Monday, 15th January. – Abbé Lamy and I call on Miss V. I arrive first; I see her alone for a while. She tells me that the Thomist Circles are a very important work and one which needs to be extended; that Jacques ought to help the Japanese and other students who will join them in her project (as regards philosophical studies); she also says that we ought to work with her, and have a house to ourselves, with some spare rooms. . .

Then the saintly Curé arrives and, later, Jacques. The saintly Curé and Miss V. talk together alone for a few moments.

He agrees with Miss V. about the work with which Our Lord has charged her. It is not a question of a religious order, but of forming 'hearths' of intense Christian life and, said the saintly Curé, "such hearths will multiply and will end by setting the world on fire"; they are to prepare apostles for the latter days.

When we were talking of the Thomist Circles, the saintly Curé said: "*Ah, St. Thomas is the apostle of modern times!*"

Miss V. S. has the Cardinal's authorisation for her work.

Saturday, 20th January. – Jacques hears Mass at Miss V's. She says to him about me what she said about one of our friends.[2]

---

1. In fact, in all the cases we knew, the vocations she thus discerned were authentic. (J.)

2. She had said to this friend that she felt Our Lord's presence in him in a very special way. (J.)

Monday, 29th January. – Jacques and I call on Miss V. (for she is always asking us to come). She has suffered very much recently. They have been offered a house in the rue Boulard for a year. They can go into it in March.

She says to us in such a touching way: "So you believe too that it is God who has brought us together?" She tells us again that we must have a house with the Blessed Sacrament, preferably for foreigners, who would only stay for a while. . .

Finally, she says to me personally: "Did M. Maritain tell you what I said about you?" "Yes." "I cannot explain it, but Our Lord is present in you in a special way. I do not know in what manner. The first time I saw you, I suspected it; the second time I was sure of it. It is an intimate union with the Word. You give out God. You have a very important inner mission. There are some souls who are in the same case. Those souls have a very important inner mission. I tell you this to console you. This grace renders the soul *universal*." She reverts several times to universality which is the character she sees impressed on her work. She tells Jacques that he has received particular grace, that he ought to make others share in it.

She looks at me with such kind eyes, with such a warm light in them; she asks us once again to come back. We leave her. Jean-Pierre Altermann is due to come in a few minutes.

Tuesday, 30th January. – She told me *that* to console me. Nevertheless what I feel is not a sensible consolation. *That* seems to me so gratuitous that I cannot, so to speak, mentally associate the idea of myself and the idea of such a grace. But what I do feel as a result is a sense of a greater detachment from myself, of a reduction of this ego, a diminished awareness of this personal self. And also of a more conscious and ardent attraction to Christ. As if she had opened my eyes to Him who is there and whom I did not want, or was not able, or did not dare to see.

But also, from now on, what an obligation for me to be attentive, to withdraw into the interior, and to treat Him worthily, He who, even apart from any special grace, is the guest of our soul in sanctifying grace. As to the question of this special grace which Miss V. spoke of, I do not trouble my mind about it; the Lord will make me aware of it if that is to be profitable to my soul. Don't we know well enough that he is there!

Jean-Pierre Altermann came to tell us about his visit to Miss V. There was no dilly-dallying, he says. Miss V. definitely assured him that he was called to the priesthood. "You will be a priest, you will do great things because you will say Mass. I should like to have been a boy so as to be able to say Mass. You will be a priest because God wills it. You can carry on with your art, the two will go very well together."

Jean-Pierre says to us: "She is like a swallow that has built its nest in the crown of thorns."

When he left her, he went to La Courneuve.

The saintly Curé entirely agrees with Miss V. While Jean-Pierre is telling us all this, Jacques tells him that when he went to La Courneuve, he had a talk with the saintly Curé who spoke to him about Jean-Pierre and told him: "The Blessed Virgin said to me: 'He has two ways open to him, both equally good, to be a secular priest or one in a religious order: in either case I promise him my support.'"

Jean-Pierre is to be present tomorrow (Wednesday) at

Mass in Miss V.'s flat where he is to see the Franciscan Father who is interested in her. The saintly Curé told him not to commit himself yet as regards the undertaking.

We want to see Père Dehau as soon as possible to talk to him about all this; he has been away for several weeks, preaching in Holland; and even now it is not easy to see him at leisure.

Blessed God, I want to do your will, but do not let us go astray or launch into a path which leads to a dead end. Grant that we may travel always by the broad road of your will and that we may arrive in the end at the very Source of your merciful will and not up against blank, blind walls where the devil will greet us with a sneer.

1st February. – Jacques has met Père Dehau, very much in a hurry, very preoccupied with his *incognito*. Jacques is disappointed and sorry. Tomorrow Véra and I are to see Père D. and talk to him about Miss V. S.[3]

Friday, 2nd February. – Naturally I like to be liked. But, God helping, I also like to be disliked. For when that happens, my soul becomes quite detached and it needs no other preparation to find God.

I fear humiliation; I do not seek it, but when it comes God generally gives me the grace to clasp it lovingly to my heart, and then I experience a keen spiritual joy.

---

3. No notes on this conversation in Raïssa's notebook. The fact is that Père Dehau, not knowing the situation at first hand, could only take the line of "wait and see", merely telling us to take an attitude of reserve and at all costs not to commit ourselves to anything which fettered our freedom. Such, of course, was already our intention. (J.)

Wednesday, 15th February. – Early in the afternoon, as I am settling down to write to Mère Marie-Thérèse, I feel myself suddenly plunged in silent absorption, my soul seems to withdraw into depth. Impossible to imagine, to think, to concentrate. Only the name of Jesus occupies my mind.

I hesitate a little before abandoning myself to this inward attraction, then I yield; my heart kindles more and more, absorption in God grows more intense and holds me for about half an hour, then relaxes a little, then intensifies again, lasting in all about an hour and a half. After which I suddenly find myself completely free and untrammelled and I write for a long while with the greatest of ease.

Véra has succeeded in her search for a house; we are going to live at Meudon; we have received the authorisation to have the Blessed Sacrament reserved in our oratory. A wonderful grace and unusual privilege which we owe, after God, to Mgr. Gibier who very warmly endorsed our request in Rome.

Tuesday, 5th June. – We move to 10 rue du Parc, Meudon.

Meudon, 8th June, Feast of the Sacred Heart. – First Mass in our chapel and installation of the Blessed Sacrament.[4]

God is too good! I have a little study which gives access to the chapel.[5] Here is a house where I can live like a hermit.

---

4. Our chapel was soon to be classed as semi-public on account of the "Thomist Circles" and of all the work with other people to which our house was destined. (J.)

5. We managed to have a small glazed window put in the middle of the door between the chapel and Raïssa's study. (J.)

Something beyond all my dreams! This first Mass is celebrated by Abbé Sarraute, a young priest who is saying his first Mass of the Sacred Heart. Present with us are: Prince Vladimir Ghika, Henri Ghéon, Jean-Pierre Altermann, Dr. Louis Pichet, Dr. Amieux.

After Mass Jacques tells our friends of Pierre Villard's generosity to us. It is to him we owe this house and, as a result, the possibility of having the Blessed Sacrament reserved.

Mid-June. – [After having noted down certain very painful disillusions which had been confided to us, Raïssa adds:] I do not want to judge Miss V. But everything all around her is so obscure, so contradictory, so petty, that we seem to come up every moment against illusion or untruthfulness. . . Miss V. seems to be lost among a welter of conflicting egotisms. We went to her in the utmost good faith. We are withdrawing ourselves, and our friends along with us.[6]

16th July. – Our last visit to Miss V.

---

6. A hopeless confusion arose from the opposing conceptions which all claimed to have Miss V.'s support. It was her entourage which was at fault; she was sincere but swept away, her physical weakness did not permit her to stand up to the storm. Some time after, once Dr. T. had been ordained, she went off with her friends to Japan where she led a life of poverty, devotion and self-denial. She left it, having reached the end of her strength, and returned to England where she died a holy death (20th February 1950). We have always remembered her with faithful affection.

I have discovered a letter from her (19th March 1924, according to the postmark) preserved by Raïssa, on the envelope of which my wife had written: "This letter is a relic". (J.)

17th July. – Sweet Jesus, Jesus Love, long live the holy obscurity of the Faith! Long live all light, natural and supernatural! Long live divine knowledge and holy Wisdom!

After what I saw yesterday at the Rue Boulard, I understand clearly what Jacques' vocation is: alone, or with others, he is to work in the light. He is to help to promote St Thomas. That is more necessary than anything else today. Perhaps Miss V. and Dr. T. will do the work of the doctor-priests? May God help them.

O good, O holy natural reason! Not to be afraid of using the right words! Say *oraison* when it is silent prayer, and *prière* when it is vocal prayer. Not to be afraid of *appearing proud*, but only of pride.

As for myself, I shall take this line: *I will say clearly what I think clearly*. Light and sincerity, that is what seems to be desirable above everything. Good for myself; and, in the long run, more charitable to everybody.

August. – From a letter to Mère Marie-Thérèse du Sacré Coeur:

"We have had a harsh experience and it has been particularly harsh for x (one of our friends). For everything that had been promised to him, and by which he had been attracted, was subsequently called into question again by Miss V. and by the people in her entourage, Father R. (Franciscan) and the Japanese doctor, now an ecclesiastical student ... (They finally) demanded he should join a kind of Franciscan Third Order, dedicated to the formation of doctor-priests. Disillusion further increased from day to day by Miss V.'s manifold inconsistencies which it was impossible not to notice, saying one thing to one person and another to another, telling everyone what they wanted to hear, it seemed to us ... We realise now that, due no doubt to lack of enlightened direction, the poor invalid's mind is in a state of inextricable muddle ... As a result, the atmosphere that surrounds her is an atmosphere of confusion in which everything is distorted, in which the slightest words lead to misunderstandings and in which minds become exacerbated ...

"The experience we have just had has led us to cherish more than ever the obscure way of Faith, Hope and Charity; plain simple rectitude, and right reason too, for which it seems to me we do not give enough thanks to God who brings to us the first glimmerings of his light through it and makes it the foundation of every spiritual edifice. How simpleminded I am, dear Mother, to have only just made such simple discoveries! I knew all this perfectly well in theory, but everything takes on a new look in practice ..."

I have a mystical love of natural reason.

26th–30th September. – Second retreat of the Thomist Circles.
Arrival of Père Garrigou-Lagrange on the 25th.

26th September. – Mass said by Père Garrigou-Lagrange in our chapel.
At 10.30 first sermon: on the love of God.
At 3.30 second sermon: on sin.

27th September. – Mass in our house, said by Abbé Journet. Ghéon is there.
At 10.30 third sermon: brotherly love.

At 3.30 fourth sermon: the cross.

Dined with us: Noël and Robert Boulet.

28th September. – Mass in our house said by Abbé Zundel.

At 10:00 fifth sermon: on the Holy Spirit.

At 3.30 sixth sermon: on zeal.

Dine with us: Abbé Journet, Abbé Zundel, M. Gauley and Dr. Saudan.

29th September. – Mass in our chapel said by Abbé Lavaud. Jean-Pierre Altermann and Marthe Spitzer are present.

At 10:00 seventh sermon: on the Mass.

30th September. – Mass in our chapel said by Abbé Péponnet. Mass of general Communion at the Présentation.

At 9.30 very beautiful High Mass at which Prince Ghika is deacon.

Afternoon at 2 o'clock in our chapel, Père Garrigou received René Kiéger (assisted by Abbé Lallement) and Dr. Saudan (assisted by Abbé Zundel) into the Third Order of St Dominic, in the presence of most of the retreatants. Singing of the Te Deum. Then we receive the papal blessing, with a plenary indulgence for the retreatants, and venerate a relic of St Thomas.

At 2.30, study meeting: Père Garrigou talks to us about the different "states" of human nature; state of nature, state of integrity, state of grace, state of fallen nature, state of restored nature.

Then a reading by Ghéon.

At supper: Père Garrigou-Lagrange, Prince Ghika,

Ghéon, Altermann, Marie-Anne [François], Marthe Spitzer, Marie-Louise [Guillot].

1st October. – Mass in our house said by Père Garrigou-Lagrange. Prince Ghika is present.

Before leaving, Père Garrigou-Lagrange tells us how very glad he is that he has come and that he will be even happier to come back. He is very pleased with the retreat.

And we are all thoroughly satisfied.

Prince Ghika had, as his penance, to have his faults told him by Jacques.

After the departure of Père Garrigou, this curious penance for two takes place in the chapel.

And afterwards we see them both calm and happy, united by true fraternal charity.

This retreat seems to have put an end to the long trials that Prince Ghika has had to endure this summer. He has been granted permission to use the Latin Rite. He is to be ordained on the 7th October.

2nd October. – Yesterday, after supper, very urgent impulse to pray in the chapel. *Recueillement* at once sweet and painful – feeling at once the bitterness of human affections and the thirst for the love of God. My God, give me your heart! Give me your heart! Take my heart.

This lasts a long while. I do not want to leave the chapel, though I am getting sleepy.

This morning, same state; feeling that the good God wants me to be his in a more complete way, involving a great restraint in the display of affection to those I love. Not to pour out my heart on creatures, even if the affection is in the order of charity. To consider myself more as

149

belonging to God. O my God, take me, take me, may I be yours, may I be wholly yours. I feel as if God is surrounding me, enveloping me, giving me a higher idea of the dignity of the soul, an idea which ought to make it very reserved towards its neighbour, even towards those whom it has most right to love.

Not to dissipate oneself on external things.

Preserve this light for me, God of love. See that I keep this reserve. This prudence. This dignity. But at the same time make me simple and kind. May it be *your love* that goes out from my soul to my neighbour.

Today, *October 2nd*. Renewal of our vow of *oraison*.

Sunday, 7th October, Feast of the Holy Rosary. – Great joy. Ordination of Prince Vladimir Ghika at the Lazarists, in Paris, before the relics of St Vincent de Paul. The most beautiful of all was Prince Ghika himself, completely rapt in God, utterly worn out, much more victim than sacrificer; that was how he looked to us after the ordination, standing, dressed in the alb, when he was offering his hands to be kissed with a gesture worthy of Fra Angelico, it expressed so much humility and renunciation.

"Once again we felt the touch of your hand, Lord, as you were passing by."

On *Thursday, 11th October*, Prince Ghika says Mass at our house. He is still trembling under the weight of his new dignity. Jacques serves his Mass and keeps very close to him to jog his memory which sometimes fails under the stress of emotion. He is in tears when he gives us Communion, Jacques, Véra and me, and also Jean-Pierre Altermann.

20th October. – Jacques gave a lecture in Avignon on *St Thomas, apostle of modern times* (as the saintly Abbé Lamy calls him). Père Janvier, who heard it, is going about everywhere saying he is delighted with it.

15th November, St Gertrude. – Prince Ghika says Mass for us at 5 o'clock in the morning. Jacques leaves for Rome.

The 19th. – Jacques' lecture in Rome (Thomist Week). Jacques is received in private audience by the Holy Father. Obtains verbal authorisation for a private chapel.

23rd November. – At the point where St Thomas, having arrived at the ultimate expression of a metaphysical truth, puts a full stop and rests, certain minds incapable of rational certainty (e.g. Père Malvy) put a question mark and remain in suspense ... It is not scepticism. It is intellectual impotence, and yet one finds it in extremely intelligent men.

The danger for the disciples of St Thomas is to put the full stop too soon.

*

[In the year 1923 Raïssa composed a little *Rule of Life,* of which she made three copies in her own hand – one for each of us – in the form of a leaflet to be slipped into a missal or a diurnal. I still have mine in my Book of Hours. I transcribe here this "Rule of Life". (J.)]

†

Ave Maria   O Sapientia

Pax

Accept all as coming from God
Do all for God
Offer all to God.

And seek ardently
the perfection of Charity
and the love of the Cross.

I

"Vacate et videte quoniam ego sum Deus."
Every day we will give the
required time to silent prayer
with sincere humility
and in peaceful abandonment
to the divine action,
wholly yielded by love to Love.
    Then, whether at rest
or at work, whether
in silence or among
noise, we will keep close
to God by incessant prayer,
yet without neglecting
the present duty. For, as
Père de Caussade says,
the duties of each moment conceal
beneath their obscure appearances,
the truth of the divine Will,
they are like
the sacraments of the present moment.
    Work will be frequently
interspersed with ejaculatory

prayers. We will gladly
seek silence
and solitude.

II

"Thou shalt love thy neighbour
as thyself." "Omnis homo mendax."
Love of our neighbour will urge us above all
to unselfishness and mildness,
but also to sincerity and firmness.
We will make absolutely no concession
to worldly-mindedness, either to please
or from false humility,
keeping the heart for God alone,
in purity and peace.
We will remember the smallest kindness
and we will be particularly grateful
to those who do our household work.
We will never complain
of anything at table.
We will always be ready
to come to the help of our neighbour
whatever his needs, without any fear
of what men may think. But we will exclude
everything that does not conform
to the order of charity. We will avoid
any outside commitment which might distract
from the life of silent prayer and silence with God.
We will involve ourselves as little as possible
in other people's affairs, and
examine all problems
without letting our judgment be obscured
by any timidity.

III

"Jesu mitis et humilis corde
Fac cor nostrum secundum
   Cor tuum."
Living in the world,
deprived of the help that
monks and nuns find in their
rule and their vows – deprived
as well through a very special dispensation
of Providence, of the poverty
in which we lived for years –
and which God loves – we must make up
by inner fervour
and by poverty of spirit
for what we lack in outer supports.

   So let us set ourselves diligently to practise
a deep and universal humility,
to make constant acts of thanksgiving
for so many blessings received,
to live in utter trust,
wholly abandoned to God's mercy.
Let us be kindly to all creatures.
Let us refrain from judging
the innermost of souls,
and let us open our heart wide enough
to admire everywhere,
and understand as much as possible
the liberty, the breadth and the variety
of God's ways.

[After this come some directions for religious exercises in common in the chapel. And, in conclusion:]

After Supper: chapter. Spiritual reading and prayer: My God, I beseech You for our relatives and our benefactors; for our friends and our enemies; for the poor and the afflicted, for saints and sinners, for the sick and the dying, for the whole Church and for all souls; and especially for those, among the living and the dead, who have a particular need of prayers. Ave Maria.

Blessed be Jesus for the infinite mercy which led him to come and live under our roof. Domine, non sum dignus.

Lord Jesus, our house is very specially yours: you live in it and we have it through your mercy and through the charity of one of your children. May your divine grace, your love and your peace always reign in it. Amen.

And finally, two prayers of St Gertrude:

Ave candidum lilium fulgidae semperque tranquillae Trinitatis, rosaque praefulgida coelicae amenitatis, de qua nasci et de cujus lacte pasci Rex coelorum voluit, divinis influxionibus animas nostras pasce.

Glory be to You, O very sweet and very benign, O very noble and very excellent, O very joyous and very glorious, O resplendent and ever tranquil Trinity, for the scarlet wounds of my Unique Beloved.

M

4. Fourth Notebook: 1924-1926

1924

Meudon, *January*. – If, as sometimes happens, the objective causes of our pain do not seem to justify the sharpness of it, do not let us be ashamed of our suffering. Let us try and turn it to good by throwing ourselves back on God. Let us suffer *always in His presence*; and, even in the hour of temptation, do not let us hide ourselves from Him. When we feel our soul at once arid and over-sensitive, it is then that we must cry out to God. The divine Word who is beyond the reach of pain took a heart like to ours so as to be able, in suffering *for* us, to suffer *with* us! Like to ours, not in imperfection but in natural inclination. "As he took my will, so he took my sadness," St. Ambrose says magnificently. Thus Jesus knew sadness, and sadness was repugnant to his human will . . .

For us, God is, at first, Truth and then Love; for if he were not, first, Truth for us, he would be any kind of love. But he is only *that love* which is but one with the sovereign and eternally living truth.

In himself, God is Love as he is Truth. "Love in God is an absolute attribute" (it is not said only in relation to creatures). It is the proper name of the Holy Spirit.

6th March. – "Dona Spiritus Sancti sunt quidam habitus quibus homo perficitur ad prompte obediendum Spiritui Sancto." (I-II, 68, 3.)

The Gifts of the Holy Spirit are *habitus* (master qualities) which dispose the soul to prompt obedience to the Holy Spirit, consequently each one of these inner qualities *awaits,* as it were, a *special motion* of the Holy Spirit and is not exercised without a *special intervention* on the part of God.

Whereas the infused virtues, even the theological ones, are *habitus* which the will of man (with the aid of the ordinary help of God – I do not know if I am saying this right) puts into action.

"It is advisable to set forth the nature of *general help* and of *particular help* . . . to explain how, during this kind of prayer, the soul sees, in a manner, with its eyes, this particular help." (St Teresa, *Life,* ch. XIV.)

7th March, St Thomas Aquinas. – The spirit of evil makes advantageous use against the Church of all the labours in the scientific field which she no longer seems to have the strength to control, to criticise and to regulate. Nevertheless she has great scientists, but far too few of them, and atheists do not know of them or pretend not to. We need far more of them and with more comprehensive and metaphysical minds. "It is the function of Wisdom to regulate all things."

It is very hard to see error increasing and spreading

endlessly and submerging souls. All the harder when one has in one's heart the absolute conviction that the Catholic truth is truly universal and that it has the power to govern every branch of knowledge, satisfy every intelligence and fulfil the desires of every heart.

Certainly, if we are Christ's, we know that "our kingdom is not of this world," and that, if the divine Truth wished to triumph in time, nothing could be easier for Him. "I would ask my Father and He would send me twelve legions of angels . . ." One knows that and yet one ardently longs for the triumph of Christ here and now, everywhere and in everything. And this longing makes the heart impatient, demanding and afflicted.

During silent prayer, I felt that the good God wanted to calm me, which he did, in a moment, by insinuating into my soul a feeling which I might express thus: error is like the foam on the waves, it eludes our grasp and keeps re-appearing. The soul must not exhaust itself fighting against the foam. Its zeal must be purified and calmed and, by union with the divine Will, it must gather strength from the depths. And Christ, with all his merits and the merits of all the saints, will do his work deep down below the surface of the waters. And everything that can be saved will be saved. For our God has chosen to reign in humility, and it really seems as if he wishes to show himself only just as much as is necessary in order that the visible Church shall endure to the end and that the gates of hell shall not prevail against it.

Yet the calm which followed silent prayer did not, as I might have expected, wipe out the hope and desire of seeing the initiation of the task of intellectual apostolate that Jacques and I have been thinking about for long:

a *Thomist Company*. Those who belonged to it would, like the members of the Thomist Circles, make the *vow of oraison* so that 1. no one should let scientific work distract him from God but that, on the contrary, each one should have an ardent desire to serve God and souls through intellectual apostolate; 2. that such an apostolate should be conducted peaceably and prudently, and should be humble and magnanimous; 3. that its mainspring should be wholly supernatural, although the natural powers of the intellect enlightened by faith would be the very instrument of this apostolate.

Once he had been well trained in Thomism and theology, each one would devote himself to a special science (theology, philosophy, history, mathematics, physics and the other natural sciences) so as to be able to combat accumulated errors through writing and through personal influence (counselling, intellectual retreats, etc.), to make a positive contribution to research, progress and the deepening of knowledge, to work for the re-establishment in men's minds of the natural rectitude which is so propitious to the fructification of grace in their souls.

Thus, as a basis, *life of silent prayer* and *Thomist training*. Then specialisation in all the sciences with a view to intellectual apostolate. Such a work could group together those whose frail health prevents them from joining the Order of St Dominic.[1]

---

1. We hoped that one of our friends would be able to create the work of which we dreamed. In fact, it is an illusion to want to *organise* such things, one must leave them to the Holy Spirit. Moreover, I now think that, at that time, we insisted too much on the idea of an apostolate. In intellectual work, all one must have in view is truth; the rest comes as a by-product. (J.)

15th March. – God is light and love and in him the two are One.

And all Creation is light in virtue of its intelligibility (light in potency), love in virtue of its (ontological) tendency (to God).

The intelligibility of creatures becomes light in act as soon as the mirror of immaterial creatures which are intelligences (human or angelic) is placed before it. From this point of view one can admit a certain "monism". The thing known is the thing itself and not the thing plus an intelligible form added to it.

The intelligible radiation of beings is their "intentional being" – a remote participation, however imperfect it be, in the creative Idea of God.

There is inchoatively a spiritual part even in inanimate bodies, and it is the *form* which keeps them in being. Such is true idealism.

The hierarchy of beings depends on the greater or lesser part of immateriality in them.

The infinite substance of God is wholly expressed or uttered [within God] by the Word.

The substance of things is also expressed (in our case in a very piecemeal and imperfect way) by the word of immaterial creatures or of those endowed with an immaterial soul.

Just as God gives things being, without any confusion of this being with the being of God, in the same way God gives them activity, in all its degrees, from physical energy to the free and voluntary activity of men and angels, without this created activity being confounded with the divine activity.

21st March, St Benedict. – I await all from God.

For from me to Him, it seems that all the bridges are cut. But not from Him to me.

I cannot even direct, be it even in a most general and indeterminate way, my thought in silent prayer.

Direction and light from God alone.

Then the soul subtly perceives the absolute divine transcendence.

Infusion of the divine light.

Incomprehensible and unspeakable light, but which is the very one which the soul desires, to which it aspires, for which it thirsts.

Vivifying and insensible light, at the highest point of the spirit.

In this prayer the soul feels a radical distaste for its own impulses, its preferences, its desires, its sensibilities, its comprehensions.

It is entirely open to God and breathes in the incomprehensible light that comes from Him.

It reposes in the unknown will of God and lives on a wholly spiritual love.

All this is reassuring darkness
    insensible delight
    incomprehensible communion.

The soul reposes more securely in this darkness than it did in the previous illuminations induced by some creature, image, symbol or sentiment.

It seems to it that it subsists on the sole will of God.

20th April, Easter Sunday. – Went to Communion at the church. Music slightly loosens the bonds of spirit and body, and the soul catches a glimpse of the rapturous, eternal love.

It goes forward to the nuptial rhythm of the angelic procession. It has a foretaste of the joys of the spiritual nuptials.

Love! It is indeed to love that it has been predestined from the beginning of the world.

Love! which is communication in joy and delights, with fulness of bliss in unending possession.

Love which is total and reciprocal giving; easy, joyous, gushing forth eternally as an eternal life.

(Some moments of inexpressible love. Heart melted. Tears.)

The essence of love is in the communication of oneself, with fulness of joy and delight in the possession of the beloved.

The essence of friendship is in desire for the good of one's friend, strong enough to sacrifice oneself for him.[2]

---

2. Raïssa uses here the words *love* and *friendship* in their currently accepted sense, and one which corresponds to very obvious realities of experience.

The love, which is *eros* in the realm of the passions, is already, though on a lower level, *eros-agapê* in the truly human world: and it is also – I mean in an analogical and absolutely supereminent manner in which all that pertains to the passions is transcended – *eros-agapê*, "mad" boundless love, the love of total mutual self-giving (cf. the Song of Songs) in the spiritual order. (There is, no doubt, a distinction of meaning between *eros* and *agapê*, but the radical opposition people choose to make between them nowadays has no foundation.)

Friendship, which is *agapê-philia,* the love of mutual goodwill, in our human world (for the Greeks it deviated towards *eros-philia*), is also – I mean in an analogical and absolutely super-eminent manner – *agapê-philia* in the spiritual order.

It is important to understand that what, in opposition to *amor concupiscentiae,* St Thomas calls *amor amicitiae* comprises as subdivision both senses ("love" and "friendship") here mentioned – Cf. the chapter "Amour et Amitié (En marge du Journal de Raïssa)" in my *Carnet de Notes.* (J.)

God loves us with friendship by providing for all our necessities and by dying for us on the Cross.

God loves us with love by making us participate in his nature by grace – by making the sanctified soul his dwelling. By making himself known to us through supernatural Revelation. All this is proof of his love. "Was not our heart burning within us, whilst He spoke in the way, and opened to us the Scriptures?" (Luke, XXIV).

And what does He demand of us ourselves? Our heart: Praebe mihi cor tuum.

Friendship is judged sufficiently by acts: "If you love me, keep my commandments."

Wholly spiritual love – only the Holy Spirit can make the soul feel that.

How can I prove my friendship to God? By keeping his commandments.

How can I prove my love to him?

By giving myself to him from the bottom of my heart, in such a way that no other *love* ever dwells in it. In this sense, God is jealous. He is not jealous of our friendships, on the contrary, he encourages them. But he is jealous of that particular gift of the heart which is love, and which is total and exclusive in its nature. Hence the value of bodily virginity *as a sign* of the integrity of the heart.

"To be loved! What words for a living heart!" (Gobineau, *Les Pléiades*).

Of the notion of *glory* in love.

It is glorious for a living soul to conquer a living person. This conquest is the triumph of love.

Our glory, in heaven, will be to have conquered God – and it is His glory, accidental glory, to have conquered a soul.

Love (on that account) demands not only *union* of wills, but also *distinction* of persons.

Trinity of divine Persons.

*

The poet, because he gives himself in some fashion, moves in an aura of love. Love which streams out of him like a gushing force, with no definite object.

*

Religious music in some way unties the knot between body and spirit. It frees the soul, exalts it towards a more spiritual life. So does every work of art inspired by the love of God. Very rare works, for it is not a question of a small love. So does metaphysics – true metaphysics.

*

My soul can no longer accept anything from reflections, comparisons, images, symbols, savours, fervours – even though the light of God glimmers in all these things. It can no longer be nourished except by that utterly pure light, even though to the soul it be darkness and therefore surpassing all understanding.

The wedding of the soul and of God. – Delight – Music of the Angels – Exultation – Wedding procession – Celebration – Communion of spirits – Adoration. Giving.

Love.

Reciprocal giving – total, easy, joyous.

Communion in delight and gladness. Fullness of joy in possession.

30th April. – I have nothing to give you. But my heart I *have* given you. I know that by the price it has cost me. I do not yield my heart to creatures, you keep it, you hold it sweetly enchained. I give it to you and continually regive it you. This poor and wretched heart. But which is *my* heart, the most personal possession I have to dispose of. I give it you. It is the share that you demanded of me at Baptism, still more at my First Communion, and even more after Extreme Unction in 1907.

All my attraction is towards the inner treasure. What I do outwardly is now contrary to my deep life. I am truly never at rest, in peace, spiritually active except alone, in silent prayer. The rest does violence to me. Makes me live on the superficial level of myself – whereas I am drawn inwards – and in a kind of insincerity since I appear to be interested in what does not really interest me. All this wearies me and brings me nothing in compensation for my effort.

I only experience any comfort and joy when, talking to someone, I feel a certain good being done, something being done for God and for souls.

Union: "Under this grace the soul cannot doubt the presence of the divine persons in itself and is hardly ever deprived of their company."

July. – For the first time Auric brought Jean Cocteau to see us. Cocteau, shattered by the death of Radiguet and almost in despair, came to Jacques because he had been told he could make him find peace again, and find God again.

After this first visit, praying for Cocteau, God gave me a joyful assurance of his conversion. I had the same feeling when, at Jacques' request, I prayed for the conversion of Pierre Villard, who did, in fact, go to confession on the eve of the day he was killed in 1918.

God is good to encourage us like this to pray for those whom he wants to bring back to him. With that assurance from him, we bear the feeling of our own inadequacy patiently.

18th July. – Great joy in my soul this morning. At the moment of setting myself to silent prayer, intense absorption in God. In the intervals when the ligature relaxed, I quietly read Père Gardeil's article in this month's *Revue Thomiste*. And I understand clearly now that lately my *oraison*, especially that of today, has been what St Teresa calls *the sleep of the faculties*, that which succeeds the prayer of quiet and precedes *"l'oraison passive d'union"* (the passive *oraison* of union).

Pages 365 – 368 of Père Gardeil gave me particular joy. They correspond to what I know of the life of my soul. My silent prayer nowadays has nearly all the characteristics described by St Teresa. And I see that, during the years of quietude, it is a state of prayer which has often been granted me. But I did not realise it until today. And after a month of interior trials. The day before yesterday I felt a certain relief as a result of reading St John of the Cross *(Nuit passive de l'esprit,* the six first paragraphs).

*

This year we have studied a great deal, in John of St. Thomas, everything concerning grace, charity and the gift of wisdom.

*

Retreat of *September 1924* (25th – 30th September). Preached by Père Garrigou-Lagrange, as in the previous years.

Tuesday, 30th September. – End of the retreat. Morning of work with Père Garrigou. He agrees with nearly all the corrections we have asked him to make in the new edition of his book: *Perfection chrétienne et Contemplation.*

4th October. – Often, even with a director who knows you well, you get nothing but general indications, speeches which might have been written in advance.

In moments of having to take grave decisions, I have always had truly godly counsel from Père Dehau. But in the normal course of my life I feel that my sole necessity is to live in the presence of God and that, for this, continual prayer and very rigorous confession are infinitely more useful than vague "directions" which could be addressed to all souls in general and do not touch any particular one.

A process of detachment is taking place in my soul. It is becoming indifferent to the judgement of others. It jealously guards its treasure. I think I ought to enter courageously on this way of solitude which is bitter to nature, but very salutary. To live with God alone. To see only him in everything. To count for nothing what comes from men. For "every man is a liar", even when he

is a very veracious person, for he lies without meaning to
when he disappoints someone who has placed some hope in
him. He lies when he gives purely human advice to someone
who is asking for divine light. He lies when human prudence
directs him in his counsels.

Only God does not lie. The soul, in the silence of prayer,
conforms more and more to this divine veracity, to this
integrity in which there is no guile.

Before God, the soul is utterly confident. If it is in fault,
it knows that He wants to correct it and forgive it. If it asks
for divine grace, for charity, for humility, it knows that its
heavenly Father will not give it stones instead of bread.
Oh, that is the one thing necessary! To live open before
God, to implore him unceasingly to purify our heart. To
make every effort not to let ourselves pass over anything;
to keep our eyes well open to our defects, to our sins, to
make a very strict confession of them.

How good it is to live in the sole desire to please God.
As regards our neighbour, only one thing is good: the love
which is charity.

God, my God, have pity on me, allow me to live in your
presence, with an upright soul, wholly lifted towards You;
a sincere soul, drinking in your sweet Veracity; a very
humble soul, looking only to you for all its good. But a soul
that has also great confidence in its Father's goodness, and
receives the manifestations of Your Love as simply as a
child.

O my God, how could I be indifferent to that love?
How could I stop being intent on knowing whether I
have advanced even one step towards you or gone backwards? No doubt, absolute certainty is impossible in these

things since "none knoweth whether he is worthy of love or of wrath".[3] But you cannot be offended by the attentiveness with which the soul scrutinises and conjectures your dispositions towards it according to the more or less clear manifestations of your action in it. You cannot reproach it for hoping in your mercy and believing in your love for us. Certainly we can gravely deceive ourselves. But you will not impute this to our pride, you know that it may be the consequence of our human weakness and of the very obscurity of Faith.

It seems to me that you ought rather to be touched by the fervour of our thanksgiving when, even though we are not sure, we think we have perceived an effect of your love in us.

Is not our confidence more meritorious for being able to spring up in uncertainty? We long so much for your love that the faintest sign of its presence gives us more joy than the most definite joys we receive from creatures.

----

3. For a long time, during the first years, Raïssa, whose intelligence thirsted so much for certainty, suffered from doubting, not God, but herself on the very subject of the silent prayer that was the life of her life. During the silent prayer itself, no uncertainty was possible. But, subsequently, looking back on it, she was sometimes subject to a temptation, which made her very unhappy, to question herself about the value of her prayer. I found in one of her notebooks a little slip of paper, dated 18th December 1918, on which I had written for her: "I promise from now on to repel as they deserve all thoughts and temptations which tend to make me doubt what I know by experience, and by the testimony of the Priest to whom I have given the care of my soul: to know that it is truly God who works in my silent prayer. I will regard them as coming from the devil, because they attack the work of God in me and want to make me lose Trust in Him." At the bottom of this slip she had signed: Raïssa. (J.)

God, my God, I deceive myself perhaps about the degree of your love for me; but what I know very definitely is that your love is my only treasure. That, even if it goes into hiding, it is sufficient to fill my life, to console me for everything, to enlighten me, to make me happy and strong. For if I have other joys, those that come from the affection and the blessed presence of Jacques – and of Véra and of Mother – I know very well that if one day you definitely made it known to me that your love had never dwelt in my soul, all joy would be extinguished for me and I should have lost *my* reason for living.

My beloved Lord, you are my God and my Love and I have no other God than you.

9th October, St Denys. – Our soul has only one Father, who is in heaven.

A great theologian preaches Love to women, but teaches Intelligence to his disciples. The two ought to be preached and taught simultaneously.

The sweeter the experience of divine things, the more bitter the experience of human ones.

To come up against the limitations of those we admire is more painful than knowing our own defects – and it surprises us more. We have such a great need to lean on a visible perfection that we are always too hasty in thinking we have found it; until experience has opened our eyes.

Realising our own wretchedness is not so discouraging. We realise it under the merciful gaze of God. We have long experience of our own nothingness. All our hope is in God; and it is good to depend on him alone for everything.

We have always known our wretchedness and we cannot give ourselves any pretext for being disillusioned.

But, as the heart matures, it learns to see the wretchedness of men with the same gentleness that it sees our own, and to know that they stand, like us, before the fatherly eyes of God who is always ready to come to help.

If, at the outset, human experience is bitter, with the help of God it can become a source of sweetness. Otherwise it would lead the soul into the isolation of pride.

The soul must learn to live with God alone. But if its solitude is holy, when it emerges from it "to converse with men", it will bring them the suaveness of the divine Wisdom, of humility and peace.

Detached from itself as well as from all reliance on human supports, its independence will not be contemptuous. It will live in the true liberty of the children of God. And it will see all things bathed in the sweetness of the divine good-will.

21st October. – Mass said in our chapel by Père Lebbe, an admirable missionary. People attribute miracles to him. Very impressive in his perfect simplicity. A soul sharp as steel. A fervour which is obviously inextinguishable, but contained, always sober in its expression.

Jacques tells him of his desire to make contact with Chinese and Hindus . . . so as to get to know each other . . . in order to make it easier, later on, to do apostolic work among the élite of these peoples. Père Lebbe tells us that it has been his desire for the past twenty years.

I am reading the life of St Jerome. One gets the impression that in the first centuries of Christianity people believed more easily in the profusion of divine graces. Since then, we have become so timid; always on our guard, to such an extent that one might wonder whether God still continues to act in men's souls. Perhaps we exaggerate this emphasis on prudence. Perhaps we are afraid of compromising the canonised saints by recognising the merciful and generous action of God in imperfect souls. But a grace which helps us to live by turning our thoughts to divine things is not sufficient to make great saints of us. Just as we must beware of canonising anybody, and not distribute certificates of sanctity, so we must also be readily inclined to believe in the manifold manifestations of the life of grace. It *must* produce some visible effects, in spite of its invisible essence; otherwise this would be unlike God's general behaviour with us. The Word was made flesh. Our intelligence is dependent on images. Our will is moved by the reason and by the passions. In the same way, God makes himself known to us, in us, around us, by certain visible, sensible effects which beautify our life and render it tolerable. *Charity believeth all things.* Perhaps if there were more charity in our hearts, we too would be more inclined to believe in the life of charity in the hearts of others. Perhaps we do not believe enough, not effectively enough, not simply enough, in God's love for us. Nor in the profusion of his mercies, nor in the richness of his treasures; nor in the humility of his love. We do not believe enough in love. We are too prudent, with that prudence which makes people commit the worst imprudences; too constricted, too mean. Ah, if God were in our image, he would not have raised up creatures out of nothingness in order to love them and make them shine with a reflection of his glory!

24th October, St Raphaël. – We were greatly moved to hear that it was Père Clérissac who assisted poor Oscar Wilde at his death.[4]

26th October, Sunday. – Mass at the church. The children sang, and the parish priest with them: "God alone, God alone is my joy" (or words to that effect). And I wept, pierced to the heart by the sense of our misery. God alone is our joy, a truth which is often hidden from us, and it is more appropriate for us to cry out from the depths of our distress: De profundis clamavi ad te, Domine. . . The grave voice of the priest accompanying the innocent voices of the children, aroused in me, for some unknown reason, a strange compassion for all priestly hearts.

Today, meeting for Scholastic studies.

27th October. – In quite unforeseen ways, more suffering for me. The Lord is extraordinarily efficient at trampling the wine-press. When he wants to humiliate hearts, he does so without its being apparent. When he wants to isolate a soul, he does not leave it a single friend – at least the soul finds it impossible to communicate with anyone

---

4. I reproduce here a footnote to p. 234 of *Les Grandes Amitiés,* 9th edition [p. 236 in earlier editions]. (J.)

"Père Clérissac," Raïssa writes in this note, "never spoke to us about Wilde. But he told one of our friends, who repeated it to us, that he was sure that Wilde died a Catholic, for he was there at his death. In the *Revue Hebdomadaire* (November 28, 1925), Mr. Robert Ross names Father Cuthbert Dunn, of the Passionists, as having given Wilde Baptism and Extreme Unction. In this case Father Clérissac would doubtless have assisted Father Dunn." (*We Have Been Friends Together, Adventures in Grace,* Doubleday, Image Books, p. 177.)

at all and even the best friend no longer knows how to help. Quite the reverse.

27th-31st October. – I have suffered very much. God absent. The soul all crushed. Feeling this appalling void in my heart, I utter agonising cries inwardly. I feel as if there were nothing left to me but a scrap of faith, an atom of hope. I have lost all sense of liberty of heart. I feel a prisoner in a very rigid prison. This prison is open to the sky, I know that. But no one is there to raise me up from earth and I am like a bird with broken wings. I drag myself about and everything hurts me.

1st November. – Mass at home. Actually I am the first to be astonished at suffering so much when I do suffer and yet at suffering so rarely. One morning, one half-hour, of silent prayer in which I feel God's assistance sweep away all this sorrow, which nevertheless, each time it returns to me, appears with such a familiar face and so deeply anchored in my soul that it seems to me it must be the invisible companion of every moment of my life. Truly I shall always need God's consolation in order to live. For I do not call it living to suffer as I have suffered these last days. It ought rather to be called wandering on the threshold of death, experiencing nothingness, measuring the abyss of our solitude.

Veni Pater pauperum.

Bremond gives me much pain. What gifts he wastes.

Jacques has arranged a meeting with Père Gardeil to talk to him about his fine articles in the *Revue Thomiste.*[5]

5. This refers to the articles Père Gardeil published later in book form under the title *La Structure de l'Ame et l'Expérience mystique.* (J.)

How can he dare present him with so many (minor) objections? God grant he discerns what is true in them and takes account of it.

9th November. – Jacques is at Rossignol, at the grave of Ernest Psichari.

10th November. – Peaceful morning.

The demands of the contemplative life: not to seek consolation from any creature. And consolations not sought, "use them as if not using them."

If a soul introduced into the mystical life does not rigorously observe these rules, it wounds the jealous God who loves it.

And then the luckiest thing that can happen to this soul is that God, in order to keep it entirely to Himself in spite of itself, causes every creature from whom it asks consolation to fail it. Then they all become, at least in appearance, enemies. Where it seeks counsel, it finds silence. Where it seeks a friendly heart, it finds deafness. Where it seeks rest, it finds more rigid restraints than those of God's commandments – which are all lovable.

And that the soul suffers thus is a very great grace. If God loved it less, he would allow creatures to console it.

It must recognise its error as soon as possible. For in looking thus to right and left, it is following a zig-zag path which perhaps will weary God's patience.

The straight way that leads to God is infinitely short, for He is as close to us as our own soul.

The straight way is the magnanimous way, without the errors and faint-heartedness of childhood, but with the simplicity and trust of a child.

In the mystical way, with regard to creatures, God only grants the soul what it does not ask, apart from what charity itself makes it a duty for it to ask. A truth experienced a hundred times. Above all, he refuses what it desires too much. On the contrary, he appears to grant everything one asks in an impulse of charity, even material things, daily bread, fine weather.

Jacques is giving a lecture at Louvain today.

21st November. – First Mass celebrated in our house by Prince Ghika for the intention of the universal apostolate. Present were: Pierre Termier, Louis Massignon, René Grousset, Jean-Pierre Altermann, Aniouta and Stanislas Fumet, Mlle Goichon, Élie Denissoff, Albert Camilleri, Mother, Véra, Jacques and myself.

The next Mass will be said by Prince Ghika on the 21st December, feast of St Thomas the Apostle.

9th December. – Abbé Lamy came to the house to have supper and spend the night.

10th December. – Abbé Lamy said Mass in our chapel.[6]

24th December. – Abbé Lamy returned to the house; we had dinner with him. He celebrated Midnight Mass here and the Dawn Mass.

---

6. Raïssa dreamed of one day seeing intellectuals with various scientific specialisations join together in a spiritual fraternity. The individual members would continue to lead their own separate lives, but would gather at regular intervals for liturgical prayer and work and study sessions. The fraternity would be concerned above

all with philosophical and theological truth. It would take the thought of St Thomas as its guide and would be dedicated to the progress of that thought in two ways: according to the light it sheds on each individual member's particular domain and as it develops in its own philosophical and theological sphere. I found a small sheet of paper in Raïssa's Journal of 1924 (written probably in November) on which she had noted down an idea just as it came to her. On reflection, the idea defined itself quickly in the form I have indicated here, according to my recollection (when the idea first occurred to Raïssa, she thought of a "religious foundation" – actually unrealisable). I transcribe the little sheet below:

O Sapientia

The Order of Saint Thomas Aquinas

Union of prayer and study to combat theological and scientific error.

I. Vow of prayer.
II. Thomistic metaphysics and theology the foundation of intellectual development.
III. Scientific specialisation.

High mass in common every morning. Compline every evening. On high holidays and Sundays the entire service in common.

On December 9th Raïssa spoke at length to the Abbé Lamy of the association she was dreaming of. The next morning, after his mass, as if he had been given light on the subject, he encouraged her outright in the idea, and told us that he himself keenly wished for the formation of such an association.

In my opinion it would be like a third order, whose members would take the following three (private) vows: a vow of *prayer,* a vow of *purity of intention* (all for truth alone, with no concern for influencing people or for making adjustments to the tastes of the day) and a vow to *study* the works of St Thomas as thoroughly as possible. What name could the fraternity take? "The apprentices of Aquinas"? What counts is not the name, but that the group should exist some day. I confess that Raïssa's dream is still close to my heart. (J.)

25th December. – At 8.30 Abbé Lamy celebrated the third Mass of Christmas here. Then we talked for a long while until the arrival of Noële and Robert Boulet. He told us that on the 10th December, finding himself alone with Mother, he asked her when she was going to be a Catholic and she answered him amiably: "A little later on."

1925

Meudon, 23rd February. – Prince Ghika has come back from Rome as quickly as possible so as not to miss celebrating Mass in our house on the 24th, the anniversary of my father's death. This is a true token of his great charity and one which touches us very much, but Mother most of all.

24th February. – Mass said by Prince Ghika. This time it seemed to me that the question of Baptism could be raised with Mother. On such a day. Prince Ghika said a word or two to her on the subject after Mass while we were still in the chapel. When I come down to the dining-room, I find Mother as white as a sheet. I realise that she is deeply perturbed and somewhat frightened. After Prince Ghika has left, she tells me that he has spoken to her about being baptised and that her only answer has been that she would do God's will. Then he has made her promise to say the Lord's Prayer every day. She resents his having brought up the question of Baptism. I have to pacify her, to tell her that nothing is altered between us, that she is as com-

pletely free as ever, and that we shall not press her, any
more than we have done hitherto, to have herself baptised.
Then she calms down, kisses me very tenderly and I feel
that her confidence in us is entirely restored.

Since that day, a barrier seems to have fallen between
Mother and ourselves on the subject of religion. Now
Mother very often questions me about this or that point of
doctrine. I have copied out the Lord's Prayer for her in
Russian characters, and she says it every day, and even
several times a day. I have also got her a little prayer-book
in Russian. As well as the catechism my dear father[1] used.
Also the New Testament. She reads all this and shows me
more affection than she did before the 24th of February.

12th March. – Jacques looks awfully tired. Heavens,
where is all this going to end? Now yet another group of
young Catholics has loaded itself on him, demanding
intellectual direction, interviews, lectures. They are full of
zeal but want to launch into battle without sufficient
intellectual and spiritual preparation. One cannot reject
them, but perhaps they will be embarrassing disciples. Yet,
once again, how can one reject them? They have the merit
of being young, of being of the same generation as our
craziest writers and of wanting to combat them.

Most of our friends think Jacques "too kind". But *we*
think that all too often Catholics are content to enjoy their
acquired truth in peace and forget that others went to their
help when they were young and crazy themselves. . .

---

1. Usually Raïssa called her father by the Russian diminutive
Papka.

Certainly, one must keep within bounds. And that is where all the difficulty lies.

Foundation of the *Roseau d'Or*. Jacques has asked Massis, Frédéric Lefèvre and Fumet to collaborate on the managerial side: Cocteau, Ghéon, Ramuz, etc., on the editorial.

26th May, St Philip Neri. – This evening Mother said to me: "I shall read all this (some prayers in Russian) *for I must prepare myself, mustn't I*?" Blessed be God! It is a promise to receive Baptism. Words I have waited for for 19 years!

Sunday, 7th June. Feast of the Most Holy Trinity. – At mid-day, Mother said to us: "I dreamt that the Pope was standing in front of me, dressed in white. He gave Jacques something for me, something white that looked like *one* bird and was *three*. Jacques had to give it to me and I was just beside Jacques." – "O Mama," I said, "what a beautiful dream, for this very day is the feast of the Blessed Trinity." My mother did not know this and was very much moved to hear it. Her dream had made a very strong impression on her though she had not attributed any meaning to it.

15th June. – This evening, meeting in our house of the principal collaborators of the *Roseau d'Or :* Ramuz, Cocteau, Ghéon, Frédéric Lefévre, Massis, Fumet.

Telegram from Père Charles announcing his arrival this evening.

Next day, 16th June. – Yesterday Cocteau was meant to

leave early after dinner, a car was to come and fetch him to take him to the first night of the Russian Ballet. But the car was late.

Père Charles arrives before it. In the white habit he wears in the desert; the red Heart, surmounted by a cross, on his breast. He is a fine-looking man, very much at his ease. He starts straight away talking about Claudel who went to meet him at Marseilles and of their pilgrimage to Saint Maximin where Charles said Mass before the relics of St Magdalene – and at Sainte-Baume.

It makes a considerable impression. I see Jean Cocteau standing, silent, in the embrasure of the window, *gripped*. So here is God's very clear answer to our prayers, to our anxiety; for some weeks now we were wondering to which priest to send Cocteau – for the time has come – and we could not find the right one. Once again our very sweet God will have responded to a very great difficulty by a very great help.

The car arrives at 10.30, half an hour after Charles. As I am seeing Cocteau off, I invite him to come to the Mass Charles is to say in our house on the 19th, the feast of the Sacred Heart. Cocteau gives an evasive answer. But I have confidence. The moment Charles came in, I am convinced Cocteau saw the sign of his destiny appear over the heart of a man. The heart with which he signs all his letters suddenly became *the heart of Jesus*.

Same day, Tuesday 16th June. – Reverdy came to see us for the first time. We talk about Cocteau and Charles. Reverdy thinks we must not wait any longer, that Cocteau must go to Confession to Charles, and go to Communion with us on the 19th. Véra promptly telephones to the

Bishop's house at Versailles and asks, without Charles' knowledge, if he can have faculties for hearing confession in our house. This is granted. We tell Charles about it afterwards; he jibs and protests but nevertheless cannot refuse the burden we are ruthlessly putting on him.

Wednesday, 17th June. – Jacques went to see Cocteau to encourage him to go to Confession to Charles at once. A mission as delicate as it was difficult.[2] Cocteau has promised to come and *talk* to Charles tomorrow, no more.

Thursday, 18th June. – Jacques went to fetch Jean [Cocteau] at his home and brought him to ours about 4 o'clock. Cocteau talked for a long while with Charles in the drawing-room while, praying inwardly but keeping up a conversation with Noële and Robert Boulet in my little study, we anxiously awaited the result of his long interview, which, to crown our difficulties, we had to keep secret from Noële and Robert. At last we heard Charles and Cocteau go up to the chapel. Then Charles summoned Jacques. Jean went to confession, saw Jacques, then left, completely overcome.

Friday, 19th June, Feast of the Sacred Heart. – Charles said Mass in our chapel. Cocteau went to Communion with us. Ghéon, Massignon, the Fumets (invited long ago for this day) were there as well. Mother, as usual, was at Mass. One more example for her. Misericordias Domini. . .

---

2. Reverdy was there, and kept urging Cocteau violently: "How can you possibly understand anything without the Sacraments? Put on the ear-phones! Put on the ear-phones!" (J.)

2nd July. – Death of Éric Satie at the Saint-Joseph hospital. A few days ago, on June 29th, Jacques saw Satie for the last time. When Satie fell asleep, Jacques stayed beside him, praying under his breath. Then Satie woke up and said these very sweet words to Jacques: "It's good to be together like this, without saying anything, especially when one thinks alike."

12th July, Sixth Sunday after Pentecost. – For the first time Mother read the Gospel *during Mass*, and the Epistle too. And the Epistle was: St Paul to the Romans (6:3–11): Quicumque baptizati sumus in Christo Jesu. . . and the Gospel: the multiplication of the loaves, St Mark (8:1–9).

28th July. – Wrote a long letter to Sophie Belkind, who is in Palestine.

29th July, St Martha. – In the morning I say to Jacques: "I have the feeling that now we ought to go quickly, waiting any longer would be bad for Mama." Yesterday, with Véra, we were wondering which of our priest friends Mother would like to baptise her. Abbé Millot, no doubt.
At 6 in the evening, I was with Jacques in my study by the chapel – suddenly I say to him: "I'm going downstairs, I must see Mama." I find her in the dining-room, reading the Epistle of St James, her face peaceful and happy. "It's very beautiful," she says to me. I answer: "Yes, Mama, and you know many things now!" "Do you think so?" she says, and then: "Then you think I'm ready?" "Oh, my dear Mama, I do think so! What incredible happiness!" I rush upstairs to call Jacques, and he flings himself on my Mother's neck. All three of us embrace

one another, mad with joy. An hour later Véra returns from Paris and weeps for joy when she hears the marvellous news.

Mother told us that she had been anxious these past few days but that this very day all her anxieties had vanished and she had made the resolution to have herself baptised and to tell us so as soon as Véra had returned from Paris. I came downstairs an hour too soon, but truly I was impelled to.

God has answered our prayers magnificently. I have so often asked him that Mother should be converted in full health and not at the moment of the last agony.

We spent a delicious evening.

31st July. – We went to announce the good news to our dear Abbé Millot and to ask him to baptise Mother. He is tremendously happy, like the true friend he is. Knowing the whole situation, he decides to move fast and chooses earlier dates than we should have dared to ask for: Baptism, Sunday, August 2nd; First Communion, August 3rd.

There again, what sweet kindness on the part of God! The 3rd of August is also the anniversary of our First Communion, Jacques', Véra's and mine. From now on there will be four of us to give special thanks to God on that day.

Sunday, 2nd August, Ninth after Pentecost. – At 5 o'clock, Mother baptised by M. Millot.

With hearts bursting with joy and thanksgiving we go downstairs at 6 o'clock to receive friends who were already waiting quite a while for us, without our being able to tell them of the great event. Mother asked us not to speak of it yet.

In the drawing-room we find M. Bovy who was converted to Catholicism after the death of his young wife, and Maurice Sachs whom Jean Cocteau sent to Jacques to be instructed in Catholicism and whom I see for the first time.

Monday, 3rd August, Finding of the Relics of St Stephen, protomartyr. – Mass said by M. Millot. Mother's First Communion. Jacques, Véra and I go to Communion with her.

After Mass, M. Millot leaves for Lourdes where he will take our thanksgivings.

6th August, Transfiguration of Our Lord. – Maurice Sachs has decided to have himself baptised. Jean Cocteau will be his godfather and I his godmother. Jacques is sending him to Père Pressoir to complete his religious instruction.

14th August. – Mgr. Gibier comes with M. Millot to confirm Mother, also in our chapel. He did not want Mother to have to make a journey. How kind everyone has been! The ceremony took place in the afternoon. Everything was so beautiful, so bright, a celebration all round us as well as in our hearts.

What shall we render God for all these benefactions!

15th August, Assumption of the Blessed Virgin. – Second Communion of my dear Mother.

16th August. – Wrote to Maurice.

29th August. – Maurice's baptism.

In spite of everything, I am not easy in my mind. There is something obscure in this boy which disquiets me.

30th August. – Maurice's First Communion.

Lord, give me your heart! Without this gift of your love, even though you were to give me the knowledge and power of the angels and possession of the entire Creation, my heart would not find its rest nor my soul its beatitude.

Martyrdom of the heart. This has come back suddenly, started up by a very trivial cause, just when I thought myself in Paradise since Mother's baptism. All at once, I found myself plunged in an abyss of misery – in the midst of temptations so deep-seated and so searching that my heart was absolutely tormented by them. I said to God: I accept this martyrdom of the heart and all the sufferings you destine for me – as acts of thanksgiving for your infinite blessings. But do, Lord, consider my wretchedness, my frailty. And if some relief is necessary for my soul, gripped in the vice of temptation and of silence, to keep its equilibrium – grant it me.

I suffer unspeakably. I feel that my suffering is rooted in the depths of my soul, in the very sources of nature. It is like an absolutely personal, inexpressible mystery. A feeble heart which *needs* to deceive itself. A stalwart reason which *never* allows it to. Poor heart! The only resource left to it is tears. Silent tears, so bitter, so harsh. They come from the sources of being and life drains away with them.

o

With those who have chosen Him as their unique Love from their youth, the Lord is not easy-going – quite the contrary. First of all, he made them know his sweetness. Assured of their fidelity – and it is he himself who assures it – he no longer spares their heart any pain. He does not make them live as if resurrected, but as dying people and martyrs. He lets them experience all their weakness so as to manifest all His power in them as He said to St Paul. He makes them learn their lessons in tears, he does not spare them the ordeal of fire, telling them: *my grace is sufficient for thee.*

These poor souls who have espoused him in Faith enter thus into the mystery of the Redemption. And then they see that there is no reason for their martyrdom except that it makes up what is lacking in the Passion of Christ.

We do not "roll ourselves up in a ball" as Marcus Aurelius advised the Stoics, so as to offer as little surface as possible for suffering to get a grip on. Christians stretch themselves out on the Cross and expose themselves to all the blows.

My Jesus is so much my God that I cannot have any other God but him. I have truly chosen him from my youth. Henceforth he is my life. And any other life I can only call *temptation.* These temptations are very rare, it is true. But for me they have all the intensity they can have in a human heart. Beyond lies madness or death. Or a way out in sin. But my choice was made long ago and for ever; anything rather than offend the immense love of my God who is my much-loved Love, from now on.

My beloved Jacques! For more than twenty years I have seen him living with his heart always intent upon God.

All my life is at his service, at the service of his work which is all for God.

To me it is not permitted to be weak.

And I do not permit myself to be.

I must be strong without one minute of respite.

I am in the extremity of distress and I need some outside aid because God has withdrawn from me. I have hours of sufferings so terrible that I feel I am going to lose my reason.

But I do not want to remove myself from the Cross. Every day I abandon myself to whatever suffering God wills. And the Cross of Jesus carries me over all the abysses.

Sunday, 6th September. – Mass said by Prince Ghika. Mother and Maurice go to Communion with us. First visit of Jean Bourgoint.

8th September, Nativity of Our Lady. – Mother goes to Communion with us.

Letter from Paul Sabon, *urgent.* Jacques answers immediately asking him to come this very day so that he could see Père Charles. He sees him, in fact, for a long time. Charles takes him up to the chapel. He stiffens – but, on coming out, when Charles says a few words to him about the Blessed Virgin, he begins to weep.

In the evening, Jacques takes Bourgoint to see Prince Ghika. The baptism is fixed for the 7th October.[3]

---

3. When he entered the Trappist order a few years later, Jean Bourgoint became Brother Pascal, at Notre-Dame de Cîteaux. Later, while remaining under obedience to the Abbot of Cîteaux, he left for the Cameroons in August, 1964, to care for the lepers. He died there on March 11, 1966. He was buried in the lepers' village of Mokolo. (J.)

Wednesday, 9th September. –

At 2 o'clock, Prince Ghika, Père Pel.

At 3 o'clock Paul Sabon, another long conversation with Charles.

Père Pel seems very pious and humble, but not very intelligent or prudent.

Thursday, 10th September. – Paul Claudel comes at 7 o'clock to serve Père C.'s Mass.

True Christian. Strong soul. But bizarre character.

At 5 o'clock Père Dehau comes; admirable. Good conversation with him.

Friday, 11th September. – Votive Mass of the Sacred Heart. It was also on the feast of the Sacred Heart that Cocteau went to Communion.

At 7 o'clock, Reverdy.

Saturday, 12th September, Feast of the Holy Name of Mary (my 42nd birthday!). – In the afternoon, visit from Pierre Couturier who is entering the noviciate at Amiens tomorrow.[4]

Sunday, 13th September. – Confirmation of Maurice Sachs, at Versailles. Moving sermon by Mgr. Gibier. He recalls that, in 1913, in the same chapel, he confirmed Ernest Psichari. . . Those present were Père Pressoir, Véra, Éveline, Jacques and myself.

---

4. He was to become that Père Couturier so dear to writers and artists, and who loved them so much and whom we loved so much. (J.)

Maurice Sachs and Jean Bourgoint lunch with us. Bourgoint declares that he is immensely happy in our little chapel. In the evening Abbé Millot dines with us.

25th September. – Beginning of the Thomist Circles' retreat, with Père Garrigou-Lagrange.

14th October. – J.'s pilgrimage to Notre-Dame des Bois. The saintly Curé tells him: "You are the missionary of the Holy Spirit."[5]

---

5. I take the liberty of transcribing here the lines I wrote when I returned from this pilgrimage, and which Raïssa kept in her fourth notebook:

Wednesday, 14th October 1925. Pilgrimage to Notre Dame of the Woods.

On our way through the woods to the Chapel I talked to the holy curé about Cocteau, about Maurice [Sachs], about all the young people who come to the house. He said to me in an extraordinarily serious tone:

"Have no doubt that you are on the road the Lord wishes you to take.

"The Holy Virgin leads all and blesses all, she who always wants to give and who finds that we never give enough (*reach out, reach out,* she said to a poor priest at the prayers for the living.)

"Our Lord was concerned with the masses, but also and above all with his apostles. Some of these young people will shine forth in their turn. They may have slipped into evil, but their strength will serve the good. This is a task which has been much neglected in our day, when we are too easily satisfied with appearances. You are the missionary of the Holy Spirit. It will take years to give some education to these young people."

On the subject of the conflicts among poets: "Yes, you will find it very difficult to make peace here. Be satisfied with the appearance of peace, that will be a step in the right direction."

"Missionary of the Holy Spirit", that is an appellation of which I am wholly unworthy. It remains to be said that there are no limits to God's mercy, even with respect to the poorest and unsteadiest of workmen. (J.)

13th December. – Death of Henri Pierre, at the age of 24, after a long illness. He wanted to become a priest, was deeply given to God.

His mother told us, a little later, that he was placed in his coffin with *De la Vie d'Oraison* on his breast. Do pray for us now, very dear soul.

1926

Meudon, *29th January*. – The story of André Grange:

André Grange, a friend of Paul Sabon, and a victim, like him, of the Surrealists, came to see Jacques. At the first interview, Jacques gave him the *Epitome* of St. John of the Cross published by C. H.[1] And St. John of the Cross acted in a marvellous way. André Grange became inseparable from the little book and showed it to everyone. In three weeks, God had done his work in him. All he had left were a few objections, easy to overcome.

Suddenly he fell ill and sensed at once that he was going to die. On Friday, the 22nd of January (when he was to have come to see us), feeling himself very near death, he sent for the curate of his parish, had an important conversation with him, went to confession and received

_____

1. I did this because I saw he was involved in a real and profound spiritual experience, but one which seemed to be dominated by the prince of darkness. (J.)

Communion. Afterwards he expressed all his joy to the priest who was just leaving – and at the moment he was going through the door, André Grange exclaimed: *Father, how corrupt the world is!* This boy of twenty who was leaving the world was judging the world in the light of supernatural wisdom.

Jacques, warned only on the morning of that Friday, by Paul Sabon, of the gravity of André Grange's illness, went to see him in the afternoon. Grange expressed all his happiness to Jacques, as to Sabon, as to all those who came to see him that day – and this in the midst of atrocious physical sufferings. He also said to Jacques: "It is St. John of the Cross who has done it all!"

The next day, he went into delirium and never emerged from it again. He received Extreme Unction and died on Sunday at eleven o'clock at night.

This conversion and this death have put an end to Paul Sabon's last hesitations. He came and took refuge with Jacques on Monday. He was to go to confession today and should go to Communion tomorrow.[2]

He told us on Monday that when he was with the Surrealists, he was aware of the devil with all his illusions and all his deceptions.

All this proves that *the best way* for all these poor souls is the knowledge of the Catholic doctrine of divine love.

---

2. Our friend Paul Sabon died on the 12th of September, 1933. I was then away, travelling. Raïssa, hearing that he was ill and in the last extremity, begged Père Riquet to go at once to Bourg-la-Reine. He was able to assist Paul before his death, which occurred at 10.30 p.m. (J.)

Yesterday again, Sabon was saying to Jacques that St. John of the Cross has everything, and that he is never tired of reading and re-reading him.

Yesterday evening, at our house, someone asked him what had made him leave the Surrealists. *"God!"* he answered emphatically.

March. – The soul drawn down by God into its most intimate depths longs for a word, longs for a light which will increase the range of its love still more. Then it realises that there is no human word precise enough, intimate enough, adequate enough, profound enough to express the depth and the intimacy of its union with God. And then it aspires towards the Father, desiring of Him that he should engender in it His Word, the Word itself – which alone can penetrate into the innermost recesses of the soul and illuminate it in a measure befitting that love which is charity.

[Notebook No. 4 stops here.]

II

JOURNAL OF 1931

JOURNAL OF 1931

Meudon, *6th October,* Tuesday. – Jacques asks me to resume my diary which I have abandoned for so long. I shall try. If I have the time, I will note down here some important events in our life during these last years. But I will begin with the most recent: The annual retreat of the Thomist Circles was preached by Père Garrigou-Lagrange from the 25th to the 28th of September. The retreatants were particularly numerous this year; we can only find the names of 117 of them but there were at least 150. Among them, Protestants like Bauhofer who is being prepared for baptism, and his wife too (she was not at Meudon). Bauhofer was charitable enough to tell us that it was only here, during these days of retreat, that he had learnt what real prayer was. It is true that the High Mass of September 27th and the Magnificat which closed the retreat on the 28th were particularly impressive. One felt such unanimity of heart and mind, such faith, in all these retreatants, priests and laity. This unanimity also struck Willard Hill at the conference Père Garrigou gave at our house on the Sunday afternoon. Among those who made this retreat were our dear Van der Meers, including Anne-Marie who is entering the Benedictines of Oosterhout on October 12th; Charles Du Bos and his wife; Abbé Charles Journet; Abbé Lallement; Father Reeves, an English Dominican; Bullough and his wife (who is the daughter of the Duse and who told me that her mother possessed Léon Bloy's books and had read them with enthusiasm); O'Sullivan, president of the Aquinas Society of London; Dalbiez; René Schwob; Oscar Bauhofer; Mme Jean Berchem and her father, Protestants; Marek Szwarc; Cohen who is preparing himself to enter the Dominicans; Germaine and Jean Dedeken; Jean and Pierre Linn, Marie-Anne François; Henri Ghéon. . .

Jacques left yesterday for Chartres where he hopes to be able to work in peace and finish *Distinguer pour Unir*.

*

Retrospective Diary

I am going to recall my memories by going backwards.

Yesterday, 5th October. – I received a visit from Mme. Cocteau. She gave me good news of Jean who is ill with a mild attack of typhoid in Toulon.

Sunday, 4th October, Feast of St. Francis of Assisi. – Mass celebrated for Willard Hill's friend who died on the 4th October 1930. Willard was present at this Mass and went to Communion with us. He wept, thinking of the beauty of God's ways. It was through this great sorrow that his conversion began. Yesterday he had opened the

Imitation at Ch. V. of Book III; it touched him to the heart.

This same Sunday afternoon, visit from Marcel Brion and the Bonjeans. She is Jewish; we talked a great deal about Catholicism. Then visit from Jacques' mother, his sister and Éveline.

Saturday, 3rd October, Feast of St. Thérèse of Lisieux. – Jacques has drawn up a ukase destined to protect us against the invasions of our fellow men! We will try once again, and see if it is possible for us to continue to live at Meudon without losing any leisure for prayer, and with no peril of death! It matters little whether one dies in harness, provided that it is the kind of harness which is willed by God.

Friday, 2nd October, Feast of the Holy Guardian Angels. – Read this during the night of 1st–2nd October:

"When you are filled with the essence of all existence, everything you say becomes true. From all time, the poets have praised truth and virtue. Has that made their readers virtuous and truthful? But when a man stripped of self lives among us, his acts become the beating of the heart of virtue; everything he does to others betters even their most mediocre dreams; everything he touches becomes true and pure; he becomes the father of reality." (*Vie de Ramakrishna* by Romain Rolland, pp. 176–177.)

And, in a note, these words of Gandhi's:

"Our spiritual experiences are necessarily communicated, whether we wish it or not. But by our life, by our example, not by our words which are a very incomplete vehicle of them. Spiritual experiences are deeper than thought itself. . . From the mere fact that we live, our spiritual experience will overflow. . . But if you want another to receive your spiritual experience, you erect an intellectual barrier between him and you. . ."

It is true that our words are a very imperfect vehicle of spiritual experiences. But not to wish at all to communicate them through speech, that is an excess and an error of Gandhi's moralism. For us who have received the word of Christ, we know that we must both live it and preach it.

And here are these men who have received such an incomplete revelation and who make the germ of life that has been given to them fructify to the maximum. And we Catholics, to whom a truth without any admixture of error has been revealed, have got to the point of receiving lessons in spirituality; whereas we ought to be able to illuminate the whole earth with the light of Christ. Yes, I know that we have our saints who are so pure and so great, but we ought to have more of them. And our religious communities ought *all* to be more contemplative than they are. For example, what crises certain great Orders we know well are going through in that respect – Orders whose particular vocation, whether it be liturgical or apostolic, requires that contemplation should have first place? And even of those dedicated solely to contemplation, there is much one could say. I know that true and pure contemplation is very rare, even in those privileged circles. Yet the charity of the Church is always visible on earth.

Ramakrishna: "Do not worry about doctrines! What counts is the essence of existence in every man: and that is *spirituality*. You must acquire it."

How can one reconcile this great sense of the value of the *spiritual* with this doctrinal eclecticism? Perhaps this is

Raïssa
Paris, 1905

Raïssa
1. *Paris, 1902*
2. *Versailles, 1920*
3. *Meudon, 1928*

Véra
Paris, 1905

Véra
1. *Paris, 1905*
2. *Saint-Jorioz, 1926*
3. *Meudon, 1928*

Véra
Princeton, 1953

inevitable when the true doctrine is not known ... Especially as there is not, properly speaking, eclecticism in Ramakrishna, but rather contempt for all doctrine which appears as blocking the mind instead of furthering spiritualisation. "I do not like discussions. And God is beyond the powers of reasoning ..."

Admirable disinterestedness: "Let the bees plunder your heart but be careful not to keep any of them captive by the beauty of your soul!" (P. 207.)

Monday, 28th September was the last day of our retreat. At lunch, the Van der Meers; at dinner, the Linns and René Schwob.

Sunday, 27th September. – Mass in our chapel. Then High Mass of the retreat at the Presentation.

I returned home alone before the sermon so as to suffer alone and to pray without any onlookers. At first I experienced a little comfort from it, then the unspeakable anguish returned. At lunch (with the Van der Meers) I suffered so much that I had to leave the table, go up to my room and lie down: the anguish in my soul became such that I thought I should go mad or die. Then I fortified myself with the name of *Mary* which was a genuine refreshment to me. No doubt that is what the souls in Purgatory feel when we pray to the Virgin for them. Afterwards the flood of nameless misery returned, but then God sent me my dear Jacques who set to making the sign of the *Cross* all over me, as they do for Extreme Unction, and I was calmed. Contrary to all hope, I was able to go downstairs at 3 o'clock for the talk Père Garrigou-Lagrange always gives in our house during the retreat.

He spoke about St Catherine of Siena and did not fail to make theology look humble before the least act of charity. All the retreatants were able to get into the drawing-room as Sandoz had had the good idea of removing the doors. Père Garrigou did a great deal of good. At dinner, Abbé Journet, Bauhofer, Abbé Leclef, Éveline. We went to bed very late, nevertheless I held out very well.

Saturday, 26th September. – At lunch Père Dehau and Père Garrigou. Before lunch I saw Père Dehau for a few minutes but this gave me no comfort at all in the anguished state I live in, especially during the past three months. At dinner, the Bulloughs, Father Reeves, O'Sullivan, all extremely charming, cultured, distinguished and pious. Besides them, Willard Hill, René Schwob, Père Garrigou. After dinner, Miss Borton. Very good evening, of deep understanding, without fatigue. (I told Père Dehau that I had a horror in advance of the ways through which I felt God would make me pass.)

Friday, 25th September. – At 3.30 first sermon of the retreat. At dinner G. Dedeken, Yvan Lenain, Moureau, Dalbiez, René Schwob, Abbé Journet.

Thursday, 24th September, Our Lady of Mercy. – In the evening, arrival of Père Garrigou; at dinner Père Garrigou. During all these days of the retreat there was perpetual coming and going in the house. I hope all this activity was useful.

Sunday, 20th September. – In the afternoon, the Szwarcs, Jean Cattauï de Ménasce, and others I can't remember now.

Jacques was at Meudon from the 6th of September. On August 15th he went to Salzburg where he gave six lectures. In Salzburg he met the Bulloughs, Guardini, Georgii and also Ghéon. On the 22nd he left for Munich with Eschweiler and Bauhofer to meet Peterson there, in joy over his conversion to Catholicism (baptised in Rome at Christmas).[1] On Wednesday 26th he left for Konnersreuth, still with Eschweiler.

On Thursday, August 27th, he saw Thérèse Neumann at her home, in her normal state. She made a very good impression indeed on him. He asked her to pray for me, and to ask God to make his will known to us. She promised to do so.

On Friday, August 28th, Jacques saw Thérèse Neumann in her painful ecstasy, in the morning, about half-past 9 – later on about midday. Two streams of blood flowed from her eyes. The linen cloths over her head and chest were spotted with bright blood. The stigmata in the hands were very evident, but did not bleed. She was half sitting up in bed with her arms raised, her body not rigid; her face expressed acute, sorrowful compassion; she did not speak.

On Saturday, the 29th, Jacques arrived at Strasburg, where Alexandre Grunelius and Nicolas Nabokov were waiting to take him to Kolbsheim where he stayed till the 6th of September.[2]

---

1. I also met Theodore Haecker in Munich. (J.)

2. This, in the person of myself, was our first meeting with those who became our beloved godchildren Antoinette and Lexi. (Raïssa was the godmother of Alexandre Grunelius; she and I the godmother and godfather of Antoinette.) Antoinette was baptised in our chapel at Meudon, by Père Bruno on March 15th, 1932; Alexandre at the Benedictine house in the Rue Monsieur, by Abbé Altermann, on June 14th, 1933. (J.)

On July 26th Jacques and I returned from Bagnoles where we had spent a month.

Véra and I were at Saint-Paul de Vence during part of May. Met P. H. at Saint-Paul.[3]

Mother has been ill since the month of April . . .

On March 7th, 1931, Willard Hill baptised in our chapel by Père Bruno.

On March 11th, 1931, Jean Hugo baptised in Paris, by Abbé Mugnier.

Both godsons of Jacques'.

*

Continuation of Diary for 1931

9th October. – Harshness of saints who are still only at the angelic stage. When they resemble the Christ of the Passion, they will begin to know what sweetness and kindness are.

---

3. René Schwob was living in Saint-Paul when Raïssa and Véra went there for a little rest. He introduced them to his friend P. H., but the latter frightened him with his black magic and his theories about the gratuitous act, and Schwob was seeking to shelter himself behind Raïssa. Between Raïssa and P. H. there were lively religious discussions and a certain mutual sympathy developed. When P. H. sent a book of his, which had just appeared, to her at Meudon, she wrote to thank him. To which he replied that he had great respect for her and that, for that very reason, "when I feel myself worthy to do so, I shall kill you." She retorted that she would be very glad to be worthy of such great homage. Cf. below, *Complementary Fragments,* Fragment 2 (see also Fragment 1). (J.)

10th October. – "My God, give me what thou commandest and command what thou wilt." (Prayer of St Augustine.)

Met Mme McCrae at the concert. Heard Schubert's *Tragic Symphony.*

11th October, Twentieth Sunday after Pentecost. – My Jacques is at Chantilly after having been to Chartres, to finish his book. In the afternoon, visits from Marthe Spitzer, Babet, Roland-Manuel, the Linns, Marie-Louise, Éveline. Roland-Manuel tells me that Père A., completely abandoned by his religious family, bears his great dereliction in a wholly supernatural spirit, but he is shattered.

12th October. – Letter from Mme Hugo Ball; she says that her husband very much liked Jacques' books and read them often. Today Anne-Marie van der Meer enters the Benedictines at Oosterhout. Jacques returned from Chantilly.

13th October. – Jacques lunched at Gay's with Père Schmitt, Maurice Brillant, Père Bernadot [. . .] and some Dahoman Catholics, great admirers of Père Aupiais'.

15th October. – Since every man of good faith and pure morals can receive divine grace and the grace of final perseverance without visibly belonging to the Church, why the preaching of the Gospel? Why not preach only the existence of God, good faith and purity, which is accessible to every conscience?

Can we not say that souls which are saved in this way

do not collaborate actively in the salvation of the world? They are saved but they do not save . . . [4] In any case the preaching of the Gospel is necessary in order to afford souls a normal state with regard to salvation.

Pierre and Christine dine with us, the first time since their daughter's departure.

16th October, Friday. – "I have received the Cross, I have received it from Thy hand: and I will bear it unto death as Thou hast laid it on me." This is the text that the Imitation gave me today (Book III, LVI). And I recognised it and accepted it from the bottom of my soul.

24th October, St Raphaël, Archangel. – No man in the world is strictly worthy of the confidence of another man. Here, the gift always surpasses the capacity to receive. Only the heart of God can be adequate to it.

Does God want us to leave here to have greater solitude? Or to have greater solitude without going away? I no

---

4. At least, we thought, they only collaborate actively in the salvation of the world by the fervour of their personal intercession and in virtue of their personal merits (united to those of the Saviour), not in virtue of the communal work accomplished by the Body of which Christ is the Head. The (conjectural) idea we both had was that it is through *sacramental* graces, and, above all, through Baptism that souls are actively engaged in the great common (co-redemptive) work of the Mystical Body of Christ. In other words, they are so deeply rooted in this Whole that it is in the work itself accomplished by it and in the Cross itself borne by it that they participate by suffering and interceding. Cf. Charles Journet, *L'Église du Verbe Incarné,* Vol. II. pp. 326–327 and 406–407. (J.)

longer know what I want in my heart of hearts . . . Going
away would be a great adventure! What would the separation cost me? I am vitally attached to only three beings,
Jacques, Véra and Mother. There is no question of leaving
them. As to other friendships, even the deepest ones, I love
to have my hands full of them but I don't close my fists on
them; they can escape me and fly away, without affecting
any essential part of me. But I love human life in general;
all this movement of hearts and minds, all these labours,
these efforts and even this agitation; I feel that it would
cost me a great deal to cut myself off from them altogether,
I should be like a brook that had withdrawn from the
great river and become a lake. No, one must only withdraw
oneself in order to reach the ocean quicker. One must
only withdraw oneself by a greater love, for a greater
love.

In the material world, energy is released by destruction.
In the spiritual world too. But not by just any destruction.
To release spiritual energy, one must be destroyed by love,
consumed by the fire of divine charity. Nothing of what is
offered to this fire is lost and everything is lost of what is not
offered to it.

Read yesterday (*23rd October*) in the Imitation: "And
even oughtest thou to think it thy unique joy that I scourge
thee unsparingly." (Book III, Ch. XXX.)

Sunday, 25th October, Feast of Christ the King. – Mass
said by Père Bruno.

Jacques is at Bellevue. At 3 o'clock there arrived Willard
Hill, and then his friend Mme McCrae with Éveline.
Then Dr. de Vries and Abbé Boutinaud, and then Babet

Jacob. Maxime is making his profession on November the 1st.[5] Wrote to Germaine (Dedeken).

26th October. – Very tired from yesterday afternoon. Will the trouble I went to yesterday bear some fruit?

This morning once again I suffered in a way that was scarcely tolerable. Is it my purgatory I am doing like this?

But whatever does God want of me? What solitude? What death?

[Raïssa has written in the margin: I ask the same questions today: 2nd April, 1934. – (in a different ink), and today, 17th December, 1936.]

Saturday, 31st October. – Concert with René Schwob. Heard Bach's *Actus Tragicus.* Mozart's *Requiem.*

1st November. – My dear Jacques has definitely returned to Meudon, and we are now snowed under with work and I no longer have a moment to myself.

Afternoon: Yves Simon, Willard Hill, Georges Izard, the Lemaîtres, the Severinis, the Pichets, Arthur Lourié.

3rd November. – Visit from Christine who brought Mme Reiner and her daughter Mia, who has such an astonishing and quite spontaneous devotion to St Thomas Aquinas.[6]

Sunday, 8th November. – Père Riquet came with some

---

5. On entering the Abbey of En-Calcat, Maxime Jacob took the name of Clément. (J.)

6. It was to this little Mia that Raïssa dedicated her *Ange de L'École.* (J.)

twenty medical students, interns . . . Jacques gave them a little lecture on the relations between science and philosophy. There also appeared Jacques de Monléon, Sandoz, Oliver Lacombe, Willard Hill, Father Smothers, Mme McCrae, etc.

Monday, 9th November. – Visit from Père Dehau. He encourages me very much. He says that the (spiritual) operation I have undergone must have been very important, since God took charge of it himself, that he had not wanted any assistant-surgeon but that, on the other hand, he had called in the Nurse who is the Blessed Virgin herself.[7] The Father dines with us, so does Éveline whom Jacques went to Paris to fetch.

The *11th November,* at Marcel Arland's house in the country.

15th November. – At dinner, Nicolas Nabokov and his friends the Gruneliuses, also Babet and Éveline.

Sunday, 22nd November, afternoon. – Psichari's eldest sister, Willard Hill and Pearson, Éveline, Roland-Manuel, François Mauriac, Pierre van der Meer, the Linns; at dinner, the Fumets.

---

7. I find in one of my notebooks, on the same date: "Père Dehau spent the day at the house. Raïssa told him that, during all that period when she suffered so much, she felt the Blessed Virgin as it were bending over her mercifully.

" 'It is the head-surgeon operating single-handed,' he replied. 'And this presence of the Blessed Virgin that you feel, yes, that is the Nurse he calls in when he performs major operations. You're lucky . . .' " (J.)

23rd November. – Departure of Jacques for Geneva. This evening he gives a lecture in Geneva.

24th November. – Departure of Jacques for Milan. At 5 o'clock, first lecture at the University of Milan. Lectures in Milan the 25th, 26th, 27th.

On the 28th, Jacques leaves for the Carthusian Monastery at Farneta.

On the 28th and 29th, Jacques had talks with Dom Florent Miège. Jacques questioned him about our difficulties. Dom Miège was absolutely definite: "These are the chains that Our Lord has given you. You must kiss your chains. Be over-driven and eaten-up to the limit. *In* prayer. Example of Père Libermann. Do not dream of changing your life, leaving your post." He is very much against the idea of the ashram.[8] "*Do not tie yourself up with anyone.*" "Love your crosses."

And all that he said for me . . . remember it in times of trial[9] . . .

Jacques returned on the 1st December.

---

8. We were wondering at that time whether we ought not to live with some friends in a kind of Christian ashram. (J.)

9. Dom Florent seemed to be in spiritual communication with Raïssa. He had a great affection for her and spoke of her interior life with a kind of intuitive assurance. He always charged me to tell her to have complete confidence in the ways by which God was leading her. And also said that he and she were deeply united in the love of God.

I transcribe here some notes of mine, taken after a conversation with him on the morning of November 29th 1931: "I say that I impose on Raïssa a life that is crushing and which disturbs her in her life of prayer. – 'How do you know if this disturbs her? No, it is not a distraction for her, she is wholly supernatural. You need

Tuesday, 1st December. – Death of the saintly Curé, at the house of Comte Biver, about 10 o'clock at night.

We saw him on his deathbed on Thursday, December 3rd. A very simple, very poor, very bare death. Funeral service on Saturday 5th at the Infirmerie Marie-Thérèse. Burial at La Courneuve.

Sunday, 6th December. – In the afternoon, good study meeting. Jacques de Monléon gave a little lecture on knowledge, and Étienne Borne on work.

Tuesday, 8th December, Immaculate Conception. – Is it not the baptism of the Virgin? Grace, faith, the indwelling of the Blessed Trinity in her soul from the first moment of her human life?

In the evening, Mozart concert, at the Société Mozartienne, with Ghéon and his sister and Willard Hill. "Pure" music; joy and play: and the very gravity in it is angelic.

----

her help, she helps you a great deal, but she is sufficiently united to God to do it without detriment to her soul.'

"I speak of the interior trials through which she is passing. – 'That's normal, the mystical ways involve this. It is necessary. She has to go through this.'

"I tell him that she said to me: 'The good Lord wants to kill me.' 'Yes, that's exactly it, he wants to kill the ego, that's just it.'

" 'She must never take a decision in these moments of interior suffering. In those states one must continue doggedly in the path where one was.'

"In the afternoon, I speak to him again on this subject. I say: 'I am accepting that she should sacrifice herself to God, but not to me'. He answered: 'Yes, she is sacrificed. But not to you. To the cause of Our Lord. Her life is a source of blessings.' " (J.)

Raïssa's Journal

Sunday, 13th December. – Concert: Jaubert's *Le Jour*; very pleasant atmosphere, moving melodic quality. The last part seemed to me a little forced, a little long. Before the concert, visit from Roland-Manuel and Carducci who seems near conversion. Talked to Roland-Manuel about Mauriac and Jean-Pierre Altermann. The disagreement between director and directed is even more serious than I thought.

After the concert: Ghéon, Maurice Brillant and the Arneys. Jacques Arney played some pieces of his own composition which seemed to us good music. Brillant thought well of them and wants to recommend Arney to Straram. Ghéon read us his *Avare* which is immensely funny. I gave Brillant Guina Szwarc's play *Emma* to show to Baty.

Monday, 14th December. – Jacques leaves for Louvain where he gives a lecture at 3 o'clock, once again on the idea of Christian philosophy.

Tuesday, 15th December. – Jacques stopped at the Carmelite convent, at Lille, and arrived in the evening at the Salle Gaveau for the concert conducted by Désormières: splendid programme: two Bach chorales, Satie's *Parade*, Markévitch's *Rébus, Le Sacre du Printemps.*

Curious audience: *everyone* is there: Stravinsky, Lourié, Nabokov, Markévitch; Bérard, Auric and his wife, Bonjean, Jean Cocteau, Jean Desbordes, Julien Green, etc. And Max Jacob . . .

Cocteau arrives wearing enormous thick white gloves, death enters with him. Desbordes has become quite thin and pale, he looks as if he had been iller than Cocteau.

Parade has a very moving reception. What purity in that music, and what knowledge! What domination too of the will and the consciousness over the most exquisite of sensibilities.

Rébus is like everything that Markévitch has produced so far: clever and unpleasant. Much ability and little soul. *Omnirébus* of hell, says Jacques; yes, and it is a homage to Diaghilev.

Le Sacre seems to me more beautiful every time I hear it. The whole of Russia is in this music. What splendid material for even the most geometrical and apparently *deliberate* arabesques.

We see Stravinsky after this concert. He asked us to go to his concert on Thursday. We did not want to go. But we probably shall go . . .

[End of Diary for 1931.]

III

LOOSE LEAVES

1931–1960

LOOSE LEAVES

I

1931-1935

*

Meudon, *21st February 1935*. – When one is actually living through experiences one hardly ever has the time or opportunity to write about them. From time to time one jots down a thought on a piece of paper that one keeps or one destroys. I intend to recopy here what has remained scattered up to now. It's so trifling, what I have kept, and what I have said, compared to what life has given us – especially during these last years; and yet even the little I propose doing today, shall I do it? Probably I shall not have the leisure. And besides, it's tedious copying out oneself! No chronological order (or any other), my scraps of paper are usually not dated.[1]

---

1. Nevertheless several of the fragments which will be found here are dated, but this applies mainly to fragments of letters or to fragments I found in another notebook, or in envelopes – it applies also to dated entries extracted by me from notebooks or diaries and from memorandum books (tiny ones where the brief

Q

Raïssa's Journal

*

I

Undated. – After a Communion. "Caetera creatura
vilescat, ut Creator in corde dulcescat" (St Augustine).
"Noli timere, vermis Jacob. Noli timere, quia redemi te, et
vocavi te nomine tuo: meus es tu" (Isaiah).

You have drawn my weary and weeping soul to You and
you hold it in your peace and your silence, as a friend
presses a friend to his heart without saying a word, because
at that moment there is no need for speech – all is said
inwardly.

2

Undated. – Blondel. Metaphysics. Thomism.
Technical failure to appreciate the value of the intellect.

lines were jotted down hastily) which I had set aside during my
first plundering and which were subjected to a second scrutiny.
I have added these other fragments and these dated notes (of
which there are quite a number) to the "scraps of paper" which
Raïssa had placed in the "Green Notebook", and I have sometimes
grouped several dated notes in the same Fragment. I have num-
bered all these Fragments, and I have put those which were dated
in chronological order. (A first section runs from 1931 to 1935;
a second, from 1936 to 1939; a third, from 1940 to 1960.)

Raïssa destroyed many things, notebooks, exercise-books, notes
taken on loose pages, etc. If she spared the fragments gathered
together here, it is no doubt because they must have had a special
interest in her eyes. Moreover she had written "Writings to keep
perhaps" on the notebook (Green Notebook) which contains the
"Diary for 1931", and between the pages of which she inserted
later (right up to 1939) many of her "scraps of paper". A number
of these are re-copied notes but they are sometimes notes written
straight down on the spur of the moment like the dated ones
drawn from the notebooks and memorandum books. (J.)

Few men need these ultimate assurances of the mind. But it is necessary that these men should find them also in the treasure of the Church; like a golden robe one puts on only for the greatest feasts.

Speculative truth is a very high and very narrow thing: very great by reason of its loftiness, very small because it can be reached only by an extremely small number of minds.

3

Undated. – "I am in no way qualified to defend the principle of identity," said Gabriel Marcel at a meeting at Berdiaeff's, and Charles Du Bos made a gesture which signified the same denial.

I thought I heard: "I know not this man." (But like Peter they may repent.)

It is denying by reason the principle of our natural salvation by reason.

It is denying him without whom we can do nothing human, for to deny the creature is to deny the Creator (if they knew what they are doing). It is saying that the Gospel is not addressed to philosophers, even simply inasmuch as they are men – and that Christ ought to have spoken differently to these gentlemen. It is to separate oneself from all humanity and only maintain contact with a handful of philosophers arguing among themselves. If they knew what they are saying!

4

Undated. – Mysteries and laws are equally intolerable to us – and that is the whole of Catholicism.

5

Undated. – The beauty of an *obscure* poem derives also from an appearance of development or of logical sequence, *illusionary* as in dreams, but which makes the unity of the poem as it makes the unity of the dream – by the unity of the atmosphere in which the images are formed and expressed.

6

Undated. – All the contemplation of Jesus has a practical conclusion, and it is Redemption through the Cross and death.

7

Undated. – Suffering brings forth spirit into the world.

8

Undated. – Culture of a vine: Israel is surrounded by formal laws like thorns to keep out other nations and set it apart – separate it. All the elect are *separated people*.

Afterwards, the Church, the new chosen people, the faithful, are *separated* in this way by the sacraments, etc.

Practical instruction from God for working at this cultivation of his vineyard.

What we have to do is not determined by truth alone but by the particular purpose of the providential government of mankind.

There are many things we do not know concerning the pattern of life of other peoples according to God's purpose.

God gave gods (gods who turned out badly) to peoples other than Israel.

9

Undated. – Love in itself is not guilty and never can be. "I am not guilty," says Mélisande, who is conscious only of her love.

Sin is only in carnal intercourse *(opere aut cogitatione)* outside marriage – it is so on account of all that is necessary for the *education* of the spiritual man. We have to *educe* a *spiritual man,* capable of living eternally in the society of the divine Persons, from that *animal man* we are at birth. That is why there are no exceptions to the rules of chastity.

If anyone is able to educe from a human love a genuinely unselfish and spiritual love, even though the roots of this love are in the whole man, his love is pure of sin. A very rare love. And which presupposes that God's place is reserved in the centre of the soul, or at the summit of the spirit; and which is like a fulcrum God uses in human nature in order to transfigure it.

10

Undated. (Probably 1927). – Fragment of a letter (without the name of the person to whom it was written, probably Nicolas Nabokov) about Sacha Rzewuski:[2]

---

2. After his conversion, he entered the Dominican Order, in which he took the name of Ceslas.

From a memorandum book of Raïssa's: "*Thursday, 25th November 1926.* – We go to Nicolas Nabokov's to say our goodbyes to Alexandre Rzewuski who is leaving for the convent of Saint Maximin, keeping it absolutely secret from his family and his acquaintances." (J.)

"There are so few hearts who give themselves entirely to God that he takes good care not to refuse them; and indeed he asks their last drop of blood from them, as He himself did not spare his on the Cross: 'It's no laughing matter that I have loved thee!' Do you know that terrible saying of Our Lord's to St Angela of Foligno? Those who have not offered their soul in sacrifice to God cannot know what capacity for suffering and joy He gives them and to what depths He can excavate and re-excavate their heart. But Sacha is going to know it. We must pray very much for him."

11

Fragment of a letter copied out by Véra, with no date and not giving the name of the person to whom it was written (1931).

" . . . Work which is often a tragic struggle. I see Jacques at Berdiaeff's, confronted with Russian and French philosophers; at Du Bos' confronted with Gabriel Marcel, Du Bos, Mauriac, (and soon Gilson).[3]

" . . . At the Franco-Russian studio, like last Tuesday,[4] he is exposed to the opposition of Russian philosophers and French university professors and imbecile journalists (defenders of humanism they call themselves). Wherever he

---

3. These people were all our friends, but opposed to the philosophical approach which Raïssa and I held and had always held to be the only true one (the same applied to Gilson at that time, but nevertheless not for long – soon the progress of his meditation was to lead him to declare the supremacy of St. Thomas Aquinas over all the other medieval masters, however great, and to engage his own thought along the lines opened up by him). (J.)

4. 27th January 1931 (cf. *Le Songe de Descartes*). (J.)

goes, it is from him they expect the true, the truly Catholic word, whether to accept it or to attack it ferociously. (I think a Christian is always exposed to the wild beasts.) God sustains him, that is obvious. Whenever bad faith sets traps for him, whenever his gentleness seems to make him easy prey, his good faith and the forcefulness of his thinking disconcert his opponents. But as long as all the debating goes on, and the final and illuminating word has not been spoken – what a drama! The bad faith and the error displayed make a sorry spectacle. And I know that God gives wisdom and He can also withdraw it. Pray that the word of truth may never be refused to Jacques, it is almost a necessity in the circumstances in which Providence has placed him."

12

4th June 1931. – I enter into the presence of God with all my load of misery and troubles.

And He takes me just as I am and makes me to be alone with Him.

In such a way that I experience in this very peace my bitterest bitterness. *Ecce in pace amaritudo mea amarissima.*

13

To René Schwob, *3rd July 1931.* – "God is very indulgent to souls who run towards him, even if they happen to fall heavily on the way, and even if this happens to them often, provided they promptly get up again and cry out to him.

"But he detests the deliberate and willing halt. And I am talking only of venial sin when it is a fully-willed halt on the road which leads to God, a rest, a pleasure (no matter how small) without reference to God.

"These halts, these rests so dear to nature are the object of God's terrible jealousy. And all this has to be very strictly paid for. God wants us to live as if not living. The attachment he permits, the kind that is in the order of charity, is oriented towards God's good pleasure, however strong this attachment may be. It is the attachment of a soul in motion. It is still going forward. It is the motion of a free soul. Even its falls only check it for a moment – it gets up and goes on – and while it goes on, God staunches its wounds.

"The attachment which constitutes deliberate venial sin makes us behave, while it lasts, as if God did not exist. And that God cannot endure! The soul has not turned away from God, the matter of the sin is not grave, it has not Satan's weight of mortal sin. But the soul has not referred its joy to God – either because this joy is, in itself, sinful, or else because the soul takes its rest in the very fact of not referring it to God, in the very fact of forgetting this terrible God with all his demands. Oh, this is intolerable to God! And he does not cease, if he loves us, to tear us away from it, and he hunts us down mercilessly until he has torn us away from this attachment which is too small for our soul, and too great for the liking of his jealous love."

14

August 1931. – It is extraordinary how, when God wants to try us, the keenest affections and the most faithful friendships can be reduced to impotence, paralysed in their expression, subject to heedlessness ... Willy-nilly, we thus make our apprenticeship to the appalling loneliness of death.

It is an invitation to live and die nobly! With resolution, with generosity, because we know that it is with all these deaths that Paradise is made.

When suffering overwhelms you, suffer thoroughly, suffer to the depths, but suffer before God. "Let us go and weep before Him ... who has made us."

Excess of pain deadens sensibility, but it can vivify the soul. And this dead (or almost dead) spot becomes an area of rest and peace where a more generous life can be reborn. And so climbing up from landing to landing, with steps of pain thoroughly felt, with steps of love, though perhaps unaware of it, the soul is made spiritual and beneficent.

15

Undated. – In the state of fallen nature, the full flowering of nature is contrary to the life of grace.

Grace does not destroy nature. This is true only as regards the faculties; grace destroys neither the intellect, nor the will, nor the sensibility; on the contrary, it elevates, strengthens and refines them.

But it orients their acts towards eternal life and *mortifies* them as regards the life of this world.

In this world; and not *of* this world.

Can there be a mystical life without death? Essential problem.

"If the seed die not ... "

16

2nd February 1932, Candlemas. – This gathering together of inanimate creatures in the liturgy is a fruit of divine piety.

As everything is good in the degree that it has being, so everything is worthy of love in the same degree.

Piety is the tenderness of love, as zeal is its ardour.

Piety and zeal go hand-in-hand with the love of charity from top to bottom of the scale of beings.

It is the tender piety of God's children which brings together light and wax, bees and honey, water and salt, incense and oil, bread and wine in the celebration of divine worship. Humbly and lovingly, it gathers together all the scattered beauty of the world and lends it human voice and speech to express the tending of all things towards God, and what things signify, and what their mystery is in the very heart of the sacred mysteries.

17

Undated. – How answer the inevitable question of why there is suffering? To deny the existence of God gets us no further; it does not abolish suffering, and it does not lessen the mystery of our destiny. To deny God because all nature groans and travails is only to relieve God of the responsibility of a creation of such a kind that it inevitably involves suffering. It is the proof that we have such a natural love of God (inscribed in nature itself) that, even when it takes refuge in the depths of the unconscious, we still retain the desire to absolve God of all the evil men suffer.

18

21st December 1932. – To Antoinette Grunelius:

" . . . A certain very simple prayer by which we take into our heart those for whom we wish to pray; and then we offer this heart, with all its desires and anxieties to God, in order that He may come into it with all his love, give Himself.

"By this very meek aspiration, which demands only a little of one's attention and which, in its simplicity, is a total gift of oneself to God – one attracts to oneself Him who wants above all to give Himself, and set everything on fire with His love, and make every obstacle to his bounty melt away in it.

"This very simple prayer can be practised anywhere and at any time. It brings great meekness into the soul, calms all impatience, melts all hardness at the core of this double, yet single, love of God and our neighbour."

19

1933. I *will* to save my hope.

20

December 1933. – To Pierre van der Meer:

"Surely we are to be pitied, we who are tossed in the waves of everything that constitutes suffering in this world, of everything which, like ourselves, is all misery and need, we who 'seeking peace and pursuing it' can nevertheless only find it under the goad of a thousand trials, in labour, in noise and in the midst of the world.

"We walk in darkness, risking bruising ourselves against a thousand obstacles. But we know that 'God is love' and trust in God is our light. I have the feeling that what is asked of *us* is to live in the whirlwind, without keeping back any of our substance, without keeping back anything for ourselves, neither rest nor friendships nor health nor leisure – to pray incessantly and that even without leisure – in fact to let ourselves pitch and toss in the waves of the divine will till the day when it will say: '*It is enough.*'"

21

Undated. – Learn of me for I am meek and humble of heart. Learn of me the meekness which is love and the humility which is truth, and these things are eternal. About everything else you may make mistakes, the depths of your ignorance are my own abyss.

22

2nd February 1934. – After Communion, total giving of myself to Jesus, to his Love.

23

Undated. – If anyone about me could taste only a little of this arid suffering, of this slow death, or the bitterness of these tears wrung from the very source of life – then they would understand.

But I do not wish anyone such an experience.

24

1934. – Death puts an end to the sacrament of marriage – for then another marriage becomes lawful, and a new sacrament of marriage. And this is understandable because this sacrament is for temporal humanity and for the perfecting of the species.[5]

But does there then remain nothing for heaven of the union of a husband and wife, faithful to each other till death? – What remains is what *friendship* may have created of purely spiritual union between them, of similarity of soul, of equality of merits, perhaps, in a life in which everything has been in common.

25

Undated. – "O God, I salute thee, bitter bitterness full of all graces." (Tauler, *Sermon for the 5th Sunday after Trinity.*)

Ecce in pace amaritudo mea amarissima.

"Thou refuse to die with a good heart." (Tauler, *Sermons.*)

You shall announce his death till he come. (I Cor. 11:26.)
"You shall announce it *by dying,* by stripping yourself through the virtue of his death." (Tauler, *Sermons.*)

"And even oughtest thou to think it thy unique joy that I scourge thee unsparingly." (*Imitation.* – 23rd October 1931).

26

12th February 1934. – In the morning, weighed down by

---

5. For the *perfecting* of the species, that is to say in order that the highest exigencies of the natural law with regard to the human species should be recognised and supernaturally confirmed and that the rigour which is thus demanded from each one should raise the moral level of the species. (J.)

anxiety, on account of the nights of rioting last week and the general strike announced for this very day – I set myself to silent prayer as usual. And God, mercifully, took me into his great peace and kept me there a long while. And even in reassuring me for the day itself (for longer still? I do not know) he let me understand that I have to give much of my substance.

On account of the great peace in which God held me, I was able to savour this very bitter bitterness without feeling the agony which, for me, belongs to this kind of stripping away and of death.

27

Sunday, 18th February 1934. – In the morning, during *oraison,* I gave myself up to the love of God. Stretched out, as if on the cross, transfixed through the heart, as if with a lance. Immobilised by love. And Love worked in silence, excavating, probing deep, burning, taking no notice of my groans. This lasted a long time. I had to make deliberate efforts, walk about, tidy up, in order to relax the tight bonds with which God had bound me. (Impossible to conceal this from the eyes of Jacques.)

28

Saturday, 3rd March 1934, 5 o'clock. – After much anguish, I was drawn to the chapel and there, right up against the altar, Jesus allowed me to breathe. He restored serenity to my soul, reassured me, showed that everything is clear, that I must not be frightened, that he will not desert me, will not let me withdraw myself from him. I could not bring myself to leave the altar, kissing it, touching it, clinging as close as I could to him for refuge.

[Raïssa has added later – without a date, probably end of March]: All this Lent has been terrible, and most of all the Thursday, Friday and Saturday in Holy Week. And Sunday the 25th and Monday the 26th.

Agony! Agony!

29

[*April 1934.* – (From one of my notebooks.) She tells me that she thinks she is participating a little in Our Lord's agony and in his temptation at the same time. "He wants to take everything." "I must give everything." Sometimes she goes to pray and weep in the chapel, her face buried in the altarcloth.

Later, on the day of Pentecost, she admitted to me that she had asked to suffer still more. She thinks that this is asked of her on account of the state of the world . . . (J.)]

30

7th April 1934. – Astonishing story of David in *Samuel* (2:11):

After his twofold sin it is said only that *this displeased God.*

A prophet comes on his behalf to tell David this.

David promptly repents (but he keeps the wife of Uriah and Uriah is dead thanks to his guile).

And he is promptly told that he is forgiven.

Thus the New Law *appears* harsher than the Old – it is more demanding.

Thus whereas the Old Law allowed polygamy, the New does not even allow divorce.

Perhaps it is because, taking the Old Testament as a whole, it is historical – it speaks after the events – and so we have the history of God's mercies to sinners. Instead of which, taking the New Testament also as a whole, it speaks in *advance,* it proposes the ideal of sanctity, and thus it is unheard of in its exigencies.

When our history comes to be written, the history of the Church and of humanity after the advent of Christianity, people will no doubt see even more of the history of the mercies of God to sinners.

31

10th April 1934. – Cocteau had reserved a box for us for the dress rehearsal of *La Machine Infernale* (9th April), but the invitation did not say it was a box for six and Jacques and I did not realise this until we arrived at the theatre. Christian Bérard came and occupied the four empty seats beside us. He has designed the sets which are very beautiful and surround the tragedy with an atmosphere of light that makes it all the more poignant.

I am overwhelmed by Jean Cocteau's play. It is admirable. It is the best he has written, the purest, the most human, the simplest. It is true tragedy and it is interesting to compare it in that respect with the Comédie Française's *Coriolan.* Cocteau is certainly the only tragic author of our day.

What overwhelms me and fills my soul with questions (already asked, already answered; but they have to be asked again and to be answered in a more intense, more profound, more penetrating way, more vital and more outside all our standards) – what overwhelms me is not only the beauty of this work, but the very beauty of poetry and love, and of their masterpieces – it is the grandeur that beauty confers on those who are the creators of it, like gods.

And, in front of this, our crucified God who hides his beauty in death, and his love under the darkness of faith . . .

32

10th April 1934. – Apropos of Arthur Lourié's opera *Le Festin pendant la Peste.*[6]

I find it intensely human and at the same time detached from everything in its beauty. It is one of those very rare works in which art and truth, liberty and perfection, seriousness and lightness melt into the unity of a pure object.

33

12th April 1934. – Everything that is in Jacques' work we have first lived in the form of a vital difficulty, in the form of experience – problems of art and morality, of philosophy, of faith, of prayer, of contemplation.

---

6. Lourié had played this opera to us on the piano. Four years earlier – 13th February 1930 – we had had the joy of hearing his admirable *Sonate Liturgique* at the Concerts Straram. I remember that hearing this helped Guy de Chaunac (now Père Robert of the Benedictine Abbey of En-Calcat) to become aware of his religious vocation. He had come there without our knowing it, we met him by chance in the corridors, overwhelmed by the surge of *joy* this music had produced in him. (J.)

R

All this has been given to us first of all to *live*, each according to his nature and according to God's grace.

(We began by knowing through experience the absence of truth. Afterwards we began to suffer for It, etc . . .)
This goes on.

34

Same day, 12th April 1934. – When the *habitus* increase in intensity, the intelligence keeps ceaselessly hurling itself at the object, the same object, *vehementius et profundius*, says John of St Thomas.

It is thus that vital problems once solved can present themselves anew to the mind and present themselves indeed anew, with the demand for a new, deeper, more intense penetration, for a nearer and higher and more effective solution of the difficulty seen under a new aspect, general or personal.

This applies to scientific, artistic, moral and theological *habitus*.

This would also explain the necessity of temptation which is a more vehement *question* put to the soul, so that, in surmounting it, it replies with a greater love, a more clearsighted love, a deeper gift of its depths, a more conscious and generous acceptance of being a sacrifice and a holocaust, for the sake of the Lord and of souls.

To the ordeal of temptation there has been added, since the 12th of February [1934], a strange and indescribable interior pain which immobilises me almost every day for varying lengths of time and with varying intervals between the bouts – a pain which immobilises me, body and soul, in a suffering entirely spiritual, so profound, so acute, so all-embracing that I could believe that God is permitting the Prince of this world himself to press hard on my soul.

This pain was not unknown to me, but before the 12th of February it had never been as acute as this.

It began when I completely yielded up my soul to the love of God, reducing all my prayer to the breathing of this love.

35

To Jacques, *7th May 1934.*

" . . . I feel how much God loves you, and more and more. You ought to let your soul expand freely, and no longer *worry* about anything. For now you are altogether in the Heart of God, sheltered from everything. Pray for your poor little sheep who has the feeling of having something very difficult to do in going through thorns and briars. One would have to have no fleece left not to leave any of it in these narrow paths. I think that in these great torments God is busy ridding me of all this wool, otherwise stripping me still further. Each time I think that the operation is finished. And each time it begins again I see that there was still a great deal to do . . ."

36

12th May 1934. – As I tread the path which has become my habitual one without my knowing any too well why or how I come to be on it, I question God incessantly and I try to remain sensitive to his voice.

On Thursday, at the Mass of the Ascension, his answer was marvellous. At the moment when the priest raised the Host for Communion and I was going up to the altar, the sorrow and anguish that had already invaded me were suddenly dissipated as if by a fresh breeze. My heart was dilated and filled with joy, and it was in that state I went to Communion. And Jesus seemed to receive me with much love, saying to me without words, in the depths of the soul: "I see you and I have compassion for you. Fear nothing, in spite of your weakness. I am grateful to you for the effort you are making to bring me offerings that are at once human and pure."

37

Undated. – One must scrupulously observe all the laws and not be afraid of freedom.

The heart, like the spirit, goes where it lists, goes where the weight of its love draws it. And one does not really know whence it comes, nor, in spite of everything, whither it goes . . .

One does not legislate about love. Yet there is also a Commandment of love: that of loving God and our neighbour.

Because this love is the source of all love – divine love the source of all love on earth and in heaven,

all love must be transformed into Love as grapes are transformed into wine – under the press.

38

Undated. (Probably May 1934). – At the beginning of all this God also showed me that there is something new to be introduced into asceticism: running away and destroying is not the whole of perfection.

God wants us to offer him from everything and from every affection whatever there is in them of being and of beauty.

He does not want dead offerings. He wants offerings that are pure and full of life. But, of course, where purification has taken place, something has had to die. And what remains is transformed, transfigured. Affection has entered into the order of charity.

What must be removed from human love – to render it pure, beneficent, universal and divine – is not the love itself: no, what must be suppressed, or rather surpassed, is the limits of the heart. Hence the suffering – in this effort to go beyond our narrow limits. For in these limits, in *our* limits, is *our* human joy.

But we have to go beyond these limits of the heart; we have, under the action of grace and through the travail of the soul, to leave our bounded heart for the boundless heart of God. This is truly dying to ourselves. It is only when one has accepted this death that one enters, resurrected, into the boundless heart of God with all that one loves, with all the spoils of love, giving oneself up as prey to the infinite love.

Death to ourselves makes free room for the love of God. But at the same time it makes free room for the love of creatures according to the order of divine charity.

Tread one's heart oneself in the winepress. Lay one's heart oneself on the Cross.

39

Friday, 29th June 1934. – I would like to write a sequel to *Le Prince de ce Monde*. It would be *Transfiguration*. Jesus has dispossessed the Prince of this World. In hope and by right, all creation is transfigured. In point of fact, only the saints are transfigured. But nevertheless transfiguration in hope, and by right gives us a new outlook on the created and the human . . .

40

1st July 1934. – For some months now I have had the feeling that deep below the surface, almost without my being conscious of it, I am undergoing profound, important transformations, destined one day to emerge into full light and be expressed.

. . . It is certain that for some months I have been experiencing things that are in a sense new; great and difficult things. Things of a kind that need to pass through the secrecy, the ardent warmth and the sufferings of a soul in order to become one day, elsewhere perhaps, luminous truths capable of serving men. All those who live their life in faith are thus for Christ a sort of additional humanity. But, for this, there must be that *Fides* . . .

41

6th July 1934. – [Fragment of letter to an unnamed person.]

"I am still subjected to this strange morning régime of which I spoke to you. One would think the good Lord is afraid that I shall forget that the life of the Christian in this world is a death and he reminds me of it every day by this species of little death agony. I cannot find any other words to express what I go through. And life seems so much more beautiful and more dear to someone who is about to die! At such times, no doubt, abandonment to the will of God has more value.

"When these hard moments have passed (one hour, two hours, sometimes more) I often ask myself how such an experience is even possible."

42

1934. – In these terrible sufferings I can be a *little* helped by tokens of loving-kindness and friendliness, as a soul in Purgatory is helped by an act of charity performed for it. And certainly no fine reasoning could have the same effect.

This explains Job's complaints against his "friends" who nevertheless reasoned perfectly soundly.

43

1934. – [Fragment of a letter?]

. . . This faculty of operating simultaneously on two levels – that of concrete experience, unavoidable and painful, and that of abstract and liberating understanding, rooted in the same experience . . .

. . . It was the same for me and this enables me to live. Everything that can pass from the sphere of sensibility, of affection and of all experience into that of truth becomes an instrument of liberation. Veritas liberabit vos . . . But this alchemy is in itself a heavy labour. This transfiguration can bring death.

44

Montigny, *9th July 1934.* – From a letter to C. H.:
" . . . It has been really impossible up to now to talk about

myself, about this strange state in which I have been living since the month of February, and which has gone on accentuating since March. . . . How much good your letters have done me! They have reassured me, comforted me. Even the foretelling of yet harder sufferings, even to the feeling of incurring damnation, has been of use to me, because for some days I was very near that ordeal. And I was well aware that, if I was not plunged into it, this was because God had regard for my weakness. I think I might have died of it. When I am in the grip of these great anguishes, I feel as if my life were ebbing away. They are not terrors, or fears of anything, but like a very severe struggle of the soul between life and death. . . . Jacques is often with me then, he assists me like an angel of God, he prays beside me. He tells me that I give the impression of being at peace. What is going on in me goes on at the sources of life where I think no agitation can penetrate. But the pain there is at its paroxysm. All the difficulties are there in their maximum force (it seems to me). God appears to be absent.

" . . . I am conscious of collaborating. I am conscious, but obscurely, of being in great travail . . . The most painful of these experiences end in a keener desire to belong to God, to his love. But I live through them with this confused impression of something human to save, to offer, to allow to be transfigured by the Lord."

45

19th July 1934 (note written on the 21st). – *Terrible morning*. One of the most terrible of these months. Conflict between earth and heaven, between this *unique* life "whose

joy my eyes shall no longer see" and the eternal life hidden
in the divine darkness. Jacob wrestled with the Angel in the
night. The eternal (spiritual) life, I understand this now,
can appear as an enemy, risen up against our soul, our
unique root-possession. It fights against us in order to be
conquered, that is to say *won*. Thus it is God who triumphs
in the triumph of Jacob. For *that* was Jacob's victory: he
won God by letting himself be vanquished by him. If God
had been vanquished in this struggle, Jacob would not have
asked him for his blessing. The sign of God's victory is in
Jacob's lameness. And Jacob won God by letting himself be
mortified in his flesh.

46

1934. – We are God's food. Utterly terrible to be assimilated by him.

47

Montigny, *Sunday, 5th August 1934*. – I prayed, saying:
"It is of my substance I must make a gift to God, so that he
can transform it."

And I read in my missal, after Mass (Eleventh Sunday
after Pentecost):

Honora Dominum de tua substantia (which I think can be
translated otherwise than by: "honour the Lord by the
offering of your goods"! . . .)

And, in a general way, this Mass of the eleventh Sunday
fits in well with my prayer of yesterday, and of today, and
with the circumstances . . .

48

Meudon, *7th November 1934,* 7 p.m. – Weekly confession.
Now I am back here, strange confidence with respect
to very great and difficult things. Profound, delicious
peace. Confidence as to the utility of the sufferings of these
nine last months (especially since the 12th of February).
Confidence for a soul who is dear to me.

Profound, happy calm.

In a total renunciation, feeling of the easiness of the gift
to God, to Jacques, to all . . .

49

Thursday, 22nd November 1934. – I know now that there is
this world, and the world of Jesus – and that they are
opposed to one another.

They are reconciled only when we cross the threshold of
death.

And the transfiguration comes afterwards – for those who
have passed safely through death.

The world of Jesus is quantitatively very small: the salt of
the earth, the pinch of leaven which makes the whole dough
rise . . . It comprises those who let themselves be conformed
to Him. These are his true imitators and his co-operators in
salvation.

As to *this world*, it and all its beauty are sustained by the
world of Jesus. Until death, when salvation is wrought for
all those whom God loves and whom *he does not judge.* Love
is incapable of *judging.*

One can also say that there are two categories of men:
those who – what mystery! – are capable of assimilating
sin, and those who are not capable of doing so (by virtue of
some mystery of predestination . . .)

Those who are capable of assimilating sin, of living with sin, almost of living on it; of drawing from it a useful experience, a certain human enrichment, a development, even a perfecting, in the order of mercy and humility – of arriving, finally, at the knowledge of God, at a certain theodicy, through extreme experience of the misery of the sinner. The Russians are like this, as typified in Dostoievsky's characters. What is rare about them is that they are conscious of this capacity to profit in the end from sin. The mass of sinners have this capacity too, without knowing it.

Those who are incapable of assimilating sin, because the smallest deliberate sin is like a fishbone stuck in their throat, cannot rest till they have got rid of it by contrition and confession. These are called to be assimilated to Christ. They can accept or refuse. It is a redoubtable moment when they hear that call – it is the voice of Jesus himself.

50

Friday, 23rd November 1934. – Toscanini concert: 9th Symphony.

51

24th November 1934. – Terrible ordeal in silent prayer. Felt all the bitterness of death. God asks of me more than my life: to accept living death, existence in a barren desert. That is giving more than one's soul. Amaritudo amarissima.

Tortured, sobbing, I felt at the end, as it were, a faint whisper coming from the Lord. As if he were saying to me: "It is I, Jesus. You will find me again. Yes, you will do my will. Yes, you will accept it. Yes, you will be with me." The relief, the appeasement in which this prayer ended. But this *oraison* is all my life now. And death is proposed to me at every instant on God's side. I can accept it – and enter into the world of Jesus – or refuse it and begin to live the life of this world.

52

Sunday, 25th November (1934). – A very sweet, very restful morning, like a good sleep in which one is conscious of being asleep.

53

25th November (1934). – In some manner, I am having personal experience of that great mystery St Paul speaks of, making up *what is lacking* in the Passion of Christ.

Being the Passion of God, it is forever gathered up into the eternal. What is lacking to it is *development in time*.

Jesus suffered only during a certain time. He cannot himself develop his Passion and death in time. Those who allow themselves to become his to the point of being perfectly assimilated to him, accomplish, throughout the whole length of time, what is lacking in his Passion. Those who consent to become *flesh of his flesh*. Terrible marriage, in which love is not only strong as death but begins by being a death, and a thousand deaths.

"I will espouse thee in blood."

"I am a bridegroom of blood."

"It is a terrible thing to fall into the hands of the living God."

And Jesus's words to St Angela of Foligno:

"It's no laughing matter that I have loved thee."

There is also a *fulfilment* of the Passion which can be given only by fallible creatures, and that is the struggle against the fall, against the attraction of *this world* as such, against the attraction of so many sins which represent human happiness. That gift Jesus could not make to the Father: only we can do it. It involves a manner of redeeming the world, and of suffering, which is accessible only to sinners. By renouncing the good things of this world, which, in certain cases more numerous than one might think, sin would have procured us – by giving to God our human and temporal happiness, we give him proportionately as much as he gives us, because we give him *our all,* the widow's mite of the Gospel.

54

1934. – To Nicolas Nabokov:

"Finally, my dear Nicolas, to end where your letter begins, I will tell you that my 'yoke' and my 'cross' is what is called *dying.* If we wish to serve God, then God demands that we should die to ourselves (it matters little what methods he uses in turn to bring this about). Generous souls die quickly. But I am an endless time dying. One thinks oneself truly dead and suddenly one is born again, so to speak, quite whole. Then the work begins all over again. Once again God passes his purifying flame through all the innermost recesses of the heart, for he looks after me."

55

1934. – Human felicity has no place in my destiny.
I know very definitely that God will never allow me to

belong to myself and to seek my own happiness. He has never allowed it. I belong to Him, and through Him and with Him to those whom He wishes. It is He who chooses my intimates for me.

In the midst of all my sufferings, God has given me a very clear view of my destiny. I have a destiny, and that, in itself, is marvellous. For a destiny makes the unity, the usefulness and beauty of a life. And my destiny is not to belong to myself.

God has granted Jacques and me the same destiny and, as a viaticum, a unique and marvellous mutual affection.

56

4th December 1934. – One must stop considering the observation of religious laws, faith and even charity as guarantees of a happy life on earth . . .

It is true that divine Providence watches over us. But the natural laws themselves are the first manifestations of that Providence, the first and universal manifestation of Wisdom. God lets them operate and produce all their consequences. Miracles are rare. The only assurance of privilege that we have is that *all things work together for the good of them that love God* (St Paul); but that *all* includes all calamities and all tribulations.

In certain exceptional vocations which demand the concurrence of certain material circumstances, Providence does, it is true, appear, as it were, particularly favourable, granting extraordinary graces such as charisms and miracles. But what is more frequent than these favours is, on the contrary, the apparent harshness with which God's closest friends are treated. There is not only visible martyrdom, there is the daily and hidden martyrdom of God's faithful — of those who are called not only to the active imitation of Christ, but to be assimilated by Him to Himself, to become flesh of his flesh, an additional humanity in which is fulfilled *what is lacking* (see St Paul) in the Passion of the Saviour. These are souls of singular generosity, and who have, indeed, been providentially prepared by divine grace for this redemptive vocation.

57

1934. — [A sheet of paper on which, as if in an excess of suffering, she has hurriedly copied out most of Psalm 87.]

Oh Lord God of my salvation, I have cried day and night before thee.

Let my prayer come before thee: incline thine ear unto my cry.

For my soul is full of troubles: and my life draweth nigh unto the grave.

I am counted with them that go down into the pit: I am as a man that hath no strength.

Free among the dead like the slain that lie in the grave, whom thou rememberest no more: and they are cut off from thy hand.

Thou hast laid me in the lowest pit, in darkness, in the deeps.

Thy wrath lieth hard upon me, and thou hast afflicted me with all thy waves.

Thou hast put away mine acquaintance far from me; thou hast made me an abomination unto them: I am shut up and I cannot come forth.

Mine eye mourneth by reason of affliction: Lord, I have

called daily upon thee, I have stretched out my hands
to thee. . . .

But unto thee have I cried, O Lord, and in the morning
shall my prayer come before thee.

Lord, why castest thou off my soul? Why hidest thou
thy face from me?

I am afflicted and ready to die from my youth up.
. . .

My company is the darkness of the grave.

58

2nd February 1935. – Received Communion at home.
Very anguished morning.

16th February. – Began to read Kierkegaard's book, *Fear
and Trembling*.

Saturday, 2nd March. – Very hard morning.

[*Same day.* – (From one of my notebooks.) Raïssa suffered
atrociously this morning. All the horror of dereliction
suddenly descended on her during a quite peaceful period
of silent prayer; she opened the Old Testament, read the
Mosaic prescriptions, the rigours of the Law (the slave
beaten to death by his master, etc.), Abraham driving
Hagar away so cruelly. All these enigmas overwhelmed her
and thrust her back into the agonised darkness which, for
the last fortnight, seemed to have receded.

I feel Raïssa is *consubstantialised* to truth, so that all
words become a lie and a hurt. We are more and more
terribly alone.

No other resource, I think, than Jesus himself, Jesus in his humanity, Jesus Saviour and Saint on the roads of Palestine, whose human glance understands and heals. (J.)]

59

Thursday, 14th March 1935. – In the afternoon, went with Jacques to see the paintings from the Musée de Grenoble at the Petit Palais. Two names dominate everything in this exhibition: *Zurbaran* (Annunciation, Adoration of the Magi, Nativity), and *Henri Rousseau:* especially the Ship and those flowers in a vase which is itself like a boat.

The ship is an *absolute* work, absolutely *given*.

Saturday, 16th March. During the night wrote *Le Beau Navire:* "Rousseau . . ."[7]

60

13th April 1935. – Very hard day.

Monday, 22nd April. – Began to write on Abraham as Jacques and Abbé Journet have asked me to.

Saturday, 10th August. – Very hard day, one of the hardest since this began.

[*Same day.* – (From one of my notebooks.) Raïssa has suffered very much this week. She said to me: "One would think Jesus wants to enter into me, with all his suffering,

---

7. One of the poems in *Lettre de Nuit*. (J.)

with all the blood that drenches him -- it is unendurable . . ."
(J.)]

61

[*Monday, 12th August 1935.* – (From one of my notebooks.) Raïssa said to me: "*Jesus will be in agony till the end
of the world.*[8] There have to be souls in whom he continues
to agonise." (J.)]

Wednesday, 14th August. – Went to Communion in the
morning. A day even more terrible than the 10th. The
suffering began before Communion, diminished after,
returned again in an appalling way about 4 o'clock.

62

Monday 28th-Wednesday, 30th October 1935. – In London
with Jacques, he is giving a lecture at the Aquinas Society,
another (on "Sign and Symbol") at the Warburg Institute.
Dined with T. S. Eliot. On Wednesday at four o'clock
we returned to the Warburg Institute to see Sachsl and
Wind who had asked us to come back for a private interview. Very moving conversation which made us see that
there are deep and essentially religious aims in these erudite
researches concerning signs and symbols.

We were asked to return for a month. We would like to,
and I find London immensely attractive.

Charming evening (the 30th) with Richard O'Sullivan,
Miss Borton and Achsa.

---

8. The words in *italics* are a quotation from Pascal. (Trans.)

63

Monday, 11th November 1935. – Afternoon in Paris, at the concert given by the Strasburg Choral Society which Abbé Hoch conducts: "The Redemption", by Gounod.

The choirs are good, but this music is extremely bad, popular in the bad way, which is summed up by Max Jacob in this sentence attributed to a popular novel: "She was both a marquise and a mother."

64

Saturday, 23rd November 1935. – Yesterday evening heard Igor Stravinsky's double piano Concerto at the Salle Gaveau. He played it with his son. Admirable technically, but without the slightest inwardness; it gave me no pleasure in hearing it except such as one gets from any good professional job.

There is no *song* in this music. It does not proceed from any lyrical germ but only from a musical *idea*.

65

Monday, 16th December. – Painful morning.

Thursday, 26th December. – Visited the exhibition organised by the Gazette des Beaux-Arts. Modigliani, Chagall, Utrillo, Rousseau, Soutine, Pascin, Marie Laurencin.

I detest the Soutines that are there. (First manner, I was told, very inferior to what he has done since.) I was on the whole a little disappointed by the Modiglianis.

Charmed more than I expected to be by the Laurencins. Quite indifferent to Pascin. The three painters there that I love are Utrillo, Chagall, Rousseau. The last sometimes attains to almost absolute perfection: *l'Été, le Navire.*

Sunday, 29th December. – At 2.30 set off to go to Lourié's, with all the crockery necessary for tea. Du Bos and his wife, the Gouhiers, the Laloys and a good number of other friends come and join us there.

Lourié played the Gigue which is dedicated to Jacques. Then the melodies which were sung: settings of a sonnet of Dante's, a passage from Alexander Blok, a passage from Pushkin. Then *Procession,*[9] of which the music is admirable – movingly sung by the Kedroffs.

3rd January 1936. – Jacques leaves for New York.[10]

---

9. One of Raïssa's poems in *Lettre de Nuit.* (J.)

10. Ever since my first visit to the Institute of Medieval Studies in Toronto (January–March 1933, – Raïssa had wanted me to make this journey, in spite of the grave anxiety her health was causing then), I used to return to Toronto almost every year for two or three months. (J.)

II

1936-1939

66

Meudon, *January 1936*. – To Jacques:

"Go on loving me like this, I need a great deal of love in order to live and I know that *I* have to love 'as not loving', in St Paul's sense, and beyond St Paul's sense. What a terrible vocation! It is for that God has placed your marvellous love at my side. For with whom would I have been able to live such a vocation, except with you? And to do so, henceforth, in an extraordinary suspension of all knowledge. Yesterday, nevertheless, I was intensely conscious of the love of the Cross of Jesus and of not wanting to separate myself from that Cross, which brings the just and sinners together.

"My beloved, I believe, like you, that 'it is a sign from God to be more and more severed from human conceptions concerning the reality of God. His thoughts are not like our thoughts...' But, Jacques, to live like this is martyrdom, it is no longer to have anywhere to lay one's head...

"What is wonderful, is that I can take this rest in your heart without in any way hindering God's action in us. God is so much with you. And you are truly my only sweetness in this world."

67

Saturday, 11th January 1936. – This afternoon, in Lyons, where I arrived yesterday,[1] public rehearsal of Lourié's *Symphonie Dialectique*, conducted by Jean Witkovsky. A moving occasion. It is like the final preparations for the launching of a ship. The whole orchestra and its admirable conductor efface themselves before the work; thus one is able to grasp its difficulties, its novelty, its unusual sonorities.

Sunday, 12th January. – Concert at 5 o'clock. The *Symphonie Dialectique* is very well performed. The orchestration produces a new kind of sonority, strident and fresh, clear as a bird's song and at the same time grave.

Monday, 13th January. – Left Lyons in the morning with Arthur and Jean Mouton. Very pleasant journey. I have a book of Jouhandeau's with me, *Algèbre Morale*. Arthur admires it but declares, with the good reasons of an artist who knows the value of mystery, that "all these things ought not to be said." We travel third class and lunch in the compartment. It is all so simple and charming. I return home not feeling tired.

68

Friday, 31st January [1936]. – I disobeyed Jacques: I composed myself to pray by letting myself sink and

---

1. At the invitation of Jean Mouton, whose mother lived in Lyons, Raïssa went there for the first performance of the work. Cf. further on (82) her letter to Lourié about it. (J.)

founder, because I had had enough of letting my soul, all the same in fairly considerable pain, float on the surface, without settling, without coming to rest, even in suffering; on the whole I still preferred to suffer to the depths.

But a happy surprise awaited me: I was plunged at once into a state of silent absorption, very profound and very sweet, very pacifying and very restful. And it was as if I had been made to understand that everything is much simpler and happier than I thought.

Today I can still feel the effect of that easing, of that sweet peace. (3rd February.)

69

Thursday, 13th February 1936. – Saw Julien Green (and his sister Ann for a moment). He is enthusiastically studying Hebrew. We talk a great deal about the Bible. As he is showing me out, he says to me so seriously that it gives me quite a shock: "*Think* of me a little, Raïssa" – think, that means pray – "I need it very badly." He and his sister must also have to resign themselves to not being happy, at least in this world.

70

Meudon, *26th March 1936.* – To Julien Green:
"Dear Julien, I have impatiently awaited your book and my expectation has not been disappointed. 'Minuit' is, along with 'Les Clefs de la Mort', the work of yours I love most, I think. Here you have attained the maximum of pure tragic intensity and of that power you have to such a high degree of revealing, beyond the emotional situation

you take as your starting-point, that more than real reality, that spiritual reality which is entirely shrouded in the illusion of appearances. But to place yourself like this in the heart of the night is to be near the dawn of the spiritual day, which, to our all too feeble eyes, is like night. M. Edme and his disciple M. Agnel had a glimpse of that dawn, the one in contemplation, and the other in that love so pure that it is unaware of itself.

"But, as you so admirably say, 'this region . . . is, as a rule, inaccessible, protected by Himalayas of despair . . . within ourselves, it is not very far away, and yet it is so far that an entire lifetime is not always long enough to take us there.' To reach it one must either be unaware of all difficulties, like children, or else first accept all forms of despair – then one arrives at real peace 'where the interior man develops his powers and acts.'

" 'The night is more beautiful than the day.' One might say that all the writings of St John of the Cross are the explanation of that little sentence, and of what follows: 'The dark sky sheds its mysterious grace on the earth which sleep has rendered attentive. Everything sleeps and everything listens. Freed from the gross illusions of day, the soul aspires only to invisible things . . .' What an admirable poem you have written there, Julien! I am quite intimidated at giving the impression of trying to comment on such thoughts, which, moreover, do not stop at sublime theory, but, in the case of M. Edme and M. Agnel, go so far as to produce that evangelical disposition of heart which makes us understand that 'greater love hath no man that this, that he lay down his life for his friends.' And that marvellous Elizabeth, too, will have been saved by M. Agnel.

"Your book has great literary beauty. And it is also a

generous book which brings a glimmer of hope to those
who still only know reasons for despairing.

"Believe me, dear Julien, when I tell you how much joy
I have had in reading you – and accept my very affectionate
gratitude."

71

Tuesday, 31st March 1936. – Terrible morning.

Wednesday, 1st April. – Communion. Still this very
painful state.

Friday, 10th April. – Jacques arrived home in the
evening. Pale and thinner. He was ill for over a month in
Toronto.
And I am also very weary, mainly through sadness, I
think.

Saturday, 25th April. – Hard day.

Sunday 26th. – Atrocious morning.

Monday 27th. – Hard morning.

Wednesday 29th. – Hard morning.

Friday, 1st May. – Communion.
Sufferings a little alleviated, but still so profound.

72

Sunday, 3rd May 1936. – Georges Cattaüi talks to us

about Bergson. He wants me to go and see him. Bergson talks about me to him with particular affection.

Tuesday, 26th May. – In the afternoon, at 3.30, went to see Henri Bergson. Moving meeting. He is 76 now; I had not seen him for thirty years. But it seems that these years, instead of separating us, have brought us closer together. I will try and make notes of what he said. In any case, Jacques and I can go and see him again.[2]

Dined in Paris with Jacques and Arthur.

Tried to distract ourselves by going to the cinema. How sad to want to distract oneself!

73

Saturday, 30th May 1936. – Went to the Opéra. Bruno Walter conducted Don Juan. Wonderful evening.

Wednesday, 3rd June. – Communion. Still such great interior difficulties.

Friday, 5th June. – Communion. Torturing morning.

Saturday, 6th June. – Day of calmness and strength.

74

Friday, 12th June 1936. – At 1.30, final rehearsal of the

---

2. We did indeed go back – greatly moved by his affectionate welcome and by what he said to us about Christianity. On Raïssa's visit on May 26th, cf. *We Have Been Friends Together* (*Adventures in Grace*), Doubleday, Image Books, New York, p. 338. (J.)

Concerto.[3] I think all is going well. At the rehearsal were the Thibaudeau ladies who are leaving tonight, the Severinis who have just arrived from Rome, Davenson,[4] the Laloys, Père Doncoeur, the Monléons, etc. I have come back home to have a rest and get dressed for tonight.

In the evening, first public performance of Arthur Lourié's *Concerto Spirituale,* conducted by Münch. Conducting the choirs, Vlassov and Yvonne Gouverné, at the piano Yvonne Lefébure. Great success. Magnificent

---

3. It was Raïssa who had succeeded in getting this particularly important work of Arthur Lourié's performed. To do so, she had spared herself no effort, using all the strength of her will to break down the wall of silence erected by the jealousies and clannishness of the musical world round this composer whom she regarded, with good reason, as the greatest musician of our time. For months on end, seeing all sorts of people, writing letter after letter, arguing, straightening things out, stimulating, she had worked to overcome all the obstacles and to find the material resources required by the importance of the choral part in the work. The first step, of course, had been to form a committee. Subsequently, an organisation had had to be set up, the *Association of Friends of Choral Singing,* whose foundation had been decided upon at a meeting at Roland-Manuel's house, on December 16th 1933. Its first members were Maurice Brillant, Marc Chagall, Alfred Cortot, Charles Du Bos, Mme Désirée Ferry, Henri Ghéon, Yvonne Gouverné, Emmanuel Jacob, Serge Koussevitzky, Louis Laloy, Gabriel Marcel, R. and J. Maritain, François Mauriac, Mme Frédéric Moreau, Roland-Manuel, Boris de Schloezer, Vuillermoz. The President of the Association was Mauriac: the Secretary, Yvonne Gouverné; the Treasurer, Emmanuel Jacob – my much-loved godson, who, during the Occupation, was to be handed over to the Gestapo by the French police and immolated in Germany.

In a letter of June 22nd 1936, Yvonne Gouverné wrote to Raïssa: "Tell yourself from me, though you refuse to admit it yourself, that *you alone,* through your tenacity, have been the instigator of this performance, and if I say that, *it is because I am sure of it.*" (Underlined in the text.) (J.)

4. Penname of Henri Marrou (Trans.)

audience, all the musicians and critics were there. It was a very great joy to me. We were in the Lourié's box, Jacques and I and Mlle Gouverné.

Among the critics whom I know: Schloezer, Vuillermoz, Roland-Manuel, Louis Laloy, Maurice Brillant, H. Davenson, Gabriel Marcel.

Mr. Clarke came from London; he is a conductor at the B.B.C.

Toscanini was present at the concert.

75

Saturday, 12th December 1936.[5] – Terrible morning in abandonment to suffering. And very painful day.

In the afternoon, Olivier Lacombe came, also a Mohammedan Indian; in the evening, Jean Hugo.

But I was too shattered with exhaustion to go downstairs.

Monday, 14th December. – An extremely difficult day for me. All the same I get up in the evening to receive the Berdiaeffs who come to dinner. Berdiaeff explains Chestov's theogony to me.[6]

76

Meudon, *8th January 1937.* – I am slowly recovering from this great lassitude which began three or four weeks ago (after a terrible *recueillement* which left me shattered. I

---

5. We had all three sailed from Marseilles in the *Florida,* for the Argentine (with a stop at Brazil) on Sunday, 26th July 1936. Returned to Meudon on November 7th. (J.)

6. No notebook or engagement book for the year 1937. Only two "scraps of paper". (J.)

must learn to pray in another way, with a more relaxed passivity perhaps, keeping my eyes shut to whatever painful thing is taking place in me), but I have good hope of surmounting all the difficulties. New ones arise every day, in the depths of the heart; it is as if one were absolutely compelled to go all round a great mountain and climb and descend it from every approach. And one has simultaneously to act and to let God act as He pleases. Above all, docility to let Him act; not to try too hard to know what is being done. Because certain operations are terrible when one watches them. One must shut one's eyes. I have had this feeling for several days, along with a certain confidence which is given me.

77

11th November 1937. –
Identity of death and life –
Identity of opposites:
"Blessed are they that mourn. . ."

O death where is thy sting?

The road of death and the road of life
Are one road to the footsteps of love.

"He who wishes to keep his soul, shall lose it."
He who shall give his life shall be reborn more living.

From stage to stage and from form to form
The whole creature is transformed
Through death after death
    till life everlasting.

At the core of holy death is a higher life.

In the darkness of human life
A faint light glimmers
Like a star sending down its rays
From unimaginable distance:
Only with footsteps of death
Can we mount the ladder of life.[7]

78

Undated. – The night of the spirit is the sign of the maturity of the soul. The time of childish things is over, the time of playing games, of make-believe, of eloquence, of "let's pretend." – One has at last reached the point of realising one's ignorance, on the brink of the abyss which separates the creature from the Uncreated.

Then one no longer lives on anything but the alms of unknown, inapprehensible grace.

All means have proved unavailing
All ways stop *too* short.[8]
The divine night remains impenetrable
Solitude intolerable, yet necessary, inevitable.
Every word of consolation seems a lie.
And God has abandoned us.[9]

79

Undated. –

"Be still and know that I am God."
Vacate et videte. . .

---

7. Translation by a Benedictine of Stanbrook.
8. This line alludes to the so-called "short ways" or "short means" advocated by some spiritual writers. (Trans.)
9. Translation by a Benedictine of Stanbrook.

Vocation of the contemplative.

He must *be still* – cease all occupation.

And see. See God as in an eternal present. See him face to face, although under the veil of faith,

or again *remain* as Jesus said of St. John (the pure contemplative among the Apostles and Evangelists): Sic eum volo *manere* donec veniam.

But to Peter he said:
Tu me sequere.

And to St. Matthew:
Follow me, and let the dead bury their dead.

Such is the vocation of the Apostle:[10] he has to walk with his eyes fixed on Christ who goes before him. He sees him too, but as it were from the back. He sees the shoulders of Christ, laden with the cross. He has to follow, laden himself with the cross. He must always be going forward. "Go," Jesus still says to them, "and teach all nations," this embraces all space and all time.

The apostle has to live in the eternal future, not look behind him, "let the dead bury their dead."

The gift of understanding is peculiarly that of the contemplative.

The gifts of knowledge and piety, those of the apostle.

But the gift of wisdom which is both speculative and practical is equal in the two vocations.

---

10. Raïssa well knew that, in the true apostle, preaching springs from the overflow of contemplation. What she is distinguishing between here is the vocation of the *pure* contemplative and that of the apostle. (J.)

80

Undated. – What is the role of contemplatives in this world, among the troubles of mankind?

Why do special revelations seem to be limited to the interests of a single person?

It is because the role of contemplatives among us is to be mirrors of the Image of God, reservoirs of his grace and his love – the unfailing memory of the Eternal amongst us. (Voluntary mirrors and reservoirs, for it is in loving that they reflect the Image and receive the Love. A memory without which darkness would obscure the earth. A memory in which we possess the archives of sanctity, for the mystics receive the command to speak. . .)

And they must not be distracted from this function, otherwise they could not fulfil it, for instability is injurious to contemplation.

In them, the bond of time has to be weakened in order that eternity may begin. They are face to face with God, alone with Him, not yet in the evidence of Vision but in the union of friendship. And God appears to care about nothing in the world but their love and faithfulness. For them is this commandment: "Be still and know that I am God." Afterwards, love will grow apace: "Lend me your heart."

God halts contemplatives on the threshold of vision, and he shows them his face behind a thin veil.

Like mirrors one wants to preserve untarnished, he keeps them apart, sheltered from the dust and noise and agitation of the world – sometimes by setting them apart through ecstatic experience (Lucie-Christine), sometimes by calling them to solitude, sometimes by fixing them in the rigid frame of the monastic life, [sometimes by binding them, wherever they may be, to the exigencies of a constantly purified fraternal charity (Petits Frères)].[11] He speaks to their heart and their heart forgets every other voice, and opens itself and is filled with grace. Reservoirs of life for the Church, not for the world if the world rejects spiritual teaching.

In the love of this great One sheltered in God, this contemplative Mother that, in her essence, the Church is, incentives to all forms of human justice and human prosperity are contained – it is the immense *surplus* – if only men wanted to know, or at least seek, the Kingdom of God. Peace on earth to men of goodwill.[12]

Whatever the state of goodwill of men in general, the mountains of contemplation do not depend on the temporal plain. The level of the world and even of the clergy may be very low and yet great saints abound. This was so in the XVIth century, for example, which was the century of St Teresa, of St John of the Cross, of St Ignatius, of St Francis of Sales, of St Charles Borromeo, of St Philip Neri, of St Joseph Calasanctus, of St Francis Borgia, of St Francis Xavier, etc., etc.

And, on the other hand, the presence of great saints and great contemplatives does not necessarily raise the moral level of the society of their day; example: the

---

11. If I have added the words put in brackets, it is because they convey a thought Raïssa often mentioned to me and which she has herself expressed in writing in *Liturgy and Contemplation* (pp. 74–76). (J.)

12. As to war – in all its forms – it is not God who sends it: all he has to do is to abandon men to themselves. And all the "fond hopes", however intense, will not abolish war, in the general absence of faith and charity. All forms of goodwill that are only p artial will fail. (Raïssa's note.)

T

XVIIth and XVIIIth centuries which, nevertheless, abounded in mystics. The grace of sanctity is the fruit of fidelity. To be sanctified and pacified, society too must begin by being faithful. Grace is not hereditary, it is not the patrimony of any one people.

The Church is ready to instruct us in everything that concerns the truth of life, and justice. But this word of social salvation, this efficacious word, is something we have to deserve to hear. We have to be ready to leave everything in order that it should be accomplished – "Prepare ye the way of the Lord, make straight his paths." "Every valley shall be filled and every mountain and hill shall be brought low." We do not desire it, we are not ready – and the divine voice echoes in the wilderness.

81

Meudon, 19th February 1938. – The days of anguish have returned for me. But I had been warned of this several months ago. . .

Tuesday, 24th February. – [After having noted several proofs of friendship she had received, Raïssa writes:] In spite of all these kindnesses Providence has shown me, I am living through some very hard hours. But I had been warned that they would return.

82

25th March 1938. – To Arthur Lourié. (About the performance of the Symphonie Dialectique on March 24th 1938):

"I am as happy as can be, my very dear Arthur, to have

had the joy of hearing your symphony again. . . It seems to me that Münch did not bring out the grandeur of the adagio as well as Witkovsky did, but, even so, this performance was rapture for the whole soul. This time I listened in profound peace. I remember that, in Lyons, I was shattered by anxiety, worried about how the work was going to be performed, and even though I was reassured from the first bars, the agitation persisted. Yesterday I received all this music on me, in me, as one receives the rays of the sun and the sounds of the sea. I am not talking of music, you see; I wouldn't dare to do that; I only want to tell you my impressions. Well, it seemed to me that all this music, with such pure and such fresh sonorities, which has no intention of being descriptive or emotive, was like a sunrise over the sea, with the caresses of the light and the soft, mysterious noise of the waves, that come and go. Everything gradually heightened, the earth began to live, life flowed in from everywhere, near and far. A host of beings peopled the resonant space in which one was trapped, with no loophole for escape. A rapid, exquisite dialogue was exchanged, and life rose up in the heart of men, coming from the depths of the ages, with their own spontaneous song, hinted at, dropped, taken up again; astonishing in its fragility and delicacy, then in its gravity and religious amplitude. A whole world had come from your heart to ours and was advancing towards us as the day proceeds from one dawn to the next.

"Since sounds, scents and colours 'respond to each other',[13] such, more or less, was my response to your 'dia-

---

13. Allusion to Baudelaire's line: "Les parfums, les couleurs et les sons se répondent" (Trans.).

lectic'. But I am sure you will have more authoritative criticisms than mine; I only wanted to tell you my joy."

83

Thursday, 1st September 1938. – We have decided to go, all three, to the United States and stay there for two or three months.

Friday, 23rd September. – We are getting ready to go to America in complete uncertainty as to whether it will be possible to go.[14]

84

Meudon, *6th January 1939.* – To desire nothing – to love everything.

85

17th January 1939. – In the evening, the Bourdets take me to the theatre to see Lorca's play *Noces de Sang*. Simple, admirable tragedy; prose mingled with magnificent poems.

---

14. On the 30th September it appeared that the war would not break out this year (Munich agreement). We left for New York the following day, October 1st. We stayed first in Chicago with our friends John and Eleanor Nef, then at the University of Notre Dame (where we saw Charles and Zézette Du Bos again). Raïssa and Véra left by themselves (on November 14th for New York and on the 19th, on the *Ile-de-France,* for Le Havre). I sailed on December 17th and rejoined them at Meudon on December 24th in the evening. (J.)

86

Tuesday, 7th February. – Communion.

All this distracting work when, suffering in every way, I have more need than ever of resting in silence with God. Where to find strength, light and serenity? Alas, poor world, in which these words seem so unfamiliar now!

Wednesday, 15th February. – In the afternoon went to the Picasso exhibition. Still-lifes of very beautiful colouring and, naturally, great mastery of drawing and design. But it is all ice cold and leaves one indifferent.

87

Sunday, 19th March 1939, Laetare. – Mass said by Père Bruno. During Mass, understood certain things about predestination. And that, at one moment or another of our life, we have to make a choice for the world or for Christ insofar as the latter is the head of the world of grace, as opposed to *this world* of which Lucifer is the prince. Through the mercy of God, I choose Jesus.

Same Sunday, 19th March. –
> There are two human universes:
> that of nature – THIS world;
> that of grace – which is not of THIS world
> and which is not due to human nature as such.

Each of these two universes has its own time and its own eternity.

This world is, in actual fact, the world of wounded nature.

The time of this world is the joy of life, the free play of the passions, and intellectual and artistic creation.

The time of grace has for symbol the Cross, for means suffering and works of Faith: the Faith that removes mountains.

The *eternity* of the world of grace is *glory*.

It consists in the knowledge of God seen face to face in the beatific vision. It is the perfection of the love which is charity.

The eternity of THIS *world*[15] is a life of nature alone in all degrees *of hells*.[16] It is deprived of the beatific vision of God – that is what damnation is – and it is eternal.

88

Kolbsheim, *Sunday, 16th April 1939*, Low Sunday.[17] – Communion at 8.30.

Returned to the 9.30 Mass [at the Church at Ernolsheim]. At the Elevation of the Precious Blood, life given for peace.

I was at this Mass with my godchildren Lexi and Antoinette, Jacques and the Grunelius' children, all except the tiniest.

In the afternoon I told Antoinette that it was worth offering one's life for peace. But not in her case, because of the children.

---

15. For whoever has fixed himself for ever in *this world* by refusing grace at the moment of death (and for little children who died unbaptised). (J.)

16. Nature is unhappy there and divided against itself because voluntarily turned away from God (except in limbo where the souls of unbaptised children are not turned away from God and do not suffer in any way). (J.)

17. Raïssa and I had gone to Kolbsheim on April 10th (leaving Véra in Meudon) to stay with our godchildren, Alexandre and Antoinette Grunelius. Cf. p. 397 below (J.)

Monday, 17th April. – Before we left, Antoinette asked me: "Have you done it?" I knew what she was thinking of, and I said: yes. She began to cry and went down on her knees. I consoled her by telling her that perhaps the Lord would not accept it. . .

Yesterday I made my offering saying: "If it is not unfair to Jacques and Véra."

89

Meudon, *30th May 1939.* – Communion.

In the afternoon, went with Jacques to the Orangerie, to see the Musée de Montpellier exhibition. Not remarkable, this collection; except for a very fine portrait of Baudelaire by Courbet and two marvellous Zurbarans, a St. Agatha and an Archangel Gabriel which is a pure miracle.

90

Fontgombaud, *Tuesday, 25th July 1939.* – First tranquil morning here, where we arrived on the 21st.[18] *Recueillement* returned.

On Friday, before leaving Meudon, I received a marvellous letter from Pierre Reverdy about *Lettre de Nuit.*

91

29th July 1939. – Long time of absorption in God. The

---

18. Our friend Olivier Lacombe had willingly installed himself in our house at Meudon, so the Blessed Sacrament could continue to be reserved in our chapel. (J.)

soul asks itself if it must still go on for a long while beating its wings against the bars of its cage.

Shall I write any more poems?

With me, poems are not made in the midst of a continuous clamour of the imagination – but in the heart of the most naked silence when it has attained a sufficient degree of depth and purity. . . I have spent so many years in mortifying the imagination to create in myself the silence propitious to being alone with God.

92

Monday, 31st July 1939. – Finished Shalom Asch's beautiful, astounding book: *Le Juif aux Psaumes*, on the morals and spirituality of the Hassidim, in Poland, in the middle of the XIXth century.

My maternal grandfather was a Hassid too.

And my father's father was a great ascetic.

I have all that behind me.

And for me, too, the Psalms ought to be a perpetual nourishment.

This book poses the problem of "conversion" in a magnificent and poignant way.

Tact is the art of taking into account the unconscious content of the words one is about to utter and of the reactions they will arouse in one's neighbour's unconscious.

93

Thursday, 3rd August 1939. – I go out **very** little, I would have to go out in the morning – in the afternoon it is too stormy. But the morning is the best part of my life, the one from which I draw all my energies; I must at all costs preserve the solitude, silence and stillness of it.

All my happiness is to sit at my table, in front of the window looking on to the garden, and beyond to the green water of the Creuse and the forest on the opposite bank.

When everything is at peace around me and I am quiet and alone, silence with God comes and then I find in my heart everything I love on earth and in heaven. And a landscape of living waters, and a light breeze, and savour and rest and enthusiasm.

(When it is not falling headlong and being engulfed in suffering worse than death. . .)

Saturday, 12th August, 1939 – Charles du Bos died Saturday morning, August 5th.

We have lost a great friend.

But the heart is wrung above all by the thought of what this man suffered, especially in the last three years.

He died prematurely, perhaps because lack of recognition in France forced him to earn a living in the United States by working harder than he should have.

Whenever a friend dies, it is difficult not to tell one's self that one didn't love him enough, or rather that one was negligent in showing friendship and esteem and admiration.

Ah, this hard devouring life makes us niggardly in this regard – and yet it is not the dead who need our praise, our compassion, our presence.

Now they have need only of prayer.

It is the living and not the dead who need to be visited in the loneliness of the soul and the prisons of sorrow.

Jacques went to the funeral of Charles du Bos, which was held on Wednesday, August 9th. He learned that his death had been admirably serene and strong.

A few of his last words:

"Saint Augustine, Bach, Giorgione were the masters of my life . . . and Nietzsche also, the only adversary who counts. . ."

"The mark of a great life is *failure.*"

Sunday, 13th August 1939, XIth after Pentecost. – As in 1934, I feel acutely what is said in the "Communion" of this Sunday, *Honora Dominum de tua substantia.* . . Gradual: *"Lord, I have cried unto thee: O my God, be not then silent; depart not from me.* . ."

94

Fontgombaud, *14th August 1939.* – Faced with death, shall I be afraid? Ought I to be afraid? It seems to me, no. Well or ill, I have done what I could to keep on the track of my destiny. My eternal future is in the hands of God, I abandon myself to my heavenly Father. I shall go to Christ, that will be deliverance. I have a peaceful feeling about it. The Lord knows what I have suffered. If ever I felt the "comfort" of the spiritual life, that feeling has long ago left me. A spiritual destiny is a light bridge thrown across the abyss, or the peak of a rock rising above the ocean. If the bridge and the rock are proof against all hazards, the soul does not know it. She has a view of the world that makes her dizzy, whether it displays itself to her in its beauty or its madness. Because she is *separated* but not yet *withdrawn* from the world. The beauty, the intelligible consistence, the nobility, the justice of the divine world from which she receives life are essentially objects of Faith. She lives by secret motions. The object of her love is veiled.

Anyone who has not the experience of this "separation" does not know, either, the road on which he is treading; he does not know the distinction between the two worlds; he lives in confusion. Neither does anyone who has not suffered from it know what our "separated" state is like.

95

22nd August 1939. – To Albert Béguin:

"Does a poet know himself? In my own case, I know that it was not in the continual clamour of the imagination, but in the heart of silence, when that silence attained a certain degree of depth and purity, that nearly all the poems in *Lettre de Nuit* and *La Vie Donnée* were born. But naturally one enters into this silence just as one is, with all that one lives and all that one loves and perhaps with that disposition to go straight to what *is*, 'to contemplate essences through particular existences' which I hope indeed you have not been too indulgent in mentioning apropos of this little book."

96

Saturday, 26th August 1939. – Communion.

A very great grief: Olivier Lacombe, obliged to leave Meudon hurriedly on account of the emergency, writes that yesterday he had to have the Blessed Sacrament removed from our chapel. A real blow.

Sunday, 3rd September. – France, and England too, have declared war on Germany who attacked Poland on Friday September 1st.

4th September. – Here is what Véra offers us. "Today, during mass, right after holy communion, I heard this in my heart: *Do not fear, do not fear, none of you must fear. I shall protect you, I shall watch over you.*

"At the same time a great peace and absolute confidence settled in my heart. I was very tired, very weary, and all my weariness was lifted away, and I was given great physical strength.

"The words were spoken very insistently."

5th September. – Véra tells us again, before mass: "France is saved."

During mass, before holy communion, she heard these words: "Do not fear, none of you must fear, my little children, I shall watch over you. Tell your little sister that I am by her, in her, that I have gathered up all her sufferings *with great care* for the salvation of souls. I want her to know that I am always at her side."

My sister wrote these words down in a little note for me this morning, and explained that she had underlined the words "with great care" because they were spoken with greater emphasis.

What is there to say in the face of so much divine goodness! That my anguish was perhaps beyond my strength, and that God had pity on my weakness.

I cannot doubt, furthermore, the authenticity of what is happening in the soul of my little Véra – all this has been put to the test over a long period of time, and men

like Father Dehau and Father Charles [Charles Henrion]
have complete *confidence* in her.[19]

---

19. For a long time Véra had been hearing words coming from
Jesus in the depths of her heart, but this had been kept a secret
between her and her spiritual guide, Father Dehau. It was only
during the agonising weeks at the beginning of the war that she
began to talk to us of it. (Cf. my *Carnet de Notes*, Paris DDB,
1965, pp. 285–290.) In her notes of 1939 and 1940 Raïssa trans-
scribed a number of these messages; I quote only a few of them
here:

1939

7th September. – After I had taken communion Véra offered me
this: "Last night, when I was praying especially for my little sister,
I heard these words in my heart: *I need her prayer.*

"This morning, I was awakened very gently by these words:
Tell your little sister to have unshakeable confidence.

"During mass, after communion: *You must all have unshakeable
confidence. I shall give you strength.* I also understood that the
confidence the good Lord has given us must not remain jealously
guarded in our hearts, but must be communicated insofar as that
is possible."

8th September. – From Véra: "At mass, before communion:
your confidence glorifies me, your confidence obliges me.

"When I was saying things to the good Lord. – *You have
nothing but spiritual treasures, you must offer them.*"

9th September. – From Véra: "After communion: *You must have
INDESTRUCTIBLE confidence in Me, in my love for you; tell this to
your little sister. – I shall watch over your brother, I shall protect
him.*"

25th September. – From Véra: "At church, toward the end of the
afternoon, after having passed some English soldiers: *I shall have
pity on them especially, and on all those whom you are thinking of
now and whom you will think of in the future, and on all those who
will come under your eye.*"

29th September. – From Véra: "During mass, before communion: *Tell your little sister that she is my dearly beloved daughter
and that she has nothing to fear.*"

12th October. – Véra offered us the following tonight: "On my way to the post office: *I shall protect you, I shall watch over you, I shall support you, have I not promised you this?*

"*No one should wish to avoid the cross, yours will be very merciful. Speak, speak of mercy. People do not have enough faith in my mercy. My heart is so tender toward humanity that mercy always carries the day over justice. Speak constantly of my mercy and my love; you cannot ever say enough of them.*"

26th October. – From Véra: "During mass: *Paris will not be burned.* While I was wondering to myself, yet they have said it will be burned: *What do you make of my mercy? Paris is the city of my love . . .*

"*Your little sister is to fear nothing, tell her that she is necessary to me, tell her that I gather up all her sufferings and all her agonies with great care, tell your little sister that she is necessary to me.*"

12th November. – After communion Véra heard these words: *All the soldiers are your children, you must pray for all of them.* She thought: "How can I ever accept the enemy soldiers as my children!" She was answered twice: *You must pray* FOR ALL OF THEM *as for your children.*

1940

15th January 1940. – (At Toronto, where we had just arrived). – We are beginning to know exile. And God offers us this, through Véra, so mercifully: *It is I who welcomes you to this land. I shall watch over you, I shall protect you, I shall smooth away your difficulties. For it is to do my will that you have come here.*

19th February 1940. – After mass in the Sisters' chapel, where Véra and I took communion, Véra offered me this: "Right after holy communion, in my pew; *your little sister is to fear nothing, my angels will carry her, she is my strength* (and as I didn't understand very well, Véra wrote) *because my strength is in her. Later on she will see the beautiful things I accomplish in her and by her, she will kiss my hands through eternity.*"

Yesterday, when Véra saw me suffering great anguish, she acknowledged having understood (but without inner speech) that God would choose a victim among the three of us – and that it would be myself.

18th September. – Left for Avoise where Abbé Gouin has offered us hospitality.

97

Avoise, *Saturday, 14th October 1939.* – The Cultural Relations people have asked Jacques to go to Toronto as usual on the date fixed for his lectures, then from there to the United States. He is tortured with apprehension at the thought of taking Véra and me, and exposing us to the risks of a sea journey in wartime and furthermore to the rigorous Canadian winter. But if he goes, we want to go with him.

98

October 1939. – Sometimes the very merciful strength that envelops me is, as it were, suddenly withdrawn from me. And then I find myself so alone, so wretched, so abandoned that I wonder by what miracle I keep alive and on my feet; for my soul and my mind are then, as it were, drawn out of me and only my will remains with me and enables me to live and act. These are appalling times. I say times because even though this only lasts an hour it seems as if it were never going to end. Then everything I have to do or to put up with seems to me impossible and intolerable.

99

Sunday, 5th November 1939. Twenty-third Sunday after Pentecost. –

At High Mass in the church at Avoise, I was gripped by a feeling I have never experienced before. It was as if the bitter taste of poverty and misery had filled my mouth and my whole being. A total and all-embracing misery, a dense wall with no chink in it to let in fresh air or the faintest glimmer of consolation.

Then I saw Marie [our Polish maid] pass by, going to take up her place in church; a humble, touching little figure, in her clothes of some dark, indeterminate colour which became even dimmer as they brushed against the benches. She too appeared to me as defenceless poverty – the image of her country, devastated Poland. Marie, a little creature alone in the world, with no relatives, with no country. No one but us – and we are probably going away!

I followed the Mass with my heart shattered with pity and bitterness, thinking of our friends over there, those in Warsaw – in Laski, no doubt tortured to death, or still alive and enduring all kinds of fearful ordeals. So these things happen! Ah, those whose names one knows always seem nearer to us! I think of my dear Sophie Landy, in religion Sister Teresa of the Carrying of the Cross. What a name! What a destiny! And Abbé Kornilovicz, and Marylski, and Mère Crapska, the blind nun, light of her community. I chew the bitter cud of their mortal anguish.

At the last a little hope shone in my heart on account of today's Introit in which the Lord promises to bring back our captives from all places . . .

100

Avoise, *11th November 1939*. – To Maurice Sachs:
"My very dear Godson, I was beginning to be worried by your long silence, when your letter arrived. What is

your military situation? I thought you had been discharged. In any case, you are exceptionally well qualified to be an interpreter. And what are the conditions of your physical life? I cannot picture you sleeping on straw and I am reassured for the moment; 70 rue des Carmes can hardly be a stable. You are not to reproach me, Maurice, for worrying about one person when so many men are suffering and in danger of death. It is right and natural that we should worry first of all about those we love; and even those whom we only know by name are already closer to us by that very fact. But there is nothing exclusive about such solicitude. You remember what St James says? (I am quoting from memory): How can you claim to love God whom you do not see if you do not love your neighbour whom you see? I do not believe for one moment in the universal generosity of those who do not love those who are near to them. And, as for myself, I admit that I am living in anguish. There is too much cruelty on earth, too many people tortured and in the throes of death – how could the heart rest for a moment in any joy whatever? I feel as if my soul were living outside myself wherever people are suffering anguish, agony and death. Do not think that faith and hope are the seat of spiritual comfort. Certainly, they remove despair, but anxiety for such comfort would be more than likely to make them disappear.

"You ask me, dear Maurice, what I can still *hope* for? 'We ought to have hoped that all this would not happen!' I thank you for speaking to me with such simple frankness. And I will answer you just as simply. What I hope for, because such a hope is given me in the uttermost depths of my anguished heart, is first of all the victory of France

283

v

and England; and afterwards, and very dearly bought, a general rectification of men's minds, the return to certain fundamental truths without which a good human life and a lasting peace are impossible. No, I did not hope that all this would not happen. Alas, it was inevitable that *this* would happen. 'And we have not done according to what Thou hast commanded that we might be happy.' That is in the Bible, in Daniel. Excuse me, Maurice, for reverting once again to Scripture. But it is the book of our Faith. And moreover it is the very validity of this faith that you challenge. . . . Marcel Achard's quip must have made God himself smile. For ever since there have been men, and men have made war among themselves and suffered, there has also been belief in God. But how natural it is, in the face of excessive misfortune, to say like this good woman you told me about: 'I'm not very intelligent but all the same I ask myself what the good God is up to!' Let me add that we are not always as humble as she, and do not admit, to begin with, that our lights on these great matters are after all very limited. Oh, the question intrudes itself, as it has always done – it has been asked from Job and Dostoievsky to ourselves. But God does not leave it unanswered. There is first and foremost the answer addressed to all which is the Passion of the Son of God. Does it not signify, first, the gravity of the sin which calls for such an expiation? Then, that suffering united to love is the way to eternal life? And suffering comes from sin, or from the world; and love comes from God.

"But there is also for each one of us an individual answer; and we hear it better, as a rule, in sorrow than in joy. That is why, considering things from the point of view of eternity, the periods of calamities which sin has rendered inevitable are also times of the most abundant mercies. But this is hidden in the secret of invisible life of human souls and known only by those to whom God reveals it.

"Every act eternally unfolds its consequences. The relations of God with men are not something vague and confused in which anything at all might happen in a haphazard way. They take place in an atmosphere of exactitude and light. Mercy will have the last word. But this is because truth and charity will have first entered men's hearts by ways which, on account of our obduracy, are often difficult; and, sometimes, as today, bloodstained.

"You will tell me no doubt that all this is coherent within the whole framework of Catholic doctrine but that this doctrine presupposes just what you question – the very existence of God, which is incompatible in your eyes with human suffering.

"But this is because Catholic doctrine is, among all religious doctrines, the one that best integrates the existence of evil and suffering; the one that gives the best account of the causes of our misery and of the remedies for it.

"No doubt, the existence of God is not directly evident. The purely spiritual is never directly evident to us. God's existence is certain, but obscure, for the natural instinct of our heart. Very certain but still obscure, for Faith. Finally, it can be the object of quite rational certainties for the philosopher capable of discovering them at the end of a long chain of reasoning – a skill which is only possessed by a small number of minds. So the ways are manifold and the arguments numerous with most of the philosophers who arrive at the 'proof', as it is called, of the existence of God. The opposing argument drawn from the existence of evil and suffering is refuted in the same way.

"But the fact remains that the great and royal road accessible to all – when our good will responds to God's grace – is in the Gospel, in the life of Christ and in the life of the Saints . . . "

101

12th November 1939. – At High Mass, I well and truly understood that I must accept the almost incessant anguish and agony of my heart as my state of prayer and my part in co-operating with God's work in the world and in souls. I can make Tauler's cry my own.[20]

102

22nd December 1939. – We are leaving Avoise for Paris, and going from there to Marseilles (30th December). The *Exochorda* which was to have sailed on the 31st December is not leaving till the 4th January 1940.

---

20. See Fragment 25. (J.)

III

1940-1960

[*With our departure for America in 1940 we became up-rooted people. We were leaving behind forever everything that had constituted the nourishing soil of our life, our affections, our work. Raïssa had lost the only place — Meudon, with the presence of the Blessed Sacrament under our roof — where she felt herself a little sheltered on earth, and where, while risking dying in harness, she found, in spite of everything, exceptionally favourable conditions for that silence with God which she needed so much. And moreover, is it not normal that anyone who is journeying towards God should some day or other be deprived of the facilities for prayer which may have been given them at first for a more or less long period? She was flung into the hazards of the swirling waters of the world and found herself henceforth having to contend, and in particularly hostile circumstances, with the relentless energy of things which make man dispersed. She had to wrench by sheer force from the malevolent hours whatever time she could, however scrappy, for that contemplative prayer without which it was impossible for her to live. And, in the very midst of the whirlwind, a habitual union with God, a kind of uninterrupted contem-*

plation, along with sorrowful nostalgia for the leisure she would have needed in order to give herself up to it freely, continued to underlie everything she did, bringing to all her activities a peace that was not of this earth.

Those years in New York, when besieged by despair while the swastika was triumphing in Europe, we had all the same to keep up our spirits and those of others (and it was then that Raïssa suffered the cruellest wound, the searing of the spirit at the sight of the agony of the oppressed and persecuted, and of the horror of a world which God seemed to have abandoned) ;[1] *– those years in Rome when she had to face up to so many harassing obligations; – those years in Princeton, where a little calm had come at last, but along with it physical suffering and illness and the anguish of seeing Véra and myself ill in our turn, and where she paid for the work which monopolised me by having to endure harsh loneliness; during all that time she was wholly exiled, given, dispossessed. And while strength, peace, light and a kind of winged gaiety emanated from her, she*

---

1. Cf. the poem "Deus Excelsus Terribilis" (in *Au Creux du Rocher*); and, in this book itself, Fragment 127, also Number 4 of "Complementary Fragments" – *The Poetry of our Time*. In the Prologue to *Les Grandes Amitiés,* dated 6th July 1940, Raïssa wrote: " . . . My own life, my very imperfect life, has reached that maturity of soul which is acquired only at the price of extra-ordinary misfortune, personal or otherwise; that age at which nothing is left of childhood or of happiness in living. My life comes to this climax much less because of the trials that I myself have endured, than because of the misfortune which has fallen upon all humanity. For justice wears mourning, the afflicted are not – cannot – be consoled, the persecuted are not succoured, because God's truth is not spoken, and suddenly the world has become so little, so narrowed for the spirit, by the monotony of that lie which rules it and which almost alone makes itself heard." *We Have Been Friends Together,* Image Books, p. 11.

*plunged into a deeper and deeper solitude with her God and
she had no longer more than a very slender foothold on earth.*

*During all these years of which I have just spoken, there
could be no question of Raïssa's keeping, even very irregularly,
a record of her inner life. Those of her diaries which have not
been left blank, or almost entirely empty as so often happened,
contain nothing but notes concerning the external events, great
and small, of our life. Only from time to time does there
emerge from what constituted the basis of her life, a reflection on
her soul, a thought, a memory to nourish her heart, a truth
suddenly perceived or long meditated over, a cry perhaps, a cry
of distress, which she has noted on the wing. It is these notes,
with others found on separate sheets, in envelopes, and also
occasionally longer fragments,[2] and a few unpublished poems[3]
which I have collected together to complete the* Journal *with
writings dating from the years in question.[4]* (J.)]

103

Toronto, *Monday, 15th January 1940.* – We came safe
into port at New York, and finally reached Toronto, in spite
of the mines at Gibraltar, and the storm in the middle of the
ocean. No German ship appeared during our crossing to
stop us and examine us.

---

2. These longer fragments will be found in the last sections of
this book. (J.)

3. I have included three of these poems in the *Journal* (Fragments 118, 143, 144). (J.)

4. Owing to the discontinuity of these notes, I have had to put
a few more of my own notes in this section than in the preceding
ones. (J.)

Tuesday, 16th January 1940. – We two, Véra and I, are staying in the house of the Sisters of Saint-Joseph who have welcomed us with exquisite kindness. Jacques is at the University (St Michael's College).

104

Sunday, 11th February. – How good, simple, intelligent and charming the Sisters are here, particularly Sister Saint-Raymond!

Monday, 12th February. – One has to suffer . . .

Tuesday, 13th. – Oh! How one has to suffer!

Sunday, 18th February. – Once again the martyrdom of anguish – the desire for death.

105

Friday, 1st March 1940. – Departure for New York.
From 2nd to 25th March in New York. Easter in New York.

25th March. – Departure for Chicago, where we are living with our friends John and Eleanor Nef.
Jacques is giving lectures at the University. For me this exile is a terrible ordeal.

106

11th April. – Back again in New York.

Jacques' influence in the United States is extending. He is being asked to remain here, or at least to prolong his stay.

Invitations to Mexico and to the Argentine.[5] I am frightened and do not know what we ought to do. I would like to return to France in June but I do not want to prevent Jacques from doing the good he might do here.

22nd April. – Departure for Aurora-on-Cayuga where we shall make a short stay.

My sufferings are once again atrocious, my solitude very great. Véra sometimes comes in to say a few encouraging words to me. Jacques has not the time to.

107

Aurora, *24th April 1940.* – Véra says that she and Jacques behave to me as Abraham did to Isaac when he was going to sacrifice him. But as with Isaac, she thinks that at the last moment God will act and I shall be delivered.

25th April. – I suffer indeed like someone for whom it is impossible to take any initiative whatsoever. I am bound hand and foot like a victim prepared for sacrifice. I must say this, though I have a horror of applying these great and venerable words to my own self. I dare not move, I dare not will, for fear of preventing some good God desires to bring about through Jacques. Yesterday, I made the wish to die. But I was seized with compassion for Jacques and

---

5. I declined these invitations. (J.)

Véra whom my death would leave in such great loneliness, and I withdrew my wish . . .[6]

108

New York, *3rd May 1940.* – Yesterday (Ascension) Jacques left for Washington. After his departure, I received this morning (Finding of the Holy Cross) three letters – from Father Lavand, from Father de Menasce and from Abbé Journet – warning Jacques of what is being hatched against him in Rome. They want to catch him in fault; Franco's partisans haven't disarmed. Now they want to convict Jacques of error on the question of implicit faith. It will be done in an article by Father Cordovani in the *Osservatore,* where he will not be named but clearly identifiable. Misery! During this time Father Coughlin can talk every day to thousands of Catholics as a nazi, a racist, an anti-Semite, without incurring any penalty . . .

8th May. – Attended mass at noon at the Sisters of Perpetual Adoration. When we returned, Véra offered me this: "Fear nothing, you are to fear nothing, you are the little lambs of my heart." And when Véra said: 'And Jacques?" – "I do not separate him from you."

"Tell your little sister to lean on me with all her strength;

---

6. This wish to die can be better understood if one thinks of the offering of her life which Raïssa had made on April 16th, 1939 for the peace of the world. The war had come and it was in another way that God was taking her life – was going to leave her to the end "without a dwelling" and completely despoiled and make her taste as she said herself ("Ecce in Pace", in *Portes de l'Horizon*) "the divine bitterness of living and dying". (J.)

she is to fear nothing." And as Véra was saying to herself: "She doesn't have much strength, so it won't amount to very much," the following was said to her: "She is to give herself up completely; she is to rely even more on me for everything, and she is to fear nothing."

New York, *10th May 1940.* – The Germans are overrunning Holland, Belgium, Luxembourg. The great offensive has begun.

15th May. – Jacques returns to New York. He cables Paris for instructions.[7]

The same day, a telegram from Abbé Journet, saying: "Events remove problem entirely.[8] Remain America. I embrace and bless you."

109

2nd June. – Ghastly days. Paris will probably be occupied by the Germans today or tomorrow.

---

7. The Cultural Relations Ministry answered by confirming my mission to the United States. We had first thought of returning to France in June. But after the armistice, the occupation of half of France and the installation of the Vichy government, we decided to stay in the United States where we could act, speak and write freely, bear witness to the true feelings of our country and work as best as we could for the common cause. (I did not know at that time that as soon as the Germans arrived in Paris the Gestapo went to look for me at the Catholic Institute, but I knew well that the publication of my book *A travers le Désastre*, which I had begun to work on at once, closed the doors of my country to me.) (J.)

8. The "problem" that Abbé Journet alluded to cryptically was the scheme mentioned above, planned by certain ecclesiastics who hoped to make me doctrinally suspect. (J.)

3rd August 1940. – (anniversary of our first communion in 1906; and of mother's in 1925). – Have found a title for the memoirs I am writing: *Les Grandes Amitiés.*

14th September. – Véra and I went to buy kitchen equipment and dishes for our apartment at 30 Fifth Avenue (all the other furnishings are provided.)[9] The feeling of starting all over again . . .

110

10th December 1940. – Difficult day. In the evening, not being able to find my place in this world, I was still struggling against such great spiritual discomfort when suddenly a deep peace flooded me and enveloped me, with this luminous perception that I belonged to Jesus – that he was my place in this world. And I went quietly to sleep.

111

New York, *5th January 1941.* – Bergson died yesterday (4th January). A great sorrow for us. I think of what we owe him, of what so many others owe him.

They have written to us from France that he had been baptised[10] and that he had not wanted to announce it

---

9. Up to this time we had been living at a hotel. (J.)

10. This information was not correct. Bergson had been converted in his heart, he had the Christian faith, but he had not been baptised. As he states himself in his will, he would have asked for baptism if he had not feared to seem to be separating himself from the persecuted Jews. In conformity with his request, a priest came and prayed over his mortal remains. Raïssa made all this

publicly out of delicacy for the Jews who have suffered persecution during these last years.

Our master lost and found again.

112

Friday, 7th March 1941. St Thomas Aquinas. – Never yet have we spent this feast in such distress.

Sunday, 1st June. – Mass and Communion at St Francis Xavier. I wept so much during Mass and after, thinking of my little chapel at Meudon. There, I had a place on earth. Now I feel as if I were nowhere.

113

New York, *Sunday, 18th July 1943.* – Such a painful awakening! Heart too overcharged with suffering. Quasi-despair. – Courage and peace return after Mass and Communion.

114

Thursday, 27th September 1943. – Communion.

I have a constant wound in my heart from not being able to work, to answer letters . . . My time is split up into tiny fragments, frittered away by a multitude of little occupations which leave me no possibility of *recueillement* and no hope of silence in which thought and expression are nourished.

---

clear in the second of her articles in *Commonweal* (17th January and 29th August 1941). Cf. also *Henri Bergson, Essais et Témoignages inédits,* collected by A. Béguin and P. Thevenez, La Baconnière – Neuchâtel 1941. (J.)

115

Wednesday, 24th November 1943, St John of the Cross. –
In the evening at 8.30 at St Vincent-de-Paul, baptism
of my god-daughter Emily. Her father was there and her
son John. Jacques is her godfather. It was Père Couturier
who baptised her.[11]

116

Friday, 31st December 1943. – Jacques has done me the
honour of using, for his 19th broadcast for France, a prayer
in the form of a psalm which I recently wrote, "Prayer for
God's people"[12]. How will those who are suffering over

---

11. On the 22nd October 1942, Raïssa had received her first
letter from Emily Coleman who wrote to her after having read
Les Grandes Amitiés. Emily left everything for God and in order
to enter the Church. "She is courageous, strong," Raïssa noted on
November 19th; "she laughs and she cries. She has extraordinary
resilience." I want to pay a little tribute here to this god-daughter
whom Raïssa loved so tenderly and whose story she and I thought
was enough to justify all it had been necessary to suffer on the
highways of the world in order that, one day in New York, this
American woman torn away from Arizona and this Russian woman
and this Frenchman torn away from Meudon should meet.
Without abjuring her gifts as painter and poet, she is now dedicated
to a life of retirement and contemplation.
  Quite incapable of being parsimonious even in the choice of
patron saints, she wanted to receive at baptism the names of
Emily, Teresa, Gertrude, Lucy, Paula, Jeanne and Ignatius, which
was not at all convenient for Père Couturier, charged with admini-
stering the sacrament.
  Her son John, another very dear godchild of Raïssa, had been
baptised on the 28th August 1943. (J.)
  12. Part of the poem "Deus Excelsus, Terribilis" (which
appeared later in *Au Creux du Rocher*). As a result of an accident
which made it necessary to re-make the record, this broadcast was
not given until Sunday 23rd January 1944. (J.)

there have taken those words spoken sincerely from the bottom of my heart, but totally powerless to express the reality of their suffering? This thought makes me tremble with embarrassment.

117

Undated. (Probably 1943.) – Only theology and poetry can speak of God.

Knowledge, inspiration, and experience.

118

Undated (Probably 1943.) – [A poem: *The Dew of God.*]

> "The dew of God is a dew
> of light" (Is. 26:19.)

"The dew of the Lord is a dew of light"
In times of happiness
And fire in time of stress.
Your breath has burnt to ash
Our heart and soul;
The mind has fled and lost itself
In Your inscrutable justices.

Dispossessed, I chew the cud of anguish,
Parched with thirst for Your compassion,
For Your redemption
Of those who were taken away in chains
Up to the threshold of despair
And there were done to death.
When You join once again those scattered bones

Will they be clothed in flesh for another life?
When shall we hear the singing which brings together

opposites?

The joy-awakening melody
Will nevermore awake in me.
A sigh is all my breath
And my prayer a cry from the depth.
My spirit is absent, roving,
Lost in You,
Divided from me by fiery dew.[13]

119

New York, *25th January 1944*. – From a letter to
Jacques:[14]

"If there is one thing in the world I cannot bear, it is that
you should be unhappy. I hope with all my heart that this
'moment of sadness' which made you write that letter on
Saturday morning was only a moment. You have been
suffering from an oppressive delusion, for there is nothing in
the instability and insecurity of our life for which you are
responsible . . .

" . . . We can only give thanks to God for the gentleness
with which he has treated us up to now. And that inspires
me with so much confidence for the future! Not that I am
assured that we shall have nothing to do but live in peace
when the peace of Nations is restored, far from it. What I *am*

---

13. Translated by a Benedictine of Stanbrook.
14. This fragment was not found among Raïssa's papers. It
comes from a letter that I always keep with me as a talisman. I was
in Chicago when Raïssa wrote me this letter. (J.)

sure of is that you will always do what God will most want you to do – and that is the greatest security and stability of all – and that we shall always find ourselves where God will prefer us to be. Besides all this, I do well know, my dear beloved, that the burden of decisions rests entirely on your shoulders, like the burden of excessive work that never ceases to weigh you down. And the anxieties we are always giving you, Véra and I, because our health is so poor, add their load of trouble to all that. We have always had a great many of these afflictions in our life, they are our share in the Cross of Jesus, and in the depth of our soul we have never refused them. I hope God will grant us the grace to bear them better and better as life progresses towards death, towards life at last with God. This is the normal burden, the one that nobody can avoid. We *have* to climb those steps. But for all that is peculiar to our life, to my life with you, I give thanks to God with my whole soul. He has given me a marvellous lot! – the best that could have been destined for me. In you, I have found all the sweetness and light I needed, and still do need. Of that light [. . .] I have had the first fruits and the sweetest part. And your so dear love which has always surrounded me, helped me, given me courage to live. So do be happy too, my beloved Jacques, as much as it is possible to be in this world.

"Be of good heart, my beloved. We belong to him who has conquered the world . . ."

120

18th February 1944. – Terrible anguish on awakening. The tragic reality of Europe overwhelmed me, finding my heart defenceless, not yet armed for the daily battle which begins when I get up.

121

Tuesday, 9th May 1944. – My godson John came and talked to me tonight. I said to him:

"There is no book in the world one does not have the right to question except the Scriptures – but the Scriptures one doesn't understand."

Later I repeated this to Jacques who was so pleased with it that he wrote it down and stuck it up on the drawing-room wall (from which, of course, I removed it).

122

Friday, 7th July 1944. – We are at East Hampton since yesterday.[15] This countryside is delicious. The light is extraordinary; the trees, the grass – it all seems marvellous to me.

It is the first time since we have been in America that I feel myself "received", sheltered, resting on the earth, on things.

123

Friday, 25th August 1944. – Paris is liberated.

Friday, 10th November 1944. – Jacques left tonight for Paris in an American military plane.

---

15. We spent three months there; we were utterly exhausted and the doctor had prescribed rest (which moreover was highly relative: it was there that Raïssa finished the second volume of *Les Grandes Amitiés*). (J.)

[The object of this journey was to see our country and our friends again as soon as possible and to get first-hand information about the situation – still so sombre in France.

I returned to New York on January 1st 1945, not having succeeded in making General de Gaulle and Georges Bidault, then Minister for Foreign Affairs, renounce their project (which I had at first happily supposed to be only a fleeting notion and which I thought had been abandoned) of appointing me ambassador to the Vatican. The acceptance of the post which had been morally forced on me by their insistence and by the feeling that I could not evade a task demanded in the name of my country still at war, had reduced me to a kind of despair. All my plans for work were completely upset and I reproached myself for exposing Raïssa and Véra to fatigues which their health would not permit them to endure.

I now had to prepare for my departure to Rome whither Raïssa and Véra could not accompany me in the plane (once again an American military plane), and where I waited for them for over three months. (J.)]

124

Friday, 10th August 1945. – First day in Rome.[16] We

16. Raïssa and Véra arrived in Naples, where I was waiting for them, on the morning of August 9th; in Rome the same day late in the afternoon.

I had left New York on April 1st, leaving Raïssa the burden – very heavy for her – of buying, and sending by sea, all the things needed for the French Embassy to the Holy See (Italy was then out of stock of everything). Having arrived in Rome on April 20th, I had presented my credentials on May 10th. Raïssa and Véra, after innumerable contretemps, had finally succeeded in embarking at Boston, on the *Mariposa* on July 30th 1945. (J.)

must settle in, get our bearings a little, acclimatise ourselves.

I made a point of setting myself to silent prayer the very
first day. May I persevere in this! I used a "Selection from
the Writings of St. Bernard" which I found here.

125

Rome, *Saturday 25th April 1945*, St. Louis. – Mass and
Communion with Jacques and Véra at the Chiesa Nuova;
then High Mass at Saint-Louis-des-Français. Great beauty
of the church, the altar and the singing. Feeling of warm
welcome, of finding myself back home again. I was sitting
between Jacques and Véra. I thought: all this beauty, this
profusion of gold and profusion of movement in all the
carving and sculpture; these intricate rites in which everything has its symbolic meaning; all this is the work of love;
the love which flows from the first infusion of charity into
the Church. As to the artists who created all these forms,
they themselves were sustained, whether they had faith
or not, by the great love which keeps watch in and over
the Church.

After Mass, presentation of the ecclesiastical French
colony, in the sacristy.

126

25th November 1945. – Apropos of Aldous Huxley.[17]

---

17. Raïssa is alluding in particular to Huxley's ideas on mysti-
cism as set out in *Grey Eminence*. She reverted later, and in a
deeper way, to the thoughts expressed here (see further on
"Brief Writings," "And the Word was made Flesh"). (J.)

He does not know how close Christ and the Virgin Mary are to us – humanly. They are utterly close to us, although invisibly. They are our masters in contemplation, our models, our mediators; this is why the Christian contemplative can never and must never forget them. Their image may be absent in the act of contemplation – they are not the intermediaries of it, the union is immediate. But the grace of Christ assists us in contemplation – so do the merits of Mary.

127

24th December 1945. – To Achsa Belkind:

". . . You cannot imagine, and I do not even want to say, how deep the events of the last six years have filled my soul with dust and ashes; events to which it is not possible to reconcile oneself in any shape or manner except by naked, arid faith in the divine Wisdom and Mercy, which not only surpass our feelings, which I thought I knew – but, as I know now, surpass them in going beyond any standard of measurement, even thought of as supernatural. Human madness and human cruelty have been given permission to go to all lengths, unchecked, and, speaking of the six million massacred of whom so little is said, we counted very close friends among them: three of the Jacobs – the old mother, his daughter Babet, his son Manu (I think you met them at our house in Meudon). And Fondane and his sister and the elder brother of our friends Jean and Suzanne Marx (Suzanne became my goddaughter this spring).

"And, as you know, when one can put a name to a few of those who died in Auschwitz, in Belsen or in Dachau, and call up a face among them, the vast sorrow one feels for all the other victims itself assumes a face which haunts you with unspeakable horror and compassion.

"In spite of all this, God preserves in our souls a weight and stability of peace which I cannot understand; it is thus, no doubt, and much more powerfully still, that he preserved the souls of martyrs against despair."

128

Rome, *4th March 1946.* – I wake up in a state of profound sadness, – my heart full of tears. But I have no time to weep.

Day after day, I wait to be able to begin to work. Since I wait in vain, I decide to abandon the thought of writing altogether; by so doing I can apply myself solely to what I have to do here in this Embassy. I will resume my work when God wills me to if he ever does. . .

In my misery, curiously enough, I found no help at all, either from Jacques or from Véra – I have been very much alone. God permitted it to be like that. I have carried my tears inside me all day.

129

Tuesday, 5th March. In the morning, Véra and I were sitting on either side of the wood stove, praying silently. At one moment I felt Véra was particularly absorbed in God and she left almost at once to go to her room. She returned a little later, in tears, and holding something she had written for me and which encouraged me.

130

1st April 1946.[18] – There is a sanctity for each one of us, proportioned to our destiny and which God proposes to obtain by means which are not catalogued in any manual of perfection.

131

Palm Sunday, 14th April 1946. – Mass at Santa Sabina, celebrated for us and for our intentions by Père Marie-Alain Couturier, in St. Dominic's cell – for us alone, we three. Communion.

The sanctity and grandeur of this place – a lofty place. Where St. Dominic lived, whither have come St. Albert the Great, St. Thomas Aquinas, St. Hyacinth, St. Catherine of Siena. Magnificence of the Dominican saints who have passed through here, spiritual giants. Purity of all this beauty, perfection in full completeness, peace and silence.

This cell of St. Dominic's where we hear Mass is very small. Père Couturier says Mass with such sweet, discreet piety. We feel his heart filled with our cares. We feel his love for us.

132

Undated. (Probably 1946). – From a letter to Arthur Lourié:

" 'The joy of the eyes', yes, that helps a great deal. The

---

18. This note and most of the following ones were written on "scraps of paper". From the year 1946 (inclusive) Raïssa's diaries were left almost entirely blank. The diary for 1945 is missing; the diaries for 1957 and 1960 are absolutely empty, those for 1958 and 1959 contain only a few lines. (J.)

beauty of the Roman campagna is extraordinary, but in the end one perceives that it has a slightly glacial perfection – it satisfies the eyes, but it makes no deeper appeal.

"All the winter the light has been a spring light. The Latian hills polished like marble – all in exquisite pastels, even the grey sky has subtle tones of mauve and pink in it. A celestial palette for painters who were Angels. Everything ravishes the eye, nothing ravishes the heart. The beauty of Rome is different, it stirs up tenderness, awakens memory."

133

Sunday, 7th July 1946. – Canonisations are always like an opening towards heaven. Went today to that of Blessed Frances Xavier Cabrini, the most beautiful we have seen. [I insert here an undated description which must have been written not many days after the ceremony. (J.)]

The Canonisation of Mother Cabrini in St. Peter's

The Basilica is made for light and joy, triumph and glory.

At one moment there was nothing but the silence – no singing, no words, no applause; infinite sweetness of this smooth, white silence which spread over everything like a white velvet carpet, and during which everything that was white, the surplices, the lace, the pointed mitres, took on a marvellous velvetiness which seemed like a caress of angelic softness. And then the silvery singing began again and everything returned to activity.

Procession of the birds, the bread, the wine and the candles. The Pope on his throne. From the foot of the central altar there slowly advanced the cardinals, wearing

white surplices so that one could only see below the hem
the almost pink red, a pink lit up by fire, of their cardinal's
robe. The first carried gravely and respectfully a gilded
cage
in which stood
motionless and perfect
two canaries.

Mounting the steps of the throne,
he presented them to the Holy Father who blessed them.

The second advanced with the same slowness and gravity,
carrying a white cage in which stood, stiffly upright and
as if nonplussed, two turtle-doves.

The third, deeply absorbed in meditation, presented
two white doves with all their downy feathers fluffed
out – and the birds, once they had been accepted and
blessed, were returned in procession.

Then came prelates carrying the offering of bread on a
gold plate and those offering two little casks, one of wine
and the other of water, and the silver voices bathed the
procession in their light. Then the Pope, in his ample
falda, Prince Colonna on his right, Cardinal Mercati on
his left, surrounded by his attendants, descended the
steps of the throne, advanced to the altar of the Confession
and continued the Mass.

The Basilica is decorated with red damask which covers
all the walls from top to bottom; and the pillars are covered
with hanging lustres of delicate crystal.

On the right of the pontifical throne, the Italian nobility,
and the Sisters of the Saint's Congregation, all in black.

On the left, the diplomatic corps.

At the entrance of the Pope, borne on the sedia, the

silver trumpets sound – and you seem to be hearing the strident voice of gigantic violins.

At the Elevation of the Host, the Pope, holding it in both hands, slowly makes a half-turn to the left, faces the altar again, then makes a slow half-turn to the right; he does the same with the consecrated Chalice. Thus the whole congregation in the nave and the transept can see what it is adoring.

A little before the Communion, the Pope is brought back to the throne. He returns bareheaded, as if stripped – in a state of humility; his features, his face have a remarkable youth and delicacy; he looks defenceless. The Sacred Species are brought to him in procession from the altar of St. Peter. He awaits them standing, his face faintly flushed, yet behind the simplicity of the attitude you are aware of a deep emotion, a wholly inner attentiveness. He says the prayers which precede the Communion. He communicates himself; he takes the Precious Blood from the chalice through a gold straw. He gives Communion to those who are serving the Mass. Then he remains standing, in a state of recollection, without shutting his eyes or making any gesture while the Master of Ceremonies and the other attendants bustle round him.

134

Kolbsheim, *17th August 1946*. – Certain physical conditions are favourable to prayer, to silence with God, to intellectual work; others make them more difficult and arid.

Nevertheless it is not true that the human soul is in the body like a bird in a cage – the soul informs the body and makes it human, the bird does not inform the cage and does not make it into a living being endowed with sensibility.

But the body is not, in this life, entirely proportioned to the spiritual soul, and, because of that, it weighs heavily on it and prevents it from having all the soaring energy of which it is capable. And in circumstances where the body is weighed down by climatic conditions, by illness, by weariness, it weighs down the spirit. If, on the contrary, it finds itself in favourable physical conditions, the soul is made freer in its activity, lighter, more energetic (happier if it is not, in other respects, going through some trial). These favourable conditions can either be strictly physical or they can be of a mental order, as when the soul is stimulated to a deeper intuition of spiritual things by music, by the sight of beautiful things, whether in nature or art – similarly too (on another plane) by the knowledge of philosophical or theological truth, etc. These remarks are especially true of the supernatural life.

The resurrected body of the elect, the glorified body will no longer in any way hinder the full contemplative activity of the soul.

135

Undated. (Probably Rome, 1946.) – From a letter to Antoinette Grunelius, talking about a work of religious psychology:

"In a certain number of these pages there is a clumsy insistence on the psychology of married people. . . More-over, it all seems to me very futile; married people make their own psychology and unmarried people are out of their depth in it. Moreover it is dangerous to give as essential properties of marriage ones which only belong to marriage fulfilled in exceptional conditions of love, harmony, happiness, delicacy, intelligence, etc. These theologians appear to forget that marriage is a sacrament, even if it is not happy, even if it is not a love marriage, even if it is only a 'marriage of convenience'. A proof that its essential properties lie in its uprightness and not in the full flowering of nature, the 'dilating' (as they call it) of the soul etc. When one sees the number of celibate analysts who devote themselves to the problem of marriage, one has the feeling that it is the analysts most of all who would need to get married (a matter they ought to deal with, directly, with God and their confessor, and not in public and by indirect ways)."

136

Undated. (Probably Rome, 1946.) – Their thirst has been quenched and for a while they no longer need water, and they declare that water is useless. When the days of thirst and aridity come back, they will have to turn again to the springs. Without losing courage, let the guardians of the springs and the rivers watch over their purity; people will come back to ask them for this water.

Pure theological and philosophical doctrine is this water essential to the life of the spirit; its sources are rare and precious and if they are reserved to a few, it is not owing to some avarice from above, but to some incapacity from below. Nevertheless, many who aspire after them are turned away by those of their guides who do not love truth quite enough to attain to it – who love knowing for the sake of curiosity better than knowing for the sake of truth.

137

Undated (Probably 1947.) – What the Lord has done for me.

The gifts of God have an infinite expansion.

But they are at the same time for this or that individual.

First, God made the child Jacques Maritain be born on the 18th November 1882, in Paris.

Ten months later he made the child Raïssa Oumançoff be born on the 12th September[19] in Rostoff-on-the-Don.

At the date of Raïssa's birth, Henri Bergson, aged 23, was writing the *Essai sur les Données immédiates de la Conscience.*

Léon Bloy, born in 1846, was 37, he was then writing his book on Christopher Columbus.

Pere Clérissac, born in 1864, was 19, he was entering the Dominicans.

138

Rome, *13th April 1947.* – At the end of the world when exegesis[20] will have attained its perfection, it will be the nearest to the text of the Bible (while *interpreting* the letter), because this letter is inspired and inspiration has put into the letter treasures superior to all human knowledge. It is not the human science that will triumph over

---

19. In the Gregorian calendar. (J.)
20. Exegesis, as Raïssa conceived it, was not a separate so-called "science", vacillating from one hypothesis to another; it was a discipline of wisdom and took advantage of all the positive data and discoveries in order better to understand and interpret the letter *in the light of theology*. It is on this score that it was a true science. (J.)

the letter but the letter which will manifest itself by means
of the science.

139

Rome, *6th July 1947*. – To Emily Coleman:

"... I am going to try and answer your question: whether
Bloy is a saint? Only the Church indubitably proclaims
people to be saints. But there are also many saints who
will never be canonised. Bloy is perhaps one of those. We
pray to him, that tells you what we believe ourselves.

"During the twelve years that we knew him intimately,
we never had anything serious to reproach him with.
Imperfections, no doubt. But certainly not pride or lack
of charity. What seems like pride in him, to people who
did not see him live, is only the consciousness he had of
his gifts as a writer and of the importance of his message –
of the vocation imposed on him by God. Is not all that
real? And, since humility is truth, where is the pride?
What sometimes, in his writings, seems like a lack of
charity – to those who did not know him – is only a clumsy
way of showing his love for souls, his burning zeal for their
salvation, his immense sorrow for the wrong sin does to
God. In judging such and such a person severely he was
sometimes mistaken, but he was right to judge malice of
heart and lack of love severely. It was always love of God
that provoked his severe judgements, his fits of anger –
never self-love. Well! All that comes from a holy soul, a
living faith, a divine charity. That is what his godchildren
think of him.

"Léon Bloy was faithful to his vocation at the price of
extreme sufferings. If he had used his immense talent, his
genius, in the service of the world, he would have been

rich and honoured by the world. I am not saying – heaven knows – that all those who are rich and whom the world honours are in the service of the world. Nor am I saying that Léon Bloy's vocation is proposed to all of us! If John has a vocation of gentleness to his neighbour, like St Francis of Sales, let him follow it, and his godmother can also acknowledge that kind of sanctity – but we have no right to judge our neighbour's vocation by the characteristics of our own. Did all the saints bury themselves in silence like the recluses? Or else ought they all to preach in season and out of season like St Paul? There, pearl among goddaughters, is the ex-cathedra judgement of your little godmother who loves you with all her heart. As our darling godson John asks us the same question about Bloy, be generous and pass on this letter, which I beg you to read with saintly patience, serious consideration and a little love for her who loves you so much."

140

Cannes, *Summer 1947*. – God sees Jesus eternally crucified, and this is like an image of what suffering [the unnamed perfection which corresponds to suffering],[21] can be in the divine essence.

Suffering for the loss of souls.

If to save every soul God had only to intervene by his omnipotence which could make sin impossible without thereby violating freedom and destroying it at the root, he would have no need of the use he makes of that *eloquence* which tries to convince us and "seduce" us, that eloquence

---

21. Cf. above, pp. 87; 129.

which made him send his Son to death, and to the death of the Cross, and which makes him reiterate exceptional signs in the course of centuries so as to urge the zeal of holy souls either through locutions (innerly heard by such or such saint)[22] which are like a tireless supplication, or through apparitions of Jesus suffering, full of sorrow and anguish over the loss of souls, or through the Sacred Heart, wounded and bleeding, speaking of his Passion as still going on now, imploring people to come to Him; this is very striking since the apparitions to St Margaret-Mary. And so many Apparitions of the Blessed Virgin pleading, as at La Salette where she weeps over our sins and the penalties which await us. . .

If, in order to avoid the loss of any soul, God acted from absolute power,[23] he himself would be shattering what his Wisdom has conceived, everything could become no matter what, there would be a chaos of gratuitous entities without specific natures; the structure of His own creation would collapse.

What, in this case, would become of love itself by which souls conquer eternal life? Love which presupposes liberty of choice. (In the beatific vision the will, fulfilled in all the plenitude of its nature, adheres indefectibly to the Infinite Good whose possession it has pursued in the darkness of faith, in the ways of our mortal life; in other words God *has been chosen*.)

In acting according to his Wisdom and not his sole

---

22. It seemed to J. M. that for translation and the sake of clarity the text had to be a little developed. (Trans.)
23. This is a scholastic phrase: *de potentia absoluta,* in contradistinction to *de potentia ordinata*. (Trans.)

Omnipotence, God leaves the soul free to slip away, if it wills, from His sufficient grace; and if it does not thus abscond of its own initiative, he makes it freely accomplish good through His efficient grace; and thus never does the Lord take the initiative in the evil of perdition.

If Christ implores the saints, the souls which are voluntary victims, to give Him (through His grace itself and His own merits) this supplement of meritorious sufferings; if he charges them to make known his anxious, urgent appeal to all souls, sinful as they may be, so that they may come to Him with confidence, to Him who thirsts for their salvation; if he begs souls for this hidden impulse he produces in them Himself on condition that they do not slip away on their own initiative – it is because it is not "easy" to save souls, it is because He cannot save them in spite of themselves. He has to convince them, to entice them; which is the very work of love, of mercy, of the sacred Heart of Jesus.

141

24th August 1947. – Almost daily anguish. Our duty, like the way of all three of us, is confidence. "Fear nothing. . ."

142

Rome, *16th November 1947.*–To Abbé Maurice Pierquin: ". . . To tell the truth, we are rather surprised by the unqualified, indeed immoderate good my godson[24] speaks

---

24. Maurice Sachs. – Abbé Pierquin, a French priest living in Canada (Manitoba) who became a friend of ours after the publication of *Les Grandes Amitiés* (we never met him on earth), had written to Raïssa saying how much he had been distressed by reading *Le Sabbat*. (J.)

X

of us in other respects, and we count to his credit the good he so rightly speaks of Père Pressoir; we are grateful to him for having been able, in the midst of so many temptations and weaknesses, to avoid that of ingratitude. There is something else to his credit, which is that all the evil he has done he has not disguised as good by false theories as some authors, covered with glory and renown, have done, but he calls evil, evil; and good, if he had not the strength really to seek it, he has at least aspired to it, and he certainly suffered from not being able to attain to it.

"God alone can know the degree of his responsibility for the evil in him; as for us, who knew a little of how heavily handicapped he was by his heredity – we do not judge him. God have pity on him, dead or alive.[25] And you, very dear friend, do not refuse him your prayers. . ."

143

Princeton, *31st October 1948*.[26] – [A poem: *Prayer*.]

You are Truth – You are Sincerity,
But *each man is a liar*.
May all that is within me,

---

25. This doubt was soon dissipated; it is certain that Maurice was put to death towards the end of the war. (J.)

26. Nothing in the diaries for 1948 and 1949. The two following poems were found in envelopes.

Having resigned my office we all three left Rome on June 14th 1948 to embark at Naples on June 16th and arrived in New York on the 27th; after a few weeks at New Rochelle, staying with our friend Godfrey Schmidt, we began our stay in Princeton, where we rented the cottage of a professor who was away for a year, on August 19th 1948. (It was from September 1949 onwards that we lived at 26 Linden Lane.) (J.)

Good and evil, lie and error,
What I know and do not know,
Pray, beseech, cry to You!
If I seek to know me, I lose myself in thought –
It is You alone who know my real name,
Whether I am deserving of hatred or of love.
May Your pity rescue us through grace,
You who *work in us both to will and to act,*
You who *from a stone*
Can fashion child of Abraham,
Purify, illuminate my soul,
That it escape the power of nothingness.[27]

144

Paris, *August 1949.* – [A poem: *In the Unity of the Infinite Circle.*]

O Hidden God, Your presence overwhelms my heart,
Now is the time for me to watch with my unknowing
Under the pure and matchless star of Faith;
Now must I vigil keep before the gates of self,
Of my own self, a closely-shuttered tower
Whose secret walls my Lord Himself has shaped,
And had not any light to guide His step.
Our God of Compassion who restores what we have ruined –
I know not what He does,
Nor what He gives to me, what He obtains,
How He transforms my sin, to fashion light.
This aspect of myself which God creates in me
Only He knows, because He wills it thus.

---

27. Translated by a Benedictine of Stanbrook.

With holy darkness He enshrouds my spirit;
Far out of reach is heaven divine
Which burns within my soul to make it god-like.
This is the hour when I touch what Faith conceals;
Let us keep watch by everlasting gates
The long night through
Until the dawn when God shall tell the soul
To enter into self, and into Him.[28]

145

Princeton, *21st February 1950*. – Thirty-eighth anniversary of the baptism of our dear father, my godson, baptised by Jacques.

It is time not to think of anything but God, of eternal life.

Moving letter from a Carmelite. Ah! All these good, kind letters, one ought to be able to answer them all. What can I do?

I never forget anyone I have ever loved – and I give every appearance of neglecting my friends or forgetting them.

146

Tuesday, 3rd October 1950. – After a miserable night – the material insecurity of our life became so clearly apparent to me! – a morning when peace returned with a little God-given silence (*oraison*).

---

28. From *Patriarch Tree,* a selection of Raïssa Maritain's poetry translated by a Benedictine of Stanbrook and published by the Stanbrook Abbey Press, Worcester, England.

147

Wednesday, 11th October 1950. – Jacques, Véra and I went today to see our friends, the Benedictine nuns of Regina Laudis. Touching welcome. The Prioress sweeter than ever.

A Sister I know particularly well is none too happy, she cannot get accustomed to this foundresses' life. And besides she is perturbed by the influence of certain thinkers and theologians. . .

This trouble and agitation one gets oneself into because Catholics have not got *everything* that the Orthodox and the Protestants have that is good, beautiful and original – it's a form of concupiscence (even though its object is spiritual) which is not good; the Church, the unique, unique, holy, mystical Church, at once *visible* and *mystical*, is made up of all spiritual goods – wherever they are found.

148

Wednesday, 1st November 1950. – Proclamation of the dogma of the Assumption of Mary.

Sunday, 5th November. – Mass and Communion at St. Paul's church.

I was vividly aware, as a direct personal experience which surprised me myself, of the difference between a pious devotion and an act of Faith. For many years we have celebrated the Assumption as a great feast, without the question of believing or not believing having ever entered my mind; it was an act of piety bringing its own sweetness with it and sufficiently authorised by the

Church's recommendation. But after the dogmatic definition of the Assumption of Our Blessed Lady, this is truly a first act of Faith which is performed in the soul, accompanied by a joy that comes from a very particular spiritual energy, from a definite and joyous action of the spirit illuminated by a new light, a joy which doubtless belongs to every first act of Faith.

149

Princeton, *Thursday, 1st February 1951.* – Plato uses the word *music* in a universal way where we use the word *poetry* as being the soul of the fine arts.

This explains to me why, when I have received the first intuition of a poem, and I am writing this poem, *I listen* constantly to this intuition in me all the time I am writing, so that the expression shall be exactly faithful to the first intuition. *I listen* – so as not to *sing* a false note. I am speaking here in an analogical way.

150

Friday, 23rd February 1951. – I implore God not to separate me from Jacques and Véra in eternity. I make this prayer to God often and urgently and with all my heart – but Jacques and Véra are [here a word of eulogy which only Véra deserved and which I will not transcribe (J.)] – so an incomparable mercy of God is needed not to separate me from them in eternal life. I attach no condition to my prayer – except that the bountiful love of God will never abandon me.

I implore God to grant through his grace that Jacques

will never suffer through me – either here below or in the other world.

151

Friday, 6th July 1951. – We went to New York to visit Arthur and Ella Lourié. Arthur played us his new work, *Anathema*. Choir and eight instruments.

Monday, 9th July. – I wrote to Arthur Lourié about *Anathema*:

"How moving it is, the progress of your soul, visible in the way you have chosen and put together the texts of the Scriptures for this musical work. It is your Credo wholly and entirely expressed in the words of the Holy Spirit. . .

"All this is pure in spirit. And your music too is wholly true, wholly pure – I mean without any sin *against music*. I think God gave you the seed of this gift with the grace of baptism. So that your music is capable of expressing the experience of God in the soul as you do – not according to the formulas of 'religious art', but according to the life of the Spirit in us, and our life in Him. It is in relation to Him that you express our misery and you also express our love and his. This, Arthur, is the great talent – how much Jesus must prize it. We are profoundly happy, Jacques and I, that such music exists in you and through you."

152

Monday, 23rd July 1951. – Seeing in Mme Jeanne Ancelet-Hustache's book[29] the sufferings her husband

---

29. *Images et Reflets d'Henri* (privately printed), Bloud & Gay, 1950. (J.).

went through before he died, and reading the account of his death, I had a most extraordinary feeling, like the joy of deliverance the soul would feel in its most unspeakable depths – the joy of entering into the way of truth, of eternal life and of the vision of God.

I was for a moment in this joy as if these death-agonies had been mine and as if this joy had been – all hidden and muffled by his sufferings – that of the sick man who was dying. And perhaps it was that joy which appeared, once the sufferings were over, in the beautiful, the happy smile of one who had just attained blessed salvation and eternal life.

I wrote this to Mme Ancelet-Hustache.

153

Friday, 27th July 1951. – Re-read the Catholic Epistle of Jude.[30] What marvels in two pages. I would like to know it by heart. The wonderful faith in Jesus present and acting, in his divine pre-existence, when "the angels kept not their principality" and "forsook their own habitation" . . .; when "He saved his people from the land of Egypt". . . And Jude says that we must not insult "the Glories" (those lost angelic Glories).

And his marvellous greeting to those to whom he is writing. "Mercy and peace and love be yours in full measure."

These divine Scriptures awaken in my soul the desire to see God; the desire to depart for eternal life. It is a desire which springs from the joy of the soul – and not

---

30. Text of the Vulgate. (J.).

from the sadness of temporal life. I love this daily life too and I love my beloved Jacques and Véra and I love our friends, and all beauty: but perhaps God is beginning to call my soul and to train it to the hope of eternal life. At these moments of living faith and joy, the fear of God frightens me less. Sweet Jesus, have pity on me.

154

Undated (Probably 1951.) – "Believe me, Rabbi Moses, that when, at midnight, we lament in deep sorrow and the tears flow from our eyes, it is, in spite of everything, in joy. Such is the true character of the Hassid: to laugh and cry both at once, like children." (Quoted by Père de Menasce in *Quand Israël aime Dieu.*)

155

Princeton, *2nd January 1952.* – All Christians are called to union with God, and, in consequence, are "called"[31] to contemplation, in various degrees, according to the special

---

31. Raïssa has put the word "called" in quotation marks; because, by adding "in various degrees" she greatly modified it – and meant that in many cases the contemplation in question may be only masked (when it is the active Gifts which are predominantly exercised) – or even be reduced to fleeting touches (if the soul has not crossed the threshold of life under the habitual regimen of the gifts of the Spirit). When it is a question of contemplation in its typical forms, all are called to it *in principle*, at least in a remote manner. But, *in fact*, as Raïssa noted on the 16th February 1935 (see further on, in "Brief Writings", p. 366) and taking into account human circumstances, this call is addressed only to a few. (J.).

exercise of the various gifts of the Holy Spirit in different individuals.

But it is indeed the will of God that this spiritual union should be realised in quite various forms of life, in lines of great or minimal solitude, of imperceptible or of immense activity.

The question for each one of us is to find, to implore God to make known to us the form of Christian life that should be ours. It is in that form that God wishes us to find perfection and holiness, whatever this form of life may be externally.

156

Princeton, *12th July 1954*. – To Jeanne Linn:

"We are remaining at Princeton this summer because the doctor considers that Jacques still needs a great deal of rest.[32] Now the anguish of the illness is over, we are exceedingly sorry to be once again prevented from spending at least three months in France . . . . All year we think of the date when we shall be able to sail. Last summer I was very ill and I am still convalescing from that illness; all the same I was able to keep going and nurse Jacques – but when he was cured, I got worse, so much so that I have not even been able to get to church on Sunday. The parish priest is very kind and brings me Communion.

". . . We are not deserted here, it is true, it is only fair to say so. People have come to our help in all kinds

---

32. On the 26th March, I had fallen ill with a heart attack (coronary thrombosis). I had stayed in bed, obliged to keep perfectly still, for over two months, nursed by Raïssa (far from well herself though she hid this from me) and Véra. (J.).

of ways, and we have been very much prayed for. They have a custom here of making a present of numerous Masses to those they are fond of, and of offering Communions for them; and this has often been done by people who know Jacques only through his books. Yes, Jacques is very much loved here. . . And we deeply love this country, we know its spiritual qualities and the goodness of this people.

"But just as you say that you live with us and that you follow us into the present, we too live with you whom we love. . ."

157

Princeton, *Tuesday 25th January 1955.* – "The greatest of Christian truths is the love of truth" (Pascal).

158

Laetare Sunday 1955. – The *miracles* that the charity of God works in this world to establish, maintain and increase our Faith – miracles are not contrary to the Wisdom of God – do not invalidate the laws of nature, the laws of this world.

In this world and in the other, on earth and in heaven, the Wisdom of God reigns.

The laws of this world we pass through before death are the laws of nature – that nature of which in this life we have more or less perfect knowledge, and yet never perfect; even that which is according to nature still goes beyond the possibilities of our power of knowing, although these possibilities pertain to the nature of which we partake. Perhaps it would need an infinite length of our time in this world to know all the causes and effects of everything that is knowable in this world.

Nevertheless, supposing there existed a perfect natural knowledge, it would not be in a position to know what descends from on high – what belongs to the other world – which, it too, is ruled by the Wisdom of God, to which everything that is owes its being.

We know through Revelation the existence of the other world of which we are to have knowledge after death, according to the potentialities of the immortal soul and according to the state of grace and according to the state of glory.

There the spirit of the Angels and immortal souls know the laws of a world – created too – but created according to a mode of existence and intelligibility of which we can know nothing in our mortal life.

It is an *other world*.

This is no metaphor, no hyperbole, but a reality. A reality of which it is impossible to have knowledge in this life. – We know by Faith that another world exists, but we do not know *what* it is. – We know that the divine Wisdom is more resplendent there – that the keys of eternal life shine there – there where grace reigns – and that the vision of the Face of God in Glory illumines there the whole of creation.

There, all that we know in the trust and the darkness of Faith – souls, spirits illumined by a light unknown in this world apprehend it clearly – there we shall know it in a new light, proportioned to the reality *inaccessible* here to our intellect.

There will be revealed the divine laws which intervene

here below in miracles – there the eternal and infinite Wisdom of God will appear to us – governing a reality *created*, but so different from that of our world that nothing in this world here can give us knowledge of it.

There will be laid bare the sublime miracles of the presence of Jesus Man and God in every consecrated host, of the Immaculate Conception of the Virgin, of the miraculous virginity of the Mother of Jesus – of the resurrection of the dead, like Lazarus and the daughter of Jairus here below, and of the resurrection of bodies for our eternal life.

159

Passion Sunday 1955. – Epistle of St. Paul to the Hebrews (9:11–12). ". . . Christ, being come as High Priest of the good things to come, has entered once and for all into the sanctuary by a greater and more perfect tabernacle not made with hand of man, that is to say, not *of this creation.* . ."

But neither is this creation "made with the hand of man." God is the Creator of it. Tabernacles, in this creation, are made "with the hand of man" – but human, and animal, begetting depends on animal and human nature which is created by God.

So what does this passage in St. Paul signify? "That is to say, not of this creation" – except the *divine Incarnation of the Word*, the miraculous conception of Christ, and His birth of a Virgin – and thus the affirmation of *the other world.* . .?[33]

---

33. If by this "sanctuary" into which Christ has entered one understands, according to a current interpretation, the heaven into which he entered after his Ascension, then it is even more

160

East Hampton, *22nd July 1956*. – I have at last been able to go to Mass – the 10 o'clock.

Surprised by the singing – overwhelmed with love. Suddenly heaven seems to me quite close – Jesus quite close, eternal life quite close – beatitude only behind a veil. The Mother of God makes her nearness felt too.

The presence of Jesus in Communion sensible to faith – making itself felt through the nakedness of faith.

The other world present.

161

East Hampton, *28th August 1956*. – Letting singing and music act in oneself, letting the soul "open itself to divine things" (St. Thomas). When music produces this liberating effect, one is suddenly delivered from the constraint of effort and from distractions, from irrelevant images, and, as it were, from the distance between time and eternity. Burning love invades the soul, illumines faith. The conquered heart gives us the sweetness of tears.

162

Undated. (Probably 1956.) – Sources of peace: God and trees.

---

the affirmation of *the other world* of which Raïssa speaks, for "heaven" is the world unknown to us where, according to laws inaccessible to our mind here below, the holy angels and the blessed souls and the glorified bodies of Jesus and Mary live and act, and which after the resurrection of the flesh, will be the world of the resurrected, the "new earth" and the "new heavens". (J.)

163

Princeton, *Wednesday, 21st November 1956*, Presentation of the Blessed Virgin.

Between half-past ten and one this morning, Véra was at the hospital for a general *x*-ray examination which the doctor wanted her to have. Our dear friend Jane Somerville went with her. Jacques and I spent a terribly anxious time during those hours. I prayed with all my soul, reminding Jesus of the many sufferings Véra had passed through in her life, and the purity of her soul and her charity and her devotion, and all the anguish that my illnesses and Jacques' sufferings had caused her. . . And I had the inspiration (which I have these days) to pray to Jesus in the actual name of Véra which He loves in a very special way – to pray to him for her in her name of Véra. I told this secret to Jacques, I prayed for Véra in the name of Véra's sanctity – in the name of Jesus' Love for her.[34]

---

34. And Jesus, through one of those ambiguous consolations which announce the worst while giving a pledge of mercy, granted Raïssa the fulfilment of her prayer *for that day*. ("Everything is perfectly all right," the doctor telephoned after he had seen the photographs). But the time of great trials had come. (And it is no doubt, for that reason, that Raïssa was given the inspiration to pray as she did; by that prayer in the name of Véra's *sanctity* she was asking for Véra's cure, but, in truth, it was *strength for the accepted sacrifice* that such a prayer connoted in itself.) On May 28th 1957, Véra, attacked by cancer, had to undergo the amputation of one breast. The cancer reappeared in the form of a tumour on the hip at the end of 1958. Our little sister, after a year, much harder still than the two preceding ones, of uninterrupted and ever-increasing sufferings borne with a patience and courage that never failed, died peacefully on the 31st December 1959. (J.)

164

Undated. (Probably 1957.) – A dogma is the point of a cone whose opening widens out to the infinite. Divine reality touches us through this point.

165

Undated. (Probably 1958.) – It is perhaps not entirely true that contemplation tends essentially to silence: *Misericordias Domini in aeternum cantabo*. If in eternal contemplation singing overflows from love, why not in the contemplation that passes through time?

We breathe in God, down into the deepest
And most silent recess of the soul
And the breath we breathe out with our lips
Can be a word and song of love.

Like holy acts, words of wisdom and beauty overflow from contemplation: – the Psalms and the whole of the inspired Scripture.

It is the same with contemplation and song as it is with the river and the sea. The end, the trend of the river is to lose itself in the ocean; but if the waters overbrim their bed, it overflows to right and left. The end of the contemplative soul is to lose itself in God – but the over-brimmed heart pours itself out in songs and in acts.[35]

---

35. Raïssa's thought is thus quite clear: 1) the *end* of contemplation is loving union with God in the silence bereft of concepts and words, whereas the *end* of poetic intuition is the work produced; 2) but what is the *end* for poetic intuition can be *superabundance* (and normal superabundance, overflowing from the possession of the end or from the movement towards it) for contemplation. (J.)

Undated. (Probably 1959.) – Suffering is necessary in this world – as God has made it.

There are perhaps other worlds, answering to other ideas of the Creator.

Under a tragic sign is our life in this world.

God gave this world – before the fall of the Angels, before the fall of the parent stem of humanity: the first couple, Adam and Eve – to that great Archangel (he was good at the first instant of his creation) who, once fallen, became the dark Prince of this world.

And after that, humanity had to be redeemed, the time of this world has to be redeemed.

The redemption is achieved by suffering united to the love of God in both senses of the words – He loving us and we loving Him.

The human soul by itself has not the power of salvation, even with love united to suffering. There is no common measure between the power of the soul and eternal salvation.

And nevertheless God saves us only by an alliance with humanity.

In the first place, the alliance of the Word, the Word assuming human nature.

In the second place in every soul which accepts suffering for the love of God.

The suffering of the Word Incarnate, of the Word made true Man for the love of God – for the love of mankind too, for the love of every soul;

Y

And the union of our suffering and our love to the Passion and Love of Jesus.

Every *acceptance* of suffering (if it proceeds, not from a brute passivity or from some philosophical pride, but from humility and courtesy) is already bound to charity, beholden to divine grace.

The saints do more than accept suffering – they ask it of God for the love of God and the salvation of souls.

167

Undated. (Probably 1959.) – To be capable of receiving much from God, that is the whole of perfection.

168

Princeton, *8th February 1960.* – To Anne Green:

" . . . There was also a special bond between Véra and me, a naïve invention, a perpetual game we played with each other. Though younger than me, Véra was my little mother in this game and I was her little child. In reality, this invention was a discovery for me – the discovery of the goodness and generosity of Véra's soul and that was verified all through our life. This strangely grave game was perpetuated beyond our childhood. Without noticing it, I used to call her my little mother, right up to her death, and even now I catch myself calling her that when I talk to her, when I call her, when I pray to her. Her presence was always a strength to us, even in her last painful years. . . ."

169

18th March 1960. – To Josette Cayssials:

" . . . Your letter is as good and as clear as can be. You

do not even reproach me for my long silence. You have had faith in my friendship for you. Véra suffered for three years, more and more painfully – and I had no freedom of mind left. Her death, in a state of half-sleep, was very peaceful. God spared her the even worse sufferings she would have had to endure. The doctor was surprised and very happy about it and congratulated us on it as if on a blessing. Véra is delivered from the sorrows of this world; happy, she is henceforth united to God in light, as she has always been in her sufferings. But for us her absence is still incomprehensible; I look at her photographs and I ask her how she could have left us. I know that to be so bewildered is absurd, but our mortal senses cannot realise anything of the happiness of the other world.

"Josette, you write to me that when you are in trouble, in turmoil, you find yourself thinking: 'If only Raïssa were here . . . ' How sorry I am to be so far away, how much I wish I could help you . . .

"You tell me that *for you* 'God is often not human enough'; but this is not only 'for you'; there is a great mystery in this; God's bountiful love *(la bonté de Dieu)* is not like human kindness *(la bonté humaine.)* The divine world we can know only in what is for us 'the other world'. Human kindness, human pity are treasures, but it is through pain and suffering – and through death – that we have to pass to reach eternal beatitude. Through pain and suffering. It is the same with all moral and spiritual values as it is with the Beatitudes Christ defined in the Gospel. In the death of Christ, God shows himself at once inhuman and human – inhuman in the Passion inflicted on his Son – human in the Passion accepted by Jesus, true Man and true God – for our salvation.

"It remains true that we have need of the kindness (*bonté*) of others in order to endure life and all its difficulties . . . "

170

Undated. (Probably 1960.) –
    "*N'ayant ni guide ni lueur*
    Que la lampe ardente en mon coeur."[36]
*N'*ayant *que* . . .
This negation signifies the night of Faith. It is in a manner a lament, a groan, the longing for the vision of God which broods over the soul; something expressed in a minor key. Although charity burns in the heart
    and quickens with the light of love
    the fire of Faith and of grace.

    In the night itself all is dark
    But in it a lamp shines.
    In the burning heart shines a lamp
    A lamp shines in the burning heart
    The heart is on fire with love
    The love lights up the whole soul.

171

[Paris, *Saturday, August 27th 1960.*– From my notebook: Towards evening Raïssa repeated several times, with

---

36.   "Having neither guide nor light
            But the ardent lamp in my heart."
I have left the lines in the French translation used by Raïssa (that of Père Cyprien de la Nativité, a seventeenth-century Carmelite) in order to leave her own *N'*ayant *que* . . . which would lose its point in English. (Trans.)

a radiant smile: "I'm going to die, I'm going to die . . . "
Then she said, to console me: "It's a joke." After that
she told me she had dreamt a few days ago, "that I was
going to die and make my ascension" and that she was
very happy. "It's good to be with God, isn't it?" (J.)]

172

[*Tuesday, October 4th.* – From my notebook:
Pierre van der Meer has come from his Abbey in Holland
to see Raïssa. He is completely overwhelmed. She radiates
love. She said to him gravely, peacefully: "No one can help
me."

He blessed her. When he was going (he was already on the
stairs) she asked him to come back and say *au revoir* to her.
(J.)]

Raïssa passed in peace into the other life on November
4th 1960.

IV

COMPLEMENTARY FRAGMENTS

COMPLEMENTARY FRAGMENTS[1]

I

[*A propos of P. H.*][2]

You believe in little miracles, believe also in great ones; the history of Christianity is full of these.

Your weakness is that you can assert yourself, and exist, only by setting yourself up in opposition, so that it is always with respect to *our* good that you affirm your own. – You cannot get away from us.

Why do you choose as your chief the greatest of the vanquished in the world?

Your inventive powers are very limited, whereas love's inventive powers are infinite.

A gratuitous act is one that is *given for nothing*.

---

1. In this section I have grouped together fragments which, either because they are the first idea for an essay, or for some other reason, seemed to me ought to be set apart from the notes which make up the chronological sequence of *Loose Leaves*. On the other hand, neither did I think I should classify them among "Brief Writings". (J.)

2. For this fragment and the following one, cf. above *Journal* of 1931, p. 206, note **3**. Raïssa recounted to me her conversations with P. H.: it was certainly thus that she replied to him, and, naturally, the tone on the other side was no less lively.

There is nothing gratuitous but the gift. There is no greater gift than the gift of one's own life. That is what God himself has given. And all of us can give proof of our love only through the gift – to the point of giving our own life. Our proof "by casting out the nines" is that of blood.

Lucifer himself obeys God. And he who obeys Lucifer is ridiculous in the eyes of Lucifer.

You refuse to receive anything.

And you are not able to give anything.

God himself was willing to receive from his creature the taste of suffering.

And by virtue of that, suffering itself, this trash – has been marked with the infinite sign of love – and of salvation.

The truly desperate, God will have mercy on them – for, without their being aware of it, their despair consists in not knowing Him who is worthy of an infinite love.

One asks too much of me.

What does *one* ask of me?

– Everything.

Everything.

Our happiness is not insolent. Our joy is taken on the Cross.

On our innocence there are stains of blood.

You have asserted that the essentials of what is truly human lie in crime and vice.

There is nothing so near to crime and vice as the respectable citizen.

Innocence is rediscovered – it is nourished with our blood and the blood of God.

There is only one perfect gratuitous act – creative and saving Love.

Facing it there is the love which responds to it, the love of man for God, and for his neighbour.

The man who does not know God or ignores Him, wanting to prove to himself his independence cannot approach to a gratuitous act except by suicide.

But what then? This sole act of independence, brings death with it and deprives him for ever of all independence.

And this life which, for sole principle and sole end, had *life* is fulfilled only in death.

May 1931.

2

[Letter to P. H.]

Meudon, 5th August 1931. – Dear Mr. H., if I have not written to you sooner, it is because illness does not always provide leisure. But at last I am a little better and if I make a point of writing to you under such unfavourable conditions, when you have probably forgotten the letter to which I am going to attempt to reply, it is because this letter is too serious, too painful within you and for me, to be passed over in unresponsive silence.

Above all, do not think I am angry because you wrote to me that you will joyfully kill me one day when you are worthy to do so. On the contrary. It is I who am not worthy of so beautiful a death, and I have never received a letter which honoured me more. I assure you I am not joking. When my godfather Léon Bloy was dying, the only thing that distressed him was dying without having given testimony of his faith by shedding his blood for it. If God makes me worthy of it, I too shall be granted such a desire.

As to your book, have no fear, you have not betrayed your God. And what would a God be who could be betrayed by a sincere word? You have quite misunderstood me if you think I read your pages with an eye to getting the better of you . . . Your book which does not wish to prove *anything* does not prove anything either, and gives me no weapon against you. You call it "the marsh". If that is how you like to designate what gives it a gleam of humanity and pity, the misery it confesses and the tenderness that clothes this misery – so be it. But it is not all that which would make you "tolerable" in my eyes. What I respect in you is the man in search of an absolute love – of an object which is worth the trouble of this life.

You dispute that God is this object. You find that we have failed lamentably when put to the test. You forget that our misery, which is, after all, human, is imputable only to the refusal of grace, which men refuse, either wholly or partially, because grace demands, it is true, that we should be hard and implacable – but to ourselves. You forget, or you are unaware, that Christianity only compelled recognition through its martyrs and its doctrine, and that every day the Church offers the earth, along with the blood of her God and her saints, the doctrine of truth and love. In this there is no sickly sentimentality. *Faith is not a feeling;* it is a hard will to truth. You do not know what it demands, you do not know what it gives. It is not made for our self-indulgence. Our Kingdom is indeed not of this world. But this too needs to be understood. We must not attach ourselves to anything of this world as if it were our final end. But we must not disassociate ourselves from it. This selfish aloofness is the great crime of our shoddy civilisation. It is not in Paradise that we will have to be just and pure, this is demanded of us *today*. It is on this earth that we must give our life, through love, to God and to every man who may have need of it. Such is our faith. God offers us the means of practising it, and we refuse them. This is why it is no longer possible to live.

You implore me to understand. But I want to, with all my heart. And I think I do understand. You tell me that you are searching for love – true love – and I believe you. I know that you want to construct a world without God, and without the values of perfection which we hold as true. . . . In your place, I too would direct my search towards a new world, a world without selfishness and hypocrisy, a world so free and so pure that it would not remember any law, human or divine. (In such a view of things, the idea of law itself disappears.)

Only *I know* now that there are laws and precepts which are part of the nature of things; such is the Decalogue. I know that human life has its fulness elsewhere.

Of this world you consider only the putrescence and you make religion responsible for it, whereas this putrescence is due to the abandoning of the very laws of life.

In my turn I implore you to understand; I am not defending "Catholics", I am not defending myself. We have deserved *everything*. (Bear in mind, nevertheless, that all men equally have been, are, and will be called to be true Catholics; and that thus you too – who have not answered this call – have deserved everything.) I am defending divine truth, and the holiness of the Church which resides in its saints and not necessarily in each one of its visible members. This truth and this holiness I defend not only in the past, but at this very hour; I know that the truth I love answers every fair question. I know that there are saints among us, and I know some of them personally.

I know too that this sanctity does not move you (once again you know nothing of it). You think that perfection is altogether different and that, if one can, one should "change the direction of life, falsified and degraded by twenty centuries of Christianity."

Do you really find in the paganism that preceded those twenty centuries, the true direction of life which the blood of Christians has turned aside from its course? Is that the direction in which you want to go? Towards subjugation to the gods of the city, towards cruelty in the service of luxury, towards the slavery which alone could sustain such a civilisation? No, doubtless. It would not be worth the trouble of wanting to *change everything;* our capitalist and atheist society, itself the result of the so-called Renaissance, has almost rediscovered the tradition . . .

You think that you ought to struggle with all your might against us who believe in God. Against us, perhaps, because we have not believed enough, not lived enough according to the demands of the Faith (had we done so, it is we who would have accomplished the Revolution by means of love). Against us. Against God, no. He is the sole author of justice and mercy. I know that this is incomprehensible to you; it seems that there is no principle in common between us. But basic humanity is the same in all; that brotherhood remains to us (along with that of poetry). And I will point out to you that there are universal and human values which you cannot do without. For example, *purity*. It is a notion which you transpose widely, but, after all, in some form or other it is necessary to you. Loyalty, justice, love. And, again, that value which is opposed to "swine" (I think we are agreed on the meaning of that word) though what name you would give it I do not know. "Man", perhaps? That goes further than you think (but you ought to think about it).

It is difficult to drive God out altogether. Invariably he returns humbly disguised under one name or another; and under the name we have chosen he makes himself loved without our knowledge.

I am recommending all round the book you have ceased to like, and I await with great expectation the one you are working on now (and your poems too). But, above all, I too am preparing myself to fight, not against you, but for you, and for all those whom we cannot reach by visible means.

3

On reading Kierkegaard

("Fear and Trembling")

If I myself had not suffered anguish during a whole long year, perhaps I would not be able to read this book of Kierkegaard's in the way that I read it today.

If I understand rightly, all his work originates in an intimate religious experience; in an absolutely personal event whose content cannot be generalised; this is the feeling given to Kierkegaard that he must break off his engagement.

To construct a work from the starting-point of an intimate, religious, and incommunicable experience – this is something a Protestant can do, or a man who is not attached to any church – once the experience has been lived, what is to stop him? He is ignorant of all theological knowledge and knows no rules, except moral ones.

A Catholic must first rediscover, through living on his theological knowledge and his religious experience by dint of fidelity, love and true spirituality, the profound liberty of the sons of God – not rediscover, but arrive at this liberty. His advantage is that this liberty harmonises with the whole of truth. The disadvantage is that one usually only reaches it late.

Meudon, *16th February 1935.*

*

The example of Abraham or of Joan of Arc is a case of a faith whose object has been proposed by a special and private revelation.

And precisely since a faith of this kind is not proposed to each one of us, Kierkegaard is justified in saying, in this sense, that he has not faith (this faith thus proposed in such or such a particular object).

Moreover, in his case, he did not receive the assurance from God that his fiancée would be given back to him – whereas God had promised Abraham a posterity through Isaac.

346

Nevertheless, in consenting to this sacrifice – the breaking-off of his engagement, perhaps Kierkegaard hoped, in spite of everything, that God would be satisfied with his good-will and give him back his fiancée; – but she was not given back to him – and that no doubt is why Kierkegaard says and reiterates that he has not faith.

Meudon, *17th February 1935.*

4

The poetry of our time[3]

Time of hatred, time of suffering. Of suffering inflicted by hatred. Time of disarray. Time of death. Haggard hope does not know what to cling on to. The agony of bodies and souls covers our earth with a dome of shrieks and blood. The promises of peace will not be able to be kept. The misery let loose by misery will not be able to be succoured – till death, till death. Till hatred and the science of hatred and the power of hatred are exhausted. Till the suicide of the earth, after the earth shall have brought

---

3. These pages were evidently written in answer to a question or to an enquiry on what could be expected of the poetry of our time. (At what date? I presume in 1945, in Rome.) Were they sent to the author of the enquiry and who was this person? I cannot remember anything about it. In any case, what matters is having these words as she wrote them first off, in a spontaneous response to an irresistible inner impulse. (J.)

z

forth its full fruit of fire. And God, on His coming, will find only dead men to judge.

Our time of blood and death; of tortures, of despair, of chaos, of disconsolation, of misery, of famine, of anguish, of accursed discoveries; time of irremediable and boundless calamity, drowning every heart which cruelty has not yet devoured.

If peace gains us a few years respite from the wars to come, frivolity will soon have forgotten everything till the day of the new irruption of hell. This time, the last of our life, is the time in which your friends and ours died, totally sacrificed. Neither weakness nor gentleness, nor old age, nor childhood, nor, above all, innocence spared them from the sight of boundless horror, from unimaginable suffering, from the atrocious suffering of their limbs, of their heart, of their flesh, of their soul and their spirit: your friends, our friends, crushed, destroyed in heaps like vermin, he or she whom I see, whose face and name I know, without being able to bear the sight of their distress
and of their humiliated death
nor ever to accept what this world has done
what men have done
– God alone, He alone can receive our acceptance
the silencing of our complaint, through arid, naked faith
in His mercy, in His wisdom
unspeakably betrayed by the appearances
which are our reality,
– then, poetry! let poetry do penance, let her be silent, because she has not words for the reality of our time; let her veil her face; let her stop flirting with our sorrow; let her forget flowers, games, graces, rhetoric and eloquence; let her strip herself and humble herself if she wishes to

348

survive the unimaginable, the indescribable, the mortal darkness of our time.

Undated. (Probably 1945.)

5

Poetry is a musical language

Poetry is not only "musical", it is music. And that not because of the pleasurable sonority of the words it gathers together, but because, beyond the more or less clear or obscure literal meaning, it has a significance analogous to that of musical language.

Musical language has the power to awaken in the one who perceives it a complex spiritual activity which mysteriously corresponds to it – a power common to every language, but in the case of music, indirect. Poetry is likewise a language of indirect meaning, so much so that this is an essential property of poetry.

The musical language of Poetry is as varied as that of Music. It is not tied down to a fixed rhythm but it does not exist without rhythm. It is not attached to a single form, but it possesses a centre of creative life and attraction which makes the unity and form of the poem as of the musical work.

Undated.

V

BRIEF WRITINGS

I

On Contemplative Prayer

On Contemplative Prayer ("Oraison")[1]

29th-31st August 1922

Val d'Illiez,
Switzerland

My dear Brother in Jesus,

I am sending you the little Guide intended for the Thomist Circles which Père Garrigou-Lagrange has asked us to write. He has just approved it in principle, but, as he has not forbidden us to try to better it, we should be very grateful if you would help us to do so by pointing out corrections that should be made. Basing ourselves on St Thomas and St John of the Cross, we have tried to answer several of the questions you raise on the subject of mystical contemplation, and it seems to me that our solutions do not differ from the ones you suggest, and with which, as regards essentials, Père Garrigou-Lagrange and Mère Marie-Thérèse are also in agreement.

If I have delayed so long in writing to you, in spite of your fraternal insistence, this is because I was so tired by the journey that I had to take to my bed on arrival. It also took me a long time to get acclimatised, and finally, after

---

1. Letter to C. H.

having been better for some days, I am once again rather feeble. Moreover the labour of thinking things out and expressing them is more and more of a burden to me; my soul, of its own accord, tends inward, towards obscurity and rest in God. And my memory seems to me so empty that I wonder how I can still give Jacques the little co-operation he asks of me and which, thanks to God, neither illness or obscurity have prevented up to now.

I am telling you all this so that you will not take my long silence for indifference. Your friendship is very dear to us and I am happy that, in your heart, you do not separate me from Jacques, although I so little deserve it.

I am sorry that I have not got a copy of your letter to Canon Saudreau, since it is about him that you wanted me to write to you. I am afraid of not answering you directly enough but you will put things into shape.

After I had read your letter, I re-read the first chapters of *L'État Mystique,* and it seemed to me that Canon Saudreau does indeed make the mistake of not insisting enough on the inherent obscurity of this state, and of producing textual quotations in which the words *knowledge* and *illuminations* would at least need to be explained.

I do not know why I had ended up by thinking that, for you too, mystical *oraison* was characterised by some sort of clarity, and in spite of all I knew from other sources and Père Dehau's assurances, I was beginning to fear for my own which for several years has been quite obscure. What you have written to me has completely reassured me and I am extremely happy that my poor experience, which I only mention with embarrassment, should be confirmed by yours which inspires me with such great confidence. So I am going to sort out my little ideas for you, since you want me to, and you, in your turn, will tell me quite candidly what you think of them.

One can say that everything mystical involves a twofold aspect and a twofold definition: ontological and psychological.

Ontologically, the essence of mystical contemplation is, it seems to me, that it is produced *in virtue of union* and thus in a *passive* fashion, by a special will of God which leads him to give us, in some manner, knowledge of his love for us.

Psychologically, the essence of mystical contemplation appears to me to be an experimental knowledge of God, *"God ineffably perceived."* That's what you think, isn't it?

At the outset, God manifests himself by pouring into our soul, as St Teresa puts it, "a great interior and exterior satisfaction," a joy which resembles no other. Later he purifies us, and sacrifices us, and this is the *night* in our soul. Then once again he beatifies and in a deeper and more spiritual way. But always *he acts first and chiefly*. Our activity accompanies His sometimes more, sometimes less, sometimes happy and easy, sometimes painful; sometimes perceptibly, sometimes in a manner unknown and imperceptible to us. It cannot be annihilated, for our spiritual faculties are immortal like our soul; and, since God is Spirit and Life, our soul is all the more alive and free the more God acts in it. But of this essential life we cannot have direct knowledge. On the contrary, the intellect, the most spiritual of our faculties, seems to us to dwindle. In contemplative prayer, there is cessation of intellectual operations.

How rightly Mère Marie-Thérèse expresses herself

when she says: "When I speak of cessation of intellectual operations, it is understood that this applies to the human mode of this operation, for contemplation gives an increase of life – and what an increase! – to our intellect *qua* intellect. It is only *qua* human intellect that there is, so to speak, annihilation."

The human mode of acting gives place to the super-human mode.

The human mode consists in going from the visible to the invisible, from the senses to the spirit, and from the created to the Uncreated.

The superhuman mode has its root in God. Undoubtedly nothing exists, nothing acts without the action of God; but in the mystical life God acts by a very special infusion of his grace which leads him sometimes to enlighten our mind, sometimes to kindle our will, sometimes to strengthen our heart, or to give us simultaneously supernatural light, ardour and strength, or to let us be aware only of the destruction of our human mode of acting, of our impotence, our nothingness.

Since this is the very special work of Divine Love, it is the work of the Holy Spirit. The soul, then, lives more intensely under the regimen of the Gifts. All the gifts of the Holy Spirit prepare it for mystical union, but the gift of Wisdom is the one that makes it bring this union into being and savour it.

This gift is the most uniting because it is the most simplifying. The gift of Fear purifies and rectifies; Knowledge and Counsel shed light on good and bad actions; Piety and Fortitude help the soul to persevere; Understanding makes it adhere more firmly to faith, the truths of faith are illuminated by a more living light in a soul that is more alive. The gift of Wisdom produces the experimental, loving and ineffable knowledge of God.

What in the ascetic or active way was done "by the command of love" is done henceforth "by love itself". And not only silence with God but all our acts can be called mystical when they are performed "by love itself", that is to say by the Holy Spirit.

Passivity, in this sense, in the sense of *the first and principal action of the Holy Spirit in the mystical life,* is ontologically the essential characteristic.

Psychologically, this passivity, *passio divinorum,* is expressed not only by the ligature and (apparent) death of our natural faculties, but also, in certain cases, by the heightening of them; it is thus that, in the saints, action itself can be described as mystical.

In contemplation, this passivity manifests itself above all by ligature, powerlessness, annihilation,[2] because our faculties of knowing are utterly disproportionate to the object of contemplation, which is God in Himself. Here the intellect must recognise its incapacity, and submit to love which, through the infusion of divine Wisdom, connaturalises the soul with God and makes it know him with an obscure and ineffable certainty.

By the other Gifts, whose object is in some way more particularised, the Holy Spirit, on the contrary, heightens our faculties and proportions them to arduous, heroic, saintly acts, by setting them to work himself, by enlightening them and strengthening them.

To return to the obscurity inherent in contemplation,

---

2. Var.: by a kind of annihilation.

one can say, it seems to me, that Dionysius[3] regards it in the main ontologically and St John of the Cross psychologically.

The obscurity of which Dionysius speaks will only yield before the light of glory; it is due to the absolute disproportion which exists between the natural activity of all finite intelligence and the divine object.

The obscurity that St John of the Cross *describes* (or at least the one he most stresses) is the *purifying Night*, infinitely painful, which ceases when the soul has attained the degree of purity and holiness willed by God.

Thus (or near enough) St John of the Cross says: "the fire begins by blackening the wood; it does not set it aflame until it has dried it out". Therefore one has to pass through nights, through all the anguishes and terrors of the night, see oneself engulfed in darkness and be dried up with suffering, before the soul is truly set on fire, kindled into flame that does not consume like natural fire, the vivifying flame of eternal life.

Certainly I have nothing to say of the Night of the spirit and what follows it. It does seem, however, if one reads the mystics, that what follows is light and joy and no longer suffering and night.

But if beatifying love succeeds purifying love, it is still *God perceived "by virtue of union"* and *"ineffably perceived"*. Whether contemplation be wholly obscure or whether intellectual visions accompany it, God remains ineffable and "ineffably perceived". So that the essence of mystical contemplation is still maintained in the two definitions, ontological and psychological.

In contemplation, it is God who is perceived, through

---

3. The pseudo-Areopagite (Trans.).

the medium, it is true, of our more or less pure finite being, just as when we touch an object, it is really the object which is perceived through the medium of a more or less sensitive hand.

God is perceived as Love because he attracts and unites, makes one suffer, or gives one joy, reveals himself to the soul as its end, its repose, its beatitude. He is perceived as someone who touches us and not as someone who is seen.

The soul touched by God leaps to the search for vision and union, but though its impulse of love sweeps it towards God, it does not see him whom it touches, and its experience is blind.[4]

It experiences God's love for it, and the love with which it responds is itself like the shadow of the divine love in it; and, in a sense, these two so different loves are only one love, as two spirits that cleave to each other are one spirit: Qui adhaeret Deo unus spiritus est.

Here are my pebbles drawn from the water; they seem awfully colorless to me. What will you make of them, my dear brother! Never mind. It was good to talk to you about God, and as a result you will have prayed still another time for your sister

Raïssa

who is very deeply attached to you in Xto,

---

4. As to the question: can there be love without knowledge, St John of the Cross answers it admirably in *The Living Flame* str. 3, v. 3, ch. X. The simple knowledge of Faith is enough for infused love, whether or not this love itself produces "the knowledge of contemplation" which in its turn nourishes love. (Raïssa's note.)

2

God and Men

[*God and Men*][1]

I am coming now to take humanity quietly – for what it is. Without exclamations – regrets – sighs – and groans. In a way quite different from that of Leibnitzian optimism – all is for the best. *God knows what he permits.*

He is not like a man who regretfully permits what he cannot prevent. He has let men go their own way armed with their freedom – and they go it. They go, gamble and work, risk everything – win more or less, and perhaps will end by winning everything. God has simply reserved for himself in humanity one Man who is his Son. And this Man-God calls to himself, for his own work – which he also has to do with men's freedom – calls a small number of men – a handful in every century to work in his own way. "He who would be my disciple, let him take up *his* cross and follow me" – and that is sufficient.

To all is given the precept of charity – the duty of hope – and this word which is the foundation of hope:

"Much will be forgiven her for she has loved much."

---

1. My title. (J.)

*

The *permission* of God is not like a weakness of God – the permission is as formative as the will of God; he permits that fallible nature should fail – but these lapses themselves have their use in the development of the human being – of all humanity – of all life in this world.

If these lapses had not been permitted, humanity would have been wholly assumed from the beginning into the supernatural life, nay more, into the beatific vision – but without having freely won this.

*

In fact, and taking into account human circumstances – the call to contemplation is addressed to a few.

Meudon, *16th February 1935.*

3

On the " humanity " of Christianity

On the "humanity" of Christianity

"If any man come to me and hate not his father, and mother, and wife, and children, and brethren, and sisters, yea and his own life also, *he cannot be my disciple*" (Luke 14:26).

The demands of Christ as regards his *disciples* are absolutely inhuman; they are divine. There is no doubt about it, he who wishes to be Christ's disciple – *must hate his own life*. The image of Jesus Crucified is *for the disciple*.

But such demands are *only* for the disciples. As regards the common body of men, Christianity is *human* in the sense that it accepts men in their weakness and inconstancy, and also in their nature attached to natural goods (father, mother, etc.). They will never feel an inward call as severe as the one that St. Luke records.

All that is demanded of them is to believe, to love, and to continue to hope after they have gone astray, however wildly.

Thus it is not the sinner, the "worldly" one, who has the greatest fear of God – rather it is those who, having been chosen as disciples, know that they are, and will be, more severely treated. From these, *all* is demanded.

Undated.

4

On Poetry as Spiritual Experience

On Poetry as Spiritual Experience

Anyone who desires to know the depths of spirit, or, if you like, the spirituality of being, begins by entering into himself. And it is also in the innermost core of life, of thought, of consciousness that he encounters Poetry, if he is destined to encounter her. Above all, if he is one of those poets in whom poetic creation – the formative emotion or intuition – arises, not from the continuous clamour of the imagination, but from absorption into a silence stripped to the uttermost of forms and words, when silence attains a high degree of depth and purity.

To go back to what I have already indicated in an essay on the same subject, I will say that, in my opinion, the source of poetry, like that of all creative intuition, lies in a certain experience which one can call "knowledge", an obscure and savourous knowledge – with an altogether spiritual savour, because, at these depths, all is spirit and life. And the poet knows that he penetrates into them by an inner withdrawal of all his senses, however fleeting it be; this is the first condition of poetic conception; it is a question here of a passive absorption, as is also that quiet of which the mystics speak, not of a voluntary, active concentration (which is also required, but at other moments).

Poetry thus appears to me as the fruit of a contact of the spirit with reality in itself ineffable, and with its source which is in truth God himself in the impulse of love which leads him to create images of his beauty. Did not Boccaccio say long ago that "poetry is theology"? It is, in any case, ontology, because it is born, when it is authentic, in the mysterious sources of being. It is in them that there begins to form (like the "setting" of a fruit) the poetic knowledge in which the poet espouses the unique individuality of things. A consubstantial knowledge – poetry is the song of this knowledge. Knowledge by connaturality with the object that gave birth to it, concrete and individual knowledge so intimate, keen and profound that it strikes the poet's heart, already tense, already keyed up to break into the song of discovery, as the sleeping lark, struck by the sun, awakens, and mounts up into the sky, and sings.

The poet has plunged into the stream of spirit underlying all our habitual activity; he has felt the contact of this reality alien to any formula, in that rare and fecund absorption which in some way has to be deserved and from which he emerges quickened in his faculties, enriched with gifts.

This plunge into the spiritual depths is altogether different from the mere surrender to the automatism of the imagination, which descends no further than the Freudian level of the physiological memory, in itself the source of pure verbalism. On that level one makes lucky finds of images, but no real discovery. One can say it now – poetry has not been, and never will be, renewed by automatism, and by the mere concurrence of words. An Eluard, for example, is a great poet *in spite of* certain preconceived recipes and theories, not because of them.

The poet who is satisfied with the procedure of Freudian therapy, with this pseudo-absorption in self which is but a pure and simple abandonment of self, only makes contact with something "ready-made", only penetrates, by definition, into the region of memories embedded in the unconscious like clusters of vipers and traumatisms. Let the psychologist and the psychiatrist make discoveries there; one cannot see of what interest this is to Poetry. If automatism releases, up to a certain point, verbal imagination, this does not suffice to justify the procedure whose consequences are in other respects disastrous, because automatism unbinds what concentration and absorption in the reality of things and self together have brought to unity of life, to the creation of a new form.

Real and fecund inner withdrawal is the first gift which is made to the poet, and it is also a natural disposition in him which has to be cultivated. The poet desires this entering into himself; he seeks to persevere in it. In the same way that God draws to him those who aspire to him, Poetry waits for those who seek her and lets herself be found by those who love her.

God. Poetry. An absolutely straight and pure inner activity goes to the one and to the other – goes, sometimes, *from* the one *to* the other. The divine silence of the soul breaks out into psalms – and the quiet of the poet sometimes discovers God. But more often than not poets and artists deem – if not God and poetry, at least the demands of the One and of the other – to be in mutual opposition. They recognise, generally, the divine source of their gifts.

And poets and musicians say: "All springs are in Thee".[1]
But they regard the demands of God's law as an obstacle to
their creative freedom and obedience to this law as a
mutilation. They do not know that this law is spiritual
and consequently the liberator of our own freedom. "Those
who believe in Jesus Christ are subject to the law of God
as to a light along the path of freedom."[2] "The Law is
spiritual," says St. Paul, "but I am carnal, sold into the
slavery of sin."[3] Baudelaire knew that (and Rimbaud too,
no doubt), and he fully accepted the inner rending such
knowledge brings with it and the humility it compels.

Baudelaire accepted the universe of objective truth,
which did not scandalise him. This has become rare in the
artists of our day: the radiant sky of the metaphysical
universe is for them a dreary desert. To commit oneself
to an object immutable in its essence is for them like
departing from life. Due to prejudice, or to actual inability,
the artists, the poets, know, or want to know, only what
they are doing, or rather what is being done in them:
their emotion, the conception of the work in them, their
travail in bringing it to birth. If, by an act of humility,
they could admit the reality of the objective world of
beings and laws which the Creator of poets *also* has brought
into existence, new and manifold realms of beauty would
no doubt be discovered to them. Then they would become –
certain of them, the greatest – truly inspired men, prophets
of this world, and the spiritual experience of divine truth
would increase, harmonise and illuminate in them the
spiritual experience of the poetic state.

---

1. Ps. 87 (86).
2. Jacques Maritain, *Saint Paul: Selections from His Writings*
(McGraw-Hill, paperback edition), p. 76.
3. Rom. 7: 14.

An artist in the pure state is almost as rare a bird as an atheist in the pure state. Nevertheless, for those of them who are of absolute good faith and who think there is an insurmountable antinomy between the demands of art and those of God, God will surely have to find a place in eternal life. These labourers in the field of beauty who do not think they reject God in rejecting his Law, will have to receive their pay, at least the ones who do not receive it in this world and who in this resemble the saints. And so will the apparent antinomy be resolved. Where truth and freedom confront one another like enemies, an appeal goes up to charity – and sanctity hears it. Somewhere a weight of love and sanctity is found which adds, to a temporal good, a good of eternal value, which saves the beauty of this world that passes, which redeems the beauty created by poets and snatches it away from him who claims he has rights over all created beauty because he is the Prince of this world.

Thus, in reality, nothing beautiful is brought into existence without love being at work. The artist creates a creature which the saint snatches back from the devil, who has often collaborated in its creation by giving the poet an experience of this world, of its "pomps", of its delights. But there is no good, no beauty and no being which grace is not willing and able to save if only we range ourselves in the ranks of sinners, if only we recognise ourselves as responsible for the Blood of Christ and for the martyrdom of the saints.

New York, *21st November 1941.*

(Appeared in the review *Fontaine,* March-April 1942.
Cf. *Nova et Vetera,* April-June 1961.)

5

The Divine Transcendence

The Divine Transcendence. Ground of the Immanence or Omnipresence of God

God envelops us and penetrates us and his being is unknown to us. We know that he exists, and we do not know what his existence is.

When, liberated by death, and transformed by Grace, we appear before God, we shall know his transcendence, but it will be a total, absolute discovery.

"What eye has not seen, what ear has not heard, what has not entered into the heart of man", that is what we shall know.

Nevertheless this transcendence, this infinite omnipotence above us, far from making us distant from it, is what places us in It without distance.

Our dependence is another absolute which places us in the bosom of God, there where we live on eternal life, there where we are born, through the soul, into eternal life.

If he were not so absolutely transcendent, God would be in some way (according to a false idea of transcendence that one sometimes encounters) univocally similar to some attribute of the creature carried to the absolute, and it is by that he would be distinguished from all attributes proper to things created. He would thus be enclosed in his absolute by a kind of limit, and insofar would be remote or absent from us.

But the transcendence of the Omnipresent knows no limitation. Nothing shuts it in or encloses it. What could create a distance between Him and us? What could remove us from Him?

We are, in God, the fruit He bears and gives life to. We are in the depths of God, whatever we make of our freedom.

Immersed in Him, and He in us.

If he were not Transcendence, there would be a distance between Him and the creature, a void between the One and the other.

Everything he has made subsists in him. Like the blind fishes immersed in the great depths.

Where grace is given, a diffused light appears and spreads. Where glory is received the beatific vision shines out in splendour.

The soul feels itself more united to God by the denial of all likeness of the deity to the created, than by all the analogies of the image that the creature is of God.

Each feature of that image is a disappointment and a weariness to the soul.

The soul's repose in God is all the greater and more perfect as the number of images decreases.

The empty imagination allows God to draw up the soul to Him, and if there then remains any effort in the soul, it is a kind of aspiration towards union, towards the dissolving of all difference, towards the fusion in love (not in essence) of the created soul with the Uncreated, of the creature with the Deity.

21st February (Year not mentioned.)

6

And the Word was made Flesh

And the Word was made Flesh

Certain spiritual writers think that the highest contemplation, being free of all the images of this world, is that which does without images altogether, even that of Jesus, and into which, consequently, the Humanity of Christ does not enter.

That is a profound error, and the problem disappears as soon as one has grasped how truly and how deeply the Word has assumed human nature – in such a way that everything which is of this nature: suffering, pity, compassion, hope. . ., all these things have become, so to speak, attributes of God. – In contemplating them, it is therefore attributes of God which are contemplated; it is God himself who is contemplated.

Since apart from and below the divine perfections, the Word Incarnate possesses human qualities which are *God's* – they are the objects of a contemplation that is just as spiritual, although it includes images.[1]

---

1. *These* images are not "a disappointment and a weariness to the soul" (cf. above, p. 382) because they do not show some created *analogatum* of the deity but something of God himself – Incarnate. (J.)

And the soul must not be afraid of passing through the human states and the human pity of Jesus, and of making requests of Him and of praying for the cure of a sick person, for example – all these things being participations in the desires and the compassion of Christ, which belonged to the divine Person itself.

Undated (Probably 1958 or 1959).

7

The True Face of God
or
Love and the Law

The True Face of God
or
Love and the Law

Tried and tempted souls feel vaguely that the law, which is so hard for them to observe, cannot be identified with God who is love.

But this feeling either remains vague, or else leads to a certain contempt for the law, or else turns the soul against God who is then seen as a hard and exacting master – which is to deny God – or would be to deny God, if the soul pushed such thoughts to their final conclusion, to their logical consequences.

Well, it is salutary to *distinguish* (to speak in legal terms) *the case of God from the case of the Law.*

Only by grasping that distinction, can the soul behave as it should towards God – and towards the law.

When Jesus felt himself abandoned by God on the Cross, it was because the face of Love was then hidden from him, and the whole of his humanity was subjected to the law, without any mitigation – something which no man except the Man-God would have been able to endure without dying.

Jesus on the Cross, and very particularly at that moment of total dereliction, suffered the full rigour of the law of the transmutation of one nature into another – *as if* he had not been God; it was his humanity as such, taken from the Virgin, which had to feel the full weight of this law. For the head must experience the law that he imposes on his members. Because, having assumed human nature, he had to experience this supreme law to which human nature, called to participate in the divine nature, is subject.

And if he had not suffered from the rigour of this law, it would not have been possible to say that the Word took a heart like our own in order to feel for our sufferings.

This law of the transformation of natures – which comprises in it all moral and divine laws – is something necessary, physical, ontological if you like – God himself cannot abolish it, just as he cannot produce the absurd.

But this law – the Law – is not He – He is Love.

So when a soul suffers, and suffers from this inexorable Law of transmutation of a nature into a higher nature (and this is the meaning of all human history) – God is with this nature which he has made and which is suffering – he is not against it. If he could transform that nature into his own by abolishing the law of suffering and death, he would abolish it – because he takes no pleasure in the spectacle of pain and death. But he cannot abolish any law inscribed in being.

The face of the law and its rigour, the face of suffering and death is not the face of God; God is love.

And his love has made him behave towards men in a way that may seem capricious.

To the Ancients, like Abraham and the other Patriarchs,

he did not reveal the whole law; in that state of nature he did not even reveal to men all the moral laws inscribed in nature. Because the observation of the whole body of these laws would have supposed the perfection of human nature to be already realised – and this was not so – or else would have demanded the help of Christic graces[1] which were not yet acquired. Hence that strange liberty left to men in the state of nature – even when these men are Abram,[2] Isaac and Jacob – and then Moses and the Jews, up to the coming of Christ. And yet it was in this state that God chose Abram to be the Father of Believers.

Abram, this simple man, with a heart which never resists the voice of God. *He believes God* who speaks to him. He does what God tells him to do. He goes from sacrifice to sacrifice: first he leaves his country and his father – the hearths of Ur of the Chaldees – he accepts the nomadic life. And then he quits easy faith; it is relatively easy to believe God when he promises abundant blessings – and an immense posterity – but when the only son, the still sterile boy, has to be sacrificed, how painful it is to believe! And it would even be impossible to obey – since obedience here requires the commission of what appears to be a crime – if faith did not lead Abram as if by the hand.

Never was greater grace of faith in God given to any

---

1. All graces received by men since the fall of Adam are Christic graces. But Raïssa is speaking here of the graces of Christ *come,* or of *sacramentally Christic* graces. (J.)

2. Abraham was first called Abram; that is why Raïssa, in this passage, freely used the two names. Cf. her *Histoire d'Abraham ou les premiers âges de la conscience morale.* English translation in vol. I of *The Bridge,* published by Msgr. John Oesterreicher (Trans.).

man. And never was any man greater in his fidelity – if we except Joseph and Mary.

Thus Abraham, too, knew the hard law of the transformation of the natural man into the spiritual and divine man – but with a wide zone of human liberty in which many laws, left in shadow by God, were put in parenthesis.

And, as for us, he has revealed to us all the terrible demands of the divinisation of man.

But in order to reveal them to us, he came himself – not with the blood of goats and bulls – but with the Blood of Christ through which his Love for us is made visible.

Thus the new Law is harsher than the old Law.

But at the same time the love of God (which softens everything) is more widespread.

It is in the blood of Jesus Crucified that the Sacraments are born,

whether they purify – Baptism

whether they vivify – Penance

whether they bring growth – the Eucharist. . .

The law – all the laws – having become so clearly, and so terribly visible,

the face of the love of God thus risks being obscured.

This is why it is more necessary than ever to distinguish between Love and the Law.

When nature, called upon to obey, groans and suffers, she is not hateful to God, for quitting its own shape is a loss for all nature – a suffering for natures endowed with sensibility.

When human nature shrinks back and fails in this labour, it is not hateful to God; he loves it, he wants to save it – he does save it, provided it does not want to be separated from him, provided it recognises the need of purification for salvation: if a sinner recognises this only at the hour of his death, he is saved and goes to Purgatory to be purified.

So what one must first and foremost tell men, and go on telling them, is to love God – to know that he is Love and to trust to the end in his Love.

The law is just. The law is necessary – with the very necessity of transformation for salvation, that is to say, for eternal life with God.

But the law is not God.

And God is not the law. – He is Love.

If God has the face of the law for men – men draw back because they feel that love is more than the law – in this they are wrong only because they do not recognise the salutary necessity of the law.

But the observation of the Law without love would be of no avail for salvation.

And love can save a man even at the last second of a bad life – if, in that second, the man has found the light of love – perhaps if he has always believed that God is Love.

Souls must be delivered from that feeling of enmity they experience (passively and actively) towards God if they see him in the apparatus of laws which to them is an image hostile to love – and which masks God's true face.

The Cross – it was the Law that imposed it on Jesus; so Jesus took it in order to share the harshness of the law with us.

These things must be said to men. If these things were not said, they would draw away from God when they suffer, because the law is a thing which seems to separate us from God, and then it presents itself – if we do not think of love – as our *enemy*, and God can never present himself as an enemy.

It is, in a certain manner, opposed to love. God has made it insofar as he is the Creator of being. But insofar as he is our end and our beatitude, he calls us beyond it.

The law is proposed externally, it implies a subjection – in itself it seems to have nothing to do with mercy – nor with the equality of friendship – nor with familiarity.

It is truly a necessity; only a necessity.

Love *gives over the head of* the Law.

(It forgives.)

Love creates trust – freedom of spirit – equality – familiarity.

Undated.

TWO LETTERS ABOUT RAÏSSA

I. — A Letter from A. G.

[When our friend Antoinette Grunelius wrote me this letter the doctor had already given up all hope. J.]

Kolbsheim,
9th October 1960.

Very dear Jacques,

It was in 1937,[1] when you were staying here, that Raïssa confided something to me that I thought I ought to pass on to you now.

We had all gone to Mass together, you were sitting on the right with the men, according to the local custom, I was near Raïssa, perhaps Véra was beside me, I cannot remember now.

During Mass, Raïssa, who was kneeling, suddenly, as it were, stretched out towards God. I noticed something unusual and turned towards her – I shall always remember the expression on her face, it was not sorrowful but her

---

1. Our friend put this date through a slip of memory. The event mentioned in her letter took place on April 16th 1939, as one sees from the little memorandum book in which Raïssa noted it and which I found later (cf. above, "Loose Leaves" Fragment 88). For those who are attentive to God's ways, one may note that Edith Stein made the same offering of her life at the same period. On Passion Sunday (1939) she wrote to the Superior of the Carmel in Echt to ask her "to allow her to offer herself to the Heart of Jesus as a sacrifice of expiation for the peace of the world." And she added: ". . . I know that I am nothing, but Jesus wishes it, and no doubt He will address the same appeal to many other souls." Cf. Jean de Fabrègues, *La Conversion d'Edith Stein*, Wesmael-Charlier, p. 119. (J.)

397

look inexpressibly conveyed the giving of her whole being. I did not, of course, make any allusion to what I had seen by chance, without meaning to, but in the course of the day Raïssa confided to me that she had offered herself to God.

She asked me not to tell you about it unless she should happen to die. It seemed to me, dear Jacques, that you ought to know now. I do not think I have betrayed her wish, because, if she did not tell you, it was so as not to cause you anguish, and because, on the contrary, knowing her secret may be a light for you in these hours of agony. . .

II. — A Letter from O. L.

[*I thank our friend Olivier Lacombe for having authorised me to publish this letter full of delicate affection. It brings out certain features of Raïssa's life which have been alluded to in the Journal only quite indirectly; and at the same time, it confirms that general law according to which when action is joined to an authentically contemplative life, the latter does not pass into the service of action, but overflows in action. (J.)*]

25th July 1963.

Very dear Jacques,

Reading *Raïssa's Journal* in proof touches me profoundly. I do not need to tell you that, do I?

It was at the beginning of 1926, as you will perhaps remember, that I began to be a frequent visitor to your home in Meudon. Up to then, I had only known you through your books. But from then on, right up to that cruel summer of 1939 when the war obliged me, in your absence, to have the Blessed Sacrament removed from the chapel, and, practically speaking, to put the final full stop to those blessed years, I was privileged to be the attentive, discreet and affectionate witness of the principal events of which the "Meudon period" is filled to bursting point.

Certainly the secret of the King was well kept there, even from familiars, however transparent the walls of that house you so generously threw open.

Thus my emotion, in its respectful faithfulness, is aroused in quite a new way by discovering, through her Journal, what Raïssa's deep spiritual life was at that time, as well as before and after. Besides myself, many others will thank you for the infinitely precious gift which is made to us from beyond death. Personally, I feel very unworthy to receive it, but it raises up and strengthens our souls in Christ.

From a less lofty point of view, perhaps what is most striking in this Journal is the supreme self-discipline which enabled Raïssa to make herself free for the Lord in the midst of such numerous, such varied, such time-devouring human obligations, and in spite of the insecurity of constantly menaced health.

Certainly leisure moments, and, even more so, free time, were what was most lacking at Meudon for all three of you. As I write this, I am not thinking so much of some serious "crises" linked to the events of the period, when you had to mobilise a common surplus of energy for immediate action in conditions which at times bordered on the impossible. No, I am thinking of the habitual and "normal" course of your lives during the Meudon years.

Raïssa was pursuing her work as poet and writer, and her own work is not only of outstanding quality but of considerable volume.

She was collaborating with you all the time. Nothing of your abundant work has been published by you without her having followed it at different stages of development right up to the final version; and you attached a peerless value to her vigilant and penetrating judgement.

A marvellous art of making people feel welcome, which was the perfect gift of self to the visitor, to the guest sent by God in the course of the day, was practised under your roof. On Sundays at Meudon – and often on weekday evenings too – your doors and your hearts were thrown wide open. And each one came back from there, moved to the depths of the soul, by having been *accepted* and recognised personally, with a solicitous friendliness that reached the most reserved centre of himself. But it is obvious that this ability to listen, to understand others without ever forcing their confidence, demanded, particularly of Raïssa, the hostess and the heart of the home, a truly prodigal self-giving and self-effacement in the service of one's neighbour.

And then (not to mention other additional meetings, philosophical or "ecumenical") there were, once a month, the study meetings of the Thomist Circles, each of which took up a whole afternoon. There were, once a year, the spiritual retreats of those same Thomist Circles, when for some days your house was the centre of a closely-woven network in which silence with God, prayer, doctrinal preoccupations of the highest order, encounters that were decisive for the destiny of many were all interlaced.

There was the tireless search for everything the age could produce in the way of the good, the true, the beautiful. . . The care to keep abreast of the intellectual and artistic life of the day. . . The trips to Paris to keep in touch there with music, painting, poetry, and follow the movements of thought.

There was the enlightenment offered to many by editing such great series as *Le Roseau d'Or* and *Les Iles*, with all the material and spiritual burdens involved: research, reading, criticising of manuscripts, getting them printed. . .

In all these activities which were common to both of

you, Raïssa took an effective part, and a very large part. If I bring up these things which you know better than I do, it is to emphasise the harmonious unity of action and contemplation, of intense action and intense contemplation in Raïssa's life during the Meudon period.

Once again, dear Jacques, I say a very affectionate "thank-you" for having let me see this most precious Journal of Raïssa's before it is published.

Olivier Lacombe

[*The reason I asked Olivier Lacombe to allow me to make use of this letter is that it touches on aspects of Raïssa's life which obviously could not be the subject of notes like the ones that constitute the* Journal. *It is important to be thus reminded that, for Raïssa, the Meudon years were years of unremitting work and worry, due both to the demands of intellectual life and to those of being ever at the disposal of others and of concern for souls. The fact remains that, on the other hand, the essential for Raïssa, during all those years, the unique essential, was always to keep herself, with the aim of union with God, at the disposal of the inner summons to silent prayer. Every day she gave to* oraison *all the time this required; and her other activities, however necessary they might be in other respects, were a kind of surplus, at once secondary and overflowing. To sustain for twenty years (first at Versailles, then at Meudon) such a régime of life, and one which became heavier and heavier in its demands, not only required an unusual acceptance of self-sacrifice and an exceptional strength of soul, it was also necessary that external conditions should allow her to find – at whatever cost – the time demanded for silence with God.*

These conditions existed at Meudon. They were denied to Raïssa after our departure to America at the beginning of 1940. It then became physically impossible for her to find the time for the prolonged recueillement she needed. She suffered greatly as a result, but she accepted it without ever losing her peace. She knew that henceforth it was in the uninterrupted buzz of the tasks of daily life, or in all too brief intervals of solitude, that she must remain faithful to silent prayer. Moreover she never failed to devote the intervals in question to silence with God, however irregularly they may have occurred. Only at Princeton, at least when illness and physical suffering didn't overrule everything, was she able to re-establish a certain regularity in the intervals of time dedicated to silence with God. But where was the little study looking on to our chapel in Meudon, and from where, through a glazed aperture, she could see the tabernacle with the Blessed Sacrament close to her? In reality, however, no one had been able to rob her of her treasure. She kept it hidden in humility. And do we not know that prayer can become incessant ("the prayer of the heart," as Father Osende puts it), when the soul, according to the saying of a hermit recorded by Cassian, "prays without knowing itself that it prays".

I would like to add also, — as far as one may venture to suggest such distinctions in the complex movement of life — that I see three main periods in Raïssa's spiritual life. Raïssa, in whose conversion the example of saints and great contemplatives played a major role, entered the ways of silent prayer immediately after her baptism. It was in the peace of silence with God that, in particular, she was to read St Thomas Aquinas for the first time, and to receive the intuitive certainties which henceforth enlightened her reason. A first period was thus the time of apprenticeship and beginning – a sort of sunrise of contemplative life (1906–1916). – A second period began when, in May 1916, Raïssa decided to give to silent prayer all the time that God would request from her. This period lasted till the end of 1939. At the outset, things were made easier for her by a comparatively light schedule. But as early as 1920–1921, and especially from 1923 on, during the time we lived at Meudon, she was obliged – at what price, only Véra and I have known – to remain fully available for all that the life of oraison *demanded from now on, and in a particularly exacting manner, as well as for the harassing surplus activities of which Olivier Lacombe's letter gives us some idea. – A third period is that which lasted from 1940 to 1960, and of which I have spoken in the preceding paragraph. (J.)]*